SEIZING THE NEW DAY

BLACKS IN THE DIASPORA   Darlene Clark Hine, John McCluskey, Jr., and David Barry Gaspar   GENERAL EDITORS

SEIZING THE NEW DAY

African
Americans in
Post–Civil War
Charleston

WILBERT L. JENKINS

Indiana University Press   Bloomington and Indianapolis

Title Page Art Courtesy of the N.C. Division of Archives and History

The paper used in this publication meets the minimum
requirements of American National Standard for Information
Sciences—Permanence of Paper for Printed Library Materials,
ANSI Z39.48-1984.

Manufactured in the United States of America

Library of Congress Cataloging-in-Publication Data

Jenkins, Wilbert L., date
Seizing the new day : African Americans in post–Civil War Charleston /
Wilbert L. Jenkins.
    p.   cm. — (Blacks in the diaspora)
Includes bibliographical references and index.
ISBN 0-253-33380-6 (alk. paper)
1. Freedmen—South Carolina—Charleston—History—19th century.
2. Afro-Americans—South Carolina—Charleston—History—
19th century. 3. Afro-Americans—History—1863–1877.
4. Charleston (S.C.)—Race relations. I. Title. II. Series.
F279.C49N427   1998
305.896'073075791—dc21   97-49399

      1 2 3 4 5 03 02 01 00 99 98

CONTENTS

ally prodding me to finish the book. Thanks also go to Jo Dohoney for typing and editing the first drafts of the book manuscript. Deborah Stuart graciously edited the final draft and I am most appreciative.

Most of all, I am indebted to my wife, Mary Montaque-Jenkins, for her generosity of spirit, sharp intellect, friendship, love, and support. To her I dedicate this book.

INTRODUCTION

The history of the American South in the first decade after the Civil War has been richly documented by twentieth-century scholars. We have detailed analyses of the roles played by both black and white political leaders during Reconstruction and accounts of the lives of the Lees, the Ellisons, the De Costas, and other members of Charleston's mulatto elite. We have in-depth studies of the responses of the illiterate black masses to emancipation and Reconstruction.[1] Most of these studies, however, focus on responses at the regional and state levels; few examine the local level. To complement these earlier studies and help provide a more complete account of the black experience between 1865 and 1877, I examine here how former slaves in Charleston, South Carolina, responded to emancipation and Reconstruction during this crucial period in the transition from slavery to freedom, looking first at their day-to-day experiences under slavery. Charleston is one of the most researched cities in nineteenth-century America, but this group of working-class blacks has been virtually ignored.

Charleston holds a secondary place among the cities of the United States at the present time. With respect to population, it does not rank in the top one hundred and it is not even South Carolina's largest city. That distinction belongs to Columbia. Yet, throughout the colonial period, Charleston was the preeminent port and entrepôt of the transatlantic slave trade to British North America. Most of the nearly ninety thousand black slaves that entered South Carolina between 1672 and 1775 came through Charleston. Charleston merchants imported and sold more than 25 percent of all blacks transported to North America during that era. Beginning in the seventeenth century and ending in 1807, for almost two centuries Charleston merchants were active participants in the transatlantic slave trade.

The end of the slave trade had a dramatic effect on Charleston's size and prosperity. In 1810 it was the fifth largest United States city; by 1830, it was sixth behind New York, Philadelphia, Boston, Baltimore, and New Orleans. But it fell to twenty-sixth among United States cities by 1870 and continued this downward spiral, reaching ninety-first in population rankings in 1920. Between 1870 and 1910, Charleston's population increased by only 20 percent, from 49,000 to 59,000. Its growth was too modest to allow it to keep pace with either the younger interior cities in the New South or the growing Northern industrial centers.[2]

Despite the loss of the slave trade, exports of cotton and rice allowed Charleston to maintain its prosperity in the first few decades of the antebellum period and to achieve recognition as the top trading and shipping center of the southeastern United States. In 1820, South Carolina led all the states of the Union in the export of domestic products. Cotton and rice accounted for 96 percent of the state's exports, all emanating from the port of Charleston. In the middle of the decade, however, an economic depression began pushing Charleston from its position as the top trading and shipping center in the Southeast. The negative economic trend continued, and by the mid-1850s, Charleston's position as the manufacturing and exporting center of South Carolina had all but evaporated. The decline can be measured, for example, in the drastic drop in the total board feet of lumber being exported to both national and international ports. And, whereas in 1848, 6.5 percent of the city's population worked in manufacturing—in sawmills, rice mills, flour mills, grist mills, lumber mills, and blind, sash, and door factories; in shipyards, brickyards, tinware shops, iron foundries, umbrella factories, turpentine distilleries, and carriage and wagon shops—twelve years later, only 2.1 percent worked in manufacturing.[3]

Charleston had failed to diversify its economy and was the least industrialized of the nation's major population centers. One of the main stumbling blocks was the resistance of planters from the low country. Anxious to preserve Charleston as a peaceful home for themselves, they opposed any kind of economic growth. They feared that the development of commercial and industrial establishments would destroy the ambiance and the social order of the city by requiring an increase in the number of slaves in the industrial work force within the city and attracting free white laborers from what they regarded as the lowest rungs of white society. Some low country planters feared also that industrialization would give rise to a powerful commercial class within the city that could threaten their preeminence. During the antebellum period, these planters dominated South Carolina's legislature and controlled its executive branch unchallenged. Their power throughout the South was disproportionate to their numbers and allowed them to spearhead the secession movements of 1850 and 1860. Largely because of their efforts Charleston was known as the training ground for secessionist hotheads and the heart of the proslavery South.

Much of the power of this "plantocracy" was derived from their wealth. A great disparity existed between rich and poor in the city. In 1860, almost 5 percent of all Charlestonians had wealth worth forty thousand dollars or more, whereas only 1 percent of all Americans fit into that category. On the other end of the spectrum, about 56 percent of all

Charlestonians, compared with 25 percent of all Americans, owned no property.[4]

Charleston's enslaved population constituted about one-third of the city's total population on the eve of the Civil War. Besides working as domestics and personal servants, these people were the backbone of Charleston's industrial labor force in the antebellum years, with many employed as coopers, engineers, mechanics, shoemakers, carpenters, bricklayers, and blacksmiths. Some slaves even worked as store clerks, while others provided labor in the maritime pursuits of the city. A few were able to manage their own businesses as artisans, though all proceeds flowed to their owners.

The slaves were by no means docile. There were instances in which slaves murdered whites, and newspapers frequently carried advertisements by slaveowners seeking runaways. Slave patrols in the Charleston area were large, well organized, and very active. One of the largest slave insurrections ever plotted in American history was organized in Charleston in 1822 by Denmark Vesey, a former slave carpenter who had purchased his freedom from money he won in a lottery. The plot was betrayed, however, and Vesey and other leaders were tried and executed. But despite the failure of the insurrection and the fact that it was unusual in the history of American slavery, throughout the antebellum years many whites in Charleston were obsessed with ideas of a slave conspiracy, regarding all slaves with suspicion and fearing also free blacks, who, as 8 percent of the city's population on the eve of the Civil War, were a significant segment of that society. In fact, by the late 1850s, there was even talk of re-enslaving freed blacks and enslaving those born into freedom.[5]

After emancipation, blacks continued to play a leading role in the city's industrial order as both skilled and unskilled laborers. Many continued to work in personal service as domestics, while others used their skills to establish their own businesses. Some were employed in public work jobs as street cleaners and as construction workers on the public edifices of Charleston. Some worked as stevedores and longshoremen, receiving relatively good wages, though the work was arduous and seasonal. Others even worked in law enforcement and firefighting. Through thrift and ingenuity, a few former slaves amassed wealth and became active members of the Republican party, where they played prominent roles in local politics and helped to shape the course of Charleston's society in the post–Civil War years. Since measures such as the Black Codes and the Reconstruction Acts affected these newly freed slaves more than any other single group, an inquiry into their day-to-day experiences is essential to understanding the Reconstruction period.

Too often scholars have written of nineteenth-century Southern blacks as if they were a homogeneous group. This is a fallacy. Blacks in the South were united by race, culture, and marriage, but they differed by region, by complexion, and by social, economic, political, religious, and educational background. Throughout this work I distinguish between the diverse groups of newly freed blacks in Charleston. After the war, the city became an urban magnet that attracted energetic blacks from the surrounding rural areas. By 1875 blacks constituted nearly two-thirds of the city's population. This group, like all groups in the South, was in no sense homogeneous. Newly freed blacks differed not only by background and complexion but also by former position in an antebellum social hierarchy among slaves that placed artisans and domestic servants of the white elite on the top tier, where a disproportionate number were light skinned. Those who had been slaves in the city had experienced a degree of social, economic, and educational freedom unknown to the newly freed rural blacks. Native black Charlestonians thus were economically more entrenched in the affairs of the city and better equipped to survive as freedpeople than were the rural migrants, most of whom had been laborers on rice and cotton plantations.

Under slavery, the systems of "hiring-out" and "living-out" also provided urban slaves with more freedom of movement and more social opportunities than their rural counterparts had access to on plantations, where pass and curfew laws were always strictly enforced. And although slaves were prohibited by law from being taught to read and write and most urban slaves were illiterate, the complexities of the urban environment did create meager educational opportunities virtually unknown in rural areas. Some urban slaves were educated in secret schools organized by free blacks, and those who became literate often taught others.

The crushing defeat of the Confederacy by Union forces shattered the institution of slavery, the linchpin of the antebellum social, economic, and political system in Charleston and in the entire American South. Relations between blacks and whites were thrown into disarray and no one could say with certainty what would follow. Many white Charlestonians believed that emancipation need not drastically change the status of blacks within Southern society, but most former slaves, determined to exercise their freedom to the fullest, disagreed. To show how blacks did exercise their freedom and adapt during this chaotic period of transition from slavery to freedom, I examine the actions and attitudes of the diverse group in Charleston, looking for answers to some very specific questions. What did emancipation mean to Charleston's blacks? Did they see it as an opportunity? As something to be viewed with caution? As a cause of confusion or of hope? Did they seek new allies and social relationships or cling to old ones? How did the free black class from the antebellum period relate to the newly freed blacks? How did the newly freed urban blacks relate to their rural counterparts? What effect did emancipation have on the black family? On the black social structure?

What were the political responses of whites and blacks to Reconstruction? And finally, can we see here the origins of the twentieth-century urban black underclass?

It would be a historical error to write about blacks during Reconstruction without devoting attention to whites. As one contemporary scholar notes, "Blacks were continually interacting with, influencing, and being influenced by whites."[6] Moreover, white accounts of the actions of blacks during Reconstruction provide some of the best sources of information about what blacks were thinking and doing. The limited space I give to whites is intended to identify and explain the behaviors and attitudes of blacks. This is not a study of how blacks responded to white racism and discrimination. I see blacks as the central actors in their own lives, not as passive objects in a white-dominated society.

Too often, historians have discussed Reconstruction purely in political terms. In taking this approach, the emphasis has been on the failure of Radical Republicans to carry out the social, economic, and political changes in the South necessary to ensure black equality and independence. Consequently, Reconstruction has been too quickly labeled a failure.[7] If one were to focus on the reordering of black life that led to the formation of independent black economic, religious, and educational institutions during these years, then Reconstruction could be reevaluated from the standpoint of blacks and a more balanced account of the period would emerge. Here I look beyond politics to emphasize instead what was for blacks the crucial undertaking of the Reconstruction period: the rebuilding and reinvention of patterns of life and of social and economic interaction. For Charleston freedmen, this meant expanding their struggle, initiated under slavery, to become independent of white control. Their efforts included attempting to construct a solid economic base for themselves and their families. They pooled meager resources to establish and maintain their own schools and churches. Despite high illiteracy rates, they trained themselves in politics through active participation, consistently showing their sophistication by voting into office those who best supported their own interests. They struggled to rebuild shattered families and to legalize family relationships. At times they risked their lives to protect family members from white violence. Black Charlestonians were able to repel white violence, supported and strengthened by their numerical majority in the city's population, by a history of experience defending the rights of blacks against whites, and by the strong nucleus of free black leadership that extended from the antebellum period.

The chapters that follow provide balance to existing histories of Reconstruction by describing the efforts by the freedpeople and the historically free blacks to reconstruct their lives at the same time that whites struggled to preserve the old social order. Using their wits and their determination, Charleston blacks took an active role in the new social order, attempting to shape it to their own needs and purposes. None of the failure of social institutions to carry out and preserve social change in the postwar South can be charged to a lack of effort by the freedpeople of Charleston.

Chapter 1 describes the social, political, and economic context of blacks in Charleston before emancipation. Chapter 2 chronicles the initial reactions to emancipation and the organization of celebrations. Chapters 3 through 6 record the efforts of freedpeople under Reconstruction to become economically self-sufficient despite the war-ravaged economy, to create and maintain educational institutions, to sustain black family life and community ties, and to construct and maintain independent religious institutions. Chapter 7 looks at the role of violence in black social and political struggles to exercise and maintain both formal and informal social rights. The Epilogue describes the end of the Reconstruction era and with it the dimming of the hopes of black Charlestonians. In scarcely a decade, the sense of light and optimism that had accompanied emancipation had been reversed by the reactionary backlash that white Southerners would later hail as "Redemption." In Charleston, as elsewhere in the South, the long night of disfranchisement and enforced segregation descended upon black Americans.

SEIZING
THE
NEW DAY

THE DARK BEFORE THE DAWN

Black Charleston before Emancipation

1

To understand how blacks in the South adjusted to freedom during Reconstruction, we must first look at the experience of slavery. The thoughts, actions, and expectations of native blacks in postwar Charleston, for example, reflected the social, cultural, political, and religious context of their slave experience. Charleston's slaves were not a homogeneous lot; what they did have in common was the fact of their slavery in an urban setting. In the aftermath of the Civil War they would be joined by newly freed slaves who migrated to Charleston from nearby plantations. As slaves, these rural blacks had had many fewer social, economic, and educational opportunities than their urban counterparts.

Free blacks made up between 10 and 20 percent of the total black population of Charleston during the half century before the Civil War, but they were an integral part of the black community. The population of free blacks in Charleston in 1850, for example, was 3,441, with women outnumbering men two to one (see Appendix, table 1). The numbers decreased slightly in the ensuing decade because the city's intensely political atmosphere in the late 1850s was unfavorable to free blacks.[1] Most free blacks were poor, and in the years before and during the Civil War, the unequal numbers of men and women increased the likelihood of fraternization and marriage between free blacks and urban slaves.

Urban slave men were particularly drawn to marrying free black women because a free wife could provide economic advantages to a slave husband. Any bit of personal wealth or property he might acquire could be held by his wife, and even invested, safe from the possibility of confiscation by the slave's owner. Furthermore, all offspring of such a union would be free. It was less desirable, however, for a black man to marry a slave woman, because the offspring of that union would not be free.

Color was a distinguishing factor among free blacks. According to the 1860 census, about 75 percent of the total population of 3,232 free blacks in Charleston were mulattoes, and, as in 1850, women outnumbered men. (Mulattoes were the offspring of black-white unions and were counted officially as black.) Women made up 60 percent of the free black population in 1850 and 62 percent in 1860. The predominance of women and of lighter color grew out of the patterns of manumission. Female slaves and their mulatto children were frequently freed by white masters, in deference to wives who viewed these mistresses with distaste and made them objects of intense scrutiny. The offspring of the master begotten with female slaves were often given small endowments and slaves along with their freedom. With no such compelling reason for manumission, fewer slave men were given their freedom. The free black community was also relatively young in 1850 and 1860, with 75 to 79 percent of free blacks being under forty years old.[2]

Among free blacks, those with dark complexions tended to marry other free blacks with dark complexions, and mulattoes tended to marry other mulattoes whenever possible. But there were exceptions recorded by the Census Bureau. For example, Thomas Wright, a black barber, married Secelia, a mulatto employed as a seamstress. They had one child, Diana. William Scirven, a mulatto carpenter, married Nancy, a black woman, and they had one child, John. Marvin Gibbes, a mulatto painter, married Ann, a black woman. They had three children: John, Jane, and Tena. Thomas Fanning, a mulatto butcher, married Libby, a black woman, and they had one child, Margaret.[3]

South Carolina was unusual among Southern states before the Civil War in allowing interracial marriage. Records show marriages in antebellum Charleston not just between blacks—free or slave—and mulattoes but also between and among blacks, mulattoes, Indians, and whites.[4] For example, Isaac Praleau, a white cotton market worker, married Anna, a black woman. They had two children, Damon and Sarah. Robert Wells, a white carpenter, married Eliza, a mulatto woman, and they had three children: Marsha, James, and Florence. Abraham Taylor, a mulatto tailor, married Isabella, an Indian woman. Joseph Dereef, an Indian wood dealer, married Mary, a mulatto woman, and they had five children: Abby, Michael, Maria, Joseph, and Mary Ann.[5]

These unions were not the norm, however. Most free blacks in Charleston lived in all-black households in 1860, the first year the census provided such data. Of the 3,232 free blacks in the city, 2,829 lived in all-black households. Of these 548 all-black households, 269 were headed by two parents. With women outnumbering men by 50 percent, it is surprising that the number of two-parent free black households was this high. Among single-parent free black households, women headed 261 and men headed 18. The typical free black household included five people, a mixture of husbands and wives, children, grandparents, uncles and aunts, cousins, boarders, and sometimes friends. In these households, children were often named after their parents.[6]

To make a living, most of the city's free blacks performed unskilled and semiskilled labor; others were skilled as coopers, carpenters, blacksmiths, plasterers, and so on. A few of these artisans managed to establish their own businesses. In addition, there were free blacks who owned large amounts of property in real estate and slaves. Several also owned businesses that catered to a white clientele. This group of property owners constituted the black elite of Charleston, many of whom were mulattoes who socialized and intermarried within their own small group.[7]

Taken as a whole, Charleston's black population was always large and, between 1790 and 1850, always exceeded the size of the white population. In 1790, blacks constituted just over 50 percent of the total city population of 16,459.[8] By 1800, the total population was up to 18,924, and blacks constituted about 53 percent.[9] Throughout the next few decades, the percentage of blacks in Charleston remained fairly stable, increasing only modestly because of native births and the importation of slaves (see table 2). During the 1850s, however, cotton prices rose, sparking a demand for more slaves to be used as field hands. As a result, between seven thousand and eight thousand slaves in Charleston were sold or exported by their owners to the rural plantations. By 1860, the proportion of slaves in Charleston's population had dropped to 34 percent. Furthermore, a steady stream of white immigrants transformed Charleston from a city that was 53 percent black in 1850 to one that was 58 percent white on the eve of the Civil War.[10]

Slaves and free blacks often belonged to the same social circle in antebellum Charleston and often intermarried. A few slaves were able because of their marriages to establish strong ties to the city's free black elite. Charles Just was one such slave. He belonged to George Just, a German immigrant who built wharves. Charles married Mary Anne, a free black woman, and lived with her and their two sons, Simeon and

James, on Calhoun Street. Charles's friends in the city included such upper-class free blacks as Daniel Payne and the Ryan, Taylor, Weston, and Holloway families. He was honored by Augustus and Hannah Ryan in 1842 by being selected as a godparent to their newborn child, who was, in part, named after him. He became a well-respected member of the Cumberland Street Methodist Church, whose congregation included many free blacks. And in 1844, along with seventeen other blacks, he helped to establish the Unity and Friendship Society, an organization designed to take care of the family of each contributing member in the event of the member's death.[11]

Marriages of slave men to free black women in Charleston increased the sex ratio imbalance between slave men and slave women of marriageable age—between fifteen and forty-nine years old—and worsened the chances of slave women finding husbands in Charleston. While theoretically they could marry free black men as well as slave men, a slave woman's chances of marriage to a free black man were small, given the limited number of free black men in the city and the disadvantage to a free man of marrying a slave woman. Charleston's slave women usually experienced limited success in finding spouses from among the ranks of urban free black men. In 1850 and 1860, they had greater success among slave men in the rural hinterlands, where there was a better sex ratio balance between black men and black women of marriage age than in Charleston.

Slave men in Goose Creek, James Island, Edisto Island, Johns Island, and other outlying rural areas were only slightly outnumbered by rural slave women in the age group of fifteen to forty-nine (see table 3). In 1850, the ratio of men to women in this group was 1 to 1.15; in the city it was 1 to 1.21. By 1860 the disparity between marriage-aged slave men and marriage-aged slave women in the city had narrowed to a ratio of 1 to 1.06, which is slightly less disparity than found in the same year in the rural slave population, where the ratio was 1 male to 1.07 females (see table 4). As a result, a marriage-aged woman from the city's slave population had a better chance of marrying another urban slave in 1860 than in 1850.

There was little change between 1850 and 1860, however, in the age composition of the slave population, which remained relatively young. Nearly 85 percent of slaves in Charleston were under fifty in 1850; in 1860 the percentage was 87 (see table 4). Color was also a distinctive characteristic in the slave population in 1850 and continued to be so in 1860. In 1850, 89 percent (17,380) of Charleston's total slave population of 19,532 was black; and in 1860, 81 percent (11,257) out of a total slave population of 13,911 was black.[12] While the number of slaves who were mulattoes grew, the vast majority of Charleston's slaves continued to be of a dark hue.

Residential patterns in antebellum Charleston suggest some spatial segregation by color and status. Slaves, free blacks, and whites were distributed throughout the four city wards and Charleston Neck in 1850. The highest concentration of both slaves and whites was in ward four and Charleston Neck, probably because most slaves lived in the same house or on the same property as their owners. The highest concentration of free blacks was also in Charleston Neck (see table 5). By 1860, Charleston Neck had been annexed to the city and Charleston was organized into eight wards, with the entire population fairly evenly distributed among the wards. But, as in 1850, the highest concentration of both slaves and whites was in ward four. The fewest slaves lived in wards seven and eight. The largest number of free blacks lived in wards four, five, and six (see table 6).[13]

On the eve of the Civil War, slaves, free blacks, and whites lived side by side on many of the same streets. Most notable of these were Broad, Calhoun, Church, Coming, East Battery, East Bay, King, Meeting, Queen, St. Philip, Tradd, and Wentworth, which had a combined population of 19,622 or 45 percent of the total population of Charleston. Records show only 15 streets, none heavily populated, out of a total of 210 in Charleston in 1861 on which no black, slave or free, resided. There were also a few streets on which only free blacks and slaves lived. These were Ashe, Dereef's Court, Hester, Huger, Rumney, Thompson's Court, and Wilson.[14] Although only a small proportion of the black population lived on these streets, the locations are noteworthy because they provided opportunities for slaves and free blacks to be in constant contact, away from whites, and thus helped contribute to the development of a sense of community and freedom among blacks and enhanced the likelihood of slaves and free blacks intermarrying.

In 1850 the total number of slaveholders in Charleston was 3,381. Of this number, 191 were black—123 female and 68 male.[15] The most common slaveholding by 1850 in Charleston was two slaves. Slightly more than half of all slaveholders owned fewer than five slaves, nearly 75 percent owned fewer than eight, and 90 percent owned fewer than fifteen.[16] By 1860, the number of slaveholders in Charleston had dropped to 2,186. At this time the gap between black female and black male slaveowners was not as wide as it had been in 1850 and, within four years, black male slaveowners outnumbered black female slaveowners.[17] Patterns of slaveholding did not change significantly between 1850 and 1860. In 1860 approximately 55 percent of slaveholders owned fewer than five slaves; still nearly 75 percent owned fewer than eight, and 92 percent owned fewer than fifteen. The most common slaveholding was still two.[18] Thus, in 1860, as in 1850, a typical slaveholding unit would not have included both parties to a slave marriage, and certainly not all members of an immediate family. Furthermore, even in slaveholding units large enough to have included all members of an immediate family, the extended family—the aunts, uncles, cousins, and grandparents who formed the slaves' notion of family—would not have been part of these units. The predominance of small slaveholdings meant that most families were divided among several owners, a situation that attacked the integrity of family life and exacerbated the potential trauma of sale.[19]

Thus, slavery in Charleston and throughout the South placed a heavy burden on family life. Slaves could never consider a place of residence as a permanent home, and families could scarcely exist in bondage. Marriage contracts between blacks were not recognized by law, and furthermore, marriages between slave men and slave women rested on the consent of their white masters, who could at any time declare a marriage null and void and break up entire families.[20] The children of slaves did not belong to their parents but were the property of the mother's owner. And even though some urban slaves had the advantage of "living-out"— of living outside the master's property, an arrangement that provided a degree of privacy that was almost nonexistent in most rural areas— attachments were seldom permanent. Often, men were able to visit their wives in the urban slave quarters or even live with them and share small bits of personal property. Children usually referred to these men as their fathers, and friends regarded the slave men and women as couples. But whatever bond existed between slaves could easily be broken. All it would take for this to occur would be a master deciding to sell a marital partner or deciding to move away, taking one marital partner or family member with him. Further, in the event of an owner's death, all slaves from his estate would be susceptible to sale under the new master.

Contemporary accounts of life in the South are full of stories about forced separation among the slaves of Charleston that all underscore the unpredictability and misery of life under slavery. James Stuart, the contemporary English observer, records the case of one man, for example, who was brokenhearted because his wife and two children were purchased by one man while he was purchased by another. After two years of living in the same town as his wife and children, the man still had not seen them and feared that "he would be beaten within an inch of his life if he ventured to go even to the corner of the street" to try to do so.[21] Norrece Jones records a story told by Susan Hamlin, a house servant for Edward Fuller, about a couple who were married one night and learned the following morning that the wife had been sold. The new bride was so incensed over the turn of events that she "got in de street an' cursed de [owner] fur all she could find."[22] John Blassingame's *Slave Testimony* is filled with firsthand accounts of heart-wrenching separations. For example, one of slave woman Rosa Barnwell's twelve children was sold to a master in Texas, and when William Summerson was only seven years old, his brother and mother were sold down South. Benjamin Holmes, a slave trained as a tailor, had been sold away from his mother to Tennessee when he was still a child.[23]

Few places in the prewar South could have produced scenes of human misery more poignant than the auction block in Charleston. One slave woman, after watching her child sold away from her, wept and raved her anguish. As she ran through the crowd trying to retrieve her child and shouting, "They have sold my babe! They have sold my babe!" white bystanders hooted at her, mocking her pain.[24] At another slave sale, a distraught couple watched helplessly as their children were sold away. Grabbing at her young children, the sobbing mother cried out, "I can't leff my children! I wont leff my children!"[25] Sometimes slaves sold in Charleston were allowed brief wharf-side embraces from relatives who had come to bid them good-bye as they were transferred from the auction block to a ship bound for New Orleans. Often, however, the families of those sold at auction had no idea where a family member was going and no opportunity to say good-bye.[26]

Despite the destructive effect of slavery on the black family, Charleston's slaves celebrated marriages and lived as family units as much as the system would permit. Although slave marriages were not sanctioned by law, they occurred frequently, sometimes accompanied by much festivity. One contemporary author, Charles Lyle, describes a formal slave wedding he saw during a trip to Charleston in the 1840s. The bride was attended by bridesmaids dressed in white, and an Episcopal minister performed the ceremony.[27] Once they were married, most slaves were loyal to one another and felt mutual bonds with their children and extended families. Robert Smalls, a Charleston slave who later became a military hero and a politician, maintained that blacks from the rural hinterlands "often walk fifteen miles on Saturday night to see a cousin."[28] Charleston slaves respectfully addressed one another as sir or madam and as a matter of common courtesy always made specific inquiries after the well-being of one another's family.[29] When emancipation came, former slaves promptly moved to make their marriages legal by signing contracts and embarked on campaigns to relocate family members separated during slavery.

By the time of emancipation, slaves in Charleston and other Southern cities had already experienced a degree of freedom unknown to those living in the rural hinterland. Laws prohibiting slaves from being on the city streets without passes from their masters were rarely enforced. It was inconvenient for a master to prepare a pass every time a slave was sent on an errand, and it was also difficult to confine slaves to their quarters.[30] This freedom resulted in numerous economic opportunities for both slaves and free blacks in antebellum Charleston.[31] The milling industry, for example, relied heavily on black labor. Chisolm Mill, Bennett's Mill, and Gibbes and Williams Steam Saw Mill used unskilled, semiskilled, and skilled slaves. Of the 160 slaves employed by the West Point Rice Mill in Charleston, many were coopers, engineers, carpenters, and blacksmiths. According to the 1848 census for the city of Charleston, there was no trade from which blacks were totally excluded.[32] Slaves did the servile labor usually avoided by whites and dubbed "nigger work,"[33] but in Charleston slaves also worked in at least thirty-eight different occupations requiring them to be skilled as mechanics, shoemakers, bricklayers, and so on.[34] Slaves were used by the Charleston Bridge Company, the Charleston Gas Light Company, and the South Carolina Canal and Railroad Company.[35] Slaves cleaned and repaired the streets of the city[36] and worked as both common laborers and artisans in the federal arsenal in Charleston.[37] Even the *Charleston Courier* used slave labor in its daily operations.[38]

The busy port of Charleston, from which rice, corn, cotton, indigo, tobacco, and sugar cane were shipped daily while more products from around the world flowed in, depended on slave labor at all levels of skill, as did the seafood industry, which commanded high prices for crabs, shrimp, oysters, and lobsters. Slaves were used, of course, as wharf hands for the strenuous and brutish work of loading and unloading ships, but also they piloted steamboats and sloops that sailed as far as Washington, D.C., and served at various levels in international trade.

Most urban slaves were domestics. They usually lived in the master's house and performed the household chores. They prepared food, washed clothes, cleaned the house, and rendered personal services to the master or mistress. They also looked after the children and the elderly, as well as attended to the needs of visitors. Of course, female domestics performed the bulk of this work, but both men and women made up the household work force. Some men served as valets for the masters, while others handled the horses and carriages or cared for the grounds and gardens. The duties of the male servant often required that he run errands in the city or surrounding areas. Picking up or delivering packages and driving for the owner sometimes involved absences of many hours, even overnight. The typical workday of a domestic servant began at five in the morning and ran until curfew at nine or ten at night. But in effect domestics were always on duty, having to be ready at any time to answer a summons from the master or mistress. There were no days off, not even Sundays, which in some homes were the most active days.[39]

Throughout most of the antebellum period Charleston's occupational structure continued to expand, creating more and more employment opportunities for slaves, free blacks, native-born Southern and Northern whites, and foreign-born whites of various national backgrounds. Slave and free black workers expected these opportunities to continue to exist after the war. Those who were trained in coopering, plastering, blacksmithing, and other mechanical arts especially wanted to pursue their trades. In fact, one of the major factors drawing rural blacks into Charleston after the war was the notion that economic opportunities abounded in urban centers. But fulfillment of these expectations was simply not feasible. All of Charleston's (and South Carolina's) banking capital was destroyed in the war, and the city was left in financial and physical ruin, with many formerly wealthy whites living in poverty. Thus, while Charleston's occupational structure was broad enough to provide blacks with seemingly unlimited economic opportunity before the war, it would not continue to do so after emancipation, and all of the former slaves' visions of increased economic opportunity would not be realized in the Reconstruction period.

As long as opportunity abounded in the prewar years, however, whenever slaveowners found they had more slaves than they could employ, they were able to hire them out or to require them to find their own employment. Charles Just, for example, the slave who helped establish the Unity and Friendship Society in Charleston, accumulated substantial savings by hiring out his labor after his designated hours of work for his master. He was so successful that he managed to build up a small estate, held in the name of his free wife, Mary Anne.[40] In 1851, Robert Smalls's owner, John McKee, hired him out to work as a waiter, a stevedore, a drayman, a sailmaker, a sailor, and a pilot. In 1857, McKee gave Smalls permission to hire out his own time, and in return Smalls paid his master fifteen dollars a month for the privilege.[41] William Summerson, as a young boy, was also hired out by his master. But when he became old enough, he hired out his own labor on a steamer operating between Charleston and St. John's River, Florida, paying his master a stipulated monthly figure for the privilege.[42] During the Civil War, Mack Duff Williams hired himself out and paid his master, John Wilson, out of money he earned as a farm laborer and wood chopper on Louis Steel's farm.[43] Susan Hamilton, a slave woman, reported that most of her master's twenty-seven slaves living on St. Phillip Street did not work in the household at all but were hired out full time.[44]

Hiring-out systems in the urban South provided an unintended advantage to runaway rural slaves, who would go to Charleston and hire themselves out for any available work, as, for example, lumbermen, fishermen, wharf hands, wood cutters, canal diggers, railroad hands, or fence-rail splitters. Most hiring-out opportunities involved working for whites, either slaveholders or those who did not own slaves, but sometimes runaway slaves hired themselves out to free blacks. William Westcoat, a plantation owner, found two of his runaway slaves working on vessels owned by Charleston free blacks.[45]

The hiring-out system provided some slaves with experience in negotiating with whites for work, wages, and living quarters and thus helped them become more assertive in their actions toward whites. But the limited taste of freedom these slaves experienced filled them with expectations of expanded economic and social opportunities that were not fulfilled after legal emancipation.

Charleston's domestic slaves were so routinely ill-treated, according to contemporary accounts, that regardless of whether they had ever tasted the limited freedom of being hired out, few if any from this category of slaves remained with their former owners to work for wages after emancipation.[46] The correspondence of the period is replete with instances of slaves being mistreated by their masters or mistresses that, taken together, belie the notion that among the servant or domestic class, relations with the owners were on the whole intimate and satisfactory. One owner was so cruel that it was said to be very rare for one of his slaves to survive a whipping: "He'd lick his slaves to death."[47] An English visitor to the South reveals that during his stay in Charleston he saw a man who seemed to take delight in slapping the face and ears of his slave.[48] Fredrika Bremer learned on a trip to Charleston that a young servant girl at the house where she was boarding had been flogged by a man who helped operate the house.[49] In a detailed, firsthand account, James Stuart comments that in the Charleston boardinghouse where he lived, not a day passed without his hearing that his landlady had whipped and misused her slaves. Whenever one of the female slaves disobeyed her mistress, the mistress beat her severely, and when she no longer had the strength to continue the beating, she insisted that the barkeeper, Mr. Ferguson, finish the punishment. Stuart later discovered that his landlady beat all her slaves every day, using either her fists or a cowhide thong. Once he saw her strike a young male servant so hard behind the ear that he reeled from the blow. On Stuart's last day at the boarding house, when he asked the cook why he had tears in his eyes, the man told Stuart "he had got such a sharp blow on the cheek bone from the Mistress that it had unmanned him for the moment."[50]

The testimony of the two sisters Angelina and Sarah Grimké—two Charlestonians who became such ardent and vocal abolitionists in the South that they were eventually forced into exile—is filled with horrifying incidents of the cruel treatment of slaves in Charleston two decades before the Civil War. Sarah Grimké recalled hearing one woman say that she had had the eyes of her waiting maid slit for some petty theft. And Sarah Grimké had heard of a woman in Charleston who had starved a female slave to death. Angelina Grimké described a male slave who was "too old to work, and therefore his allowance was stopped, and he was turned out to make his living by begging."[51] Owners who did not wish to punish their slaves themselves could, for a small fee, send them to be punished at the dreaded workhouse on Magazine Street, also known as the sugar house.[52] If slaves were caught in violation of the nine o'clock evening curfew, they too were taken to the workhouse and punished, unless their owners were willing to pay a small fine.[53] The threat of punishment for violating curfew was very real, even though there was some laxness in its enforcement. Sir William Howard Russell describes on a visit to Charleston seeing a group of blacks "shuffling through the streets in all haste in order to escape the patrol and the last peal of the curfew."[54] When the Englishman James Stuart returned to his lodgings one evening after curfew, he found the male servants of the house asleep in the hallway passages with their clothes still on, having rushed home just ahead of the curfew deadline.[55]

Injuries inflicted by floggings at the workhouse were sometimes so severe that when the slaves punished there were returned home they were kept outside the house for days because the nasty odor of their wounds was too much for the inhabitants of the house to endure. And of course these mutilated and wretched slaves were hidden from visitors.[56] Angelina Grimké told grisly stories about injuries received at the workhouse. A female slave sent there by her owner was whipped so severely that one could have laid a whole finger in the gashes on her back. The same owner also sent another female slave there to be imprisoned and worked on the treadmill for several days; for nearly a month after her return to her mistress, this slave remained lame from the punishment.[57]

Fredrika Bremer, in recounting stories of the cruelties of masters to their slaves, describes one wealthy planter who so exceeded white society's acceptance of cruelty to slaves that he was put in jail for his barbarous treatment of his slaves. Bremer found it particularly disturbing that some of the vicious acts she reports had been performed by women, many of them members of the upper echelon of Charleston society.[58]

The abundant evidence of the mistreatment of slaves in and around Charleston is somewhat tempered by accounts of more humane treatment. One contemporary visitor to antebellum Charleston notes that in one family the domestic slaves appeared to be relatively at ease and that the older slaves of long tenure with the family were treated with respect. He also notes that, upon leaving on or returning from a journey, the women of another family he visited would shake hands with all the servants. This observer qualifies his remarks, however, by admitting that his view of master-slave relations might have been skewed a bit by his having observed these relations only in the best families in Charleston and by his not having observed the treatment of field hands.[59]

But for every story of a "good" master there are dozens of stories of ill treatment. A slave who once paddled a canoe carrying Fredrika Bremer was very straightforward and candid in his replies to her questions about the natures of various masters. One, he said, was a "good master! Blessed master, ma'am," but another was a "bad master, ma'am! Beats his servants. Cuts them to pieces, ma'am!"[60]

Many slaves refused to endure such injustices.[61] Some simply ran off

Antebellum-period slave cabins. Avery Research Center for African-American History and Culture, College of Charleston.

Old Slave Mort. Avery Research Center for African-American History and Culture, College of Charleston.

TO BE SOLD, on board the Ship *Bance-Island*, on tuesday the 6th of *May* next, at *Ashley-Ferry*; a choice cargo of about 250 fine healthy

NEGROES,

just arrived from the Windward & Rice Coast. —The utmost care has already been taken, and shall be continued, to keep them free from the least danger of being infected with the SMALL-POX, no boat having been on board, and all other communication with people from *Charles-Town* prevented.

Austin, Laurens, & Appleby.

N. B. Full one Half of the above Negroes have had the SMALL-POX in their own Country.

The antebellum period. An advertisement for the sale of slaves. Black Charleston Photographic Collection, College of Charleston Library.

The antebellum period. "Uncle Billy"—Billy Simmons, slave news carrier for the *Charleston Courier*. Black Charleston Photographic Collection, College of Charleston Library.

The antebellum period.
Charlotte Middleton and
nurse. Black Charleston
Photographic Collection,
College of Charleston Library.

A plantation scene in South Carolina in 1860.
South Carolina Historical Society, Charleston.

Civil War. Union officers and enlisted men of the ironclad *Passaie* attending religious services, Charleston Harbor. Black Charleston Photographic Collection, College of Charleston Library.

Civil War. Charge at Fort Wagner by the Fifty-fourth Massachusetts Colored Regiment, July 18, 1863. Black Charleston Photographic Collection, College of Charleston Library.

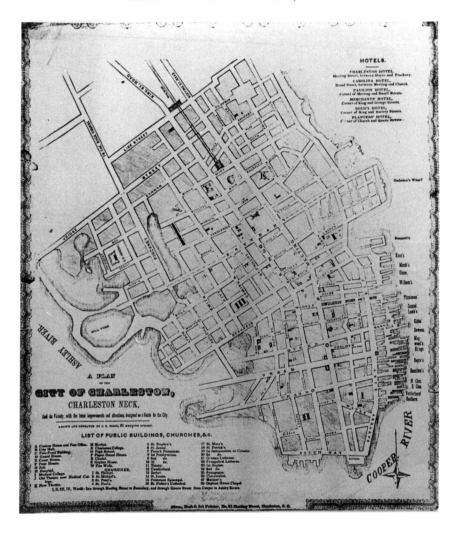

Charleston in 1842, including Charleston Neck.
South Carolina Historical Society, Charleston.

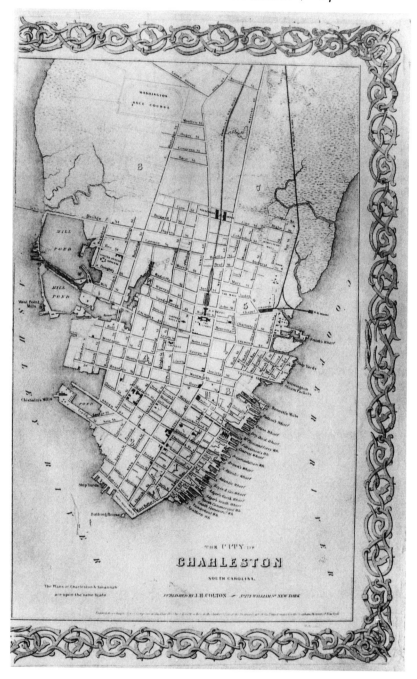

Charleston in 1855. South Carolina Historical Society, Charleston.

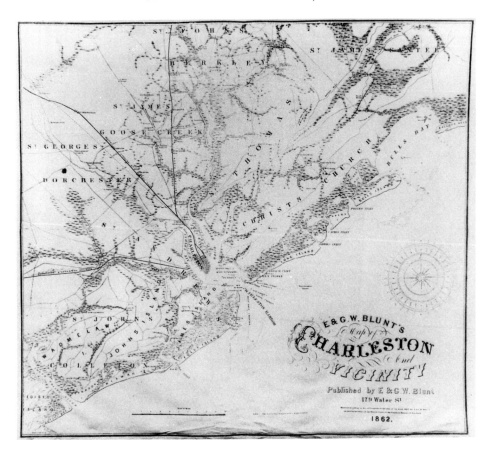

Charleston and vicinity in 1862. South Carolina Historical Society, Charleston.

and hid in the city, others tried to pass for free or white, and still others attempted to purchase their freedom and move to where they might live peacefully as free men and women. The *Charleston Courier* regularly ran stories about missing and runaway slaves during the decades before the Civil War. One story tells of a slave who managed to work on the wharves for several months, eluding capture by his owner. While the owner was trying to find the runaway, another of his slaves escaped into the congestion of town life.[62] Another slave, named Stephen, left his master's house and lived in the city with a free black woman for two years before being discovered.[63] A Charleston runaway with training as a tailor, whose owner described him as intelligent, passed as free for many years by using falsified papers.[64] Another runaway was so light skinned that his owner described him as a "bright mulatto, . . . so bright, that he can readily, as he has done before, pass himself for a white."[65] A young male slave whom J. Benwell met not long after his arrival in Charleston "was saving money for his ransom, and in two years intended to proceed to Montreal, in Canada."[66]

Charleston's black community carried a long tradition of being assertive of its rights from the prewar years into the Reconstruction years, despite stringent laws and heavy military patrols designed to quell the white minority's fears of violence and slave uprising. Much of that fear grew out of the 1822 Denmark Vesey insurrection plot. Vesey, a free black, conspired with a group of slaves, including Gullah Jack and Monday Gell, to seize the Charleston city guard and acquire control of the arsenals. Afterward, they intended to supply the slaves from the countryside and surrounding islands with weapons, set fire to the city, and slay all the whites. The leaders expected to have some three thousand blacks take part in the insurrection; but a few informers betrayed the plot and 130 blacks were arrested. After a trial, thirty-five conspirators were hanged, including Denmark Vesey and Gullah Jack, and another thirty-four were deported.[67] In the event of slave revolts, trials were not unusual, although in all other instances slaves were not accorded this right.

The Vesey conspiracy increased the fear of black uprisings and facilitated passage of a more rigorous slave code and the first in a series of Black Seamen Acts, the sole purpose of which was to isolate the city's large black population from the influence of free black sailors. Outward forms of vigilance were never again relaxed in Charleston.[68] Much of the correspondence of the time reveals white Charlestonians' preoccupation with fears of slave revolts, fears so great that, one contemporary notes, "[T]he patrol guard set as regularly every night as if an invasion were expected."[69] Almost three decades after the attempted insurrection, James Johnston Pettigrew, describing the city of Charleston to his family in North Carolina, was struck by the unusual military appearance of the city. Watchmen wore military uniforms and were extremely well armed, with night sticks, muskets, and bayonets. "Such precautions," Johnston thought, were "absolutely necessary in a city of which more than a majority of the population are slaves" and where the slaves, as residents of a seaport, were very susceptible to the corrupting influences of outsiders.[70] Five years later, another contemporary observed the same military preparedness in Charleston, where well-armed soldiers, usually in pairs, patrolled the city on horseback all night until six o'clock the next morning. In the matter of a few minutes, if need be, "the whole militia and all the independent companies of the city could be summoned with ten thousand guns for defensive purposes against the blacks."[71]

Although white fears of a black insurrection were never realized after the Vesey plot, Charleston's slaves continued to assert themselves throughout the antebellum period, using brute force, sometimes even to the point of murder. When a hotel keeper beat his slave cook, the cook retaliated by beating the hotel keeper nearly to death. The cook then fled and was never heard from again.[72] Adam Hodgson reports a conversation he had at a prison in Charleston with a slave who had succeeded in murdering his master.[73] Harrie and Janie were a slave couple who, after being whipped by their master, devised a plan to kill the whole family by poisoning them. They almost succeeded. One morning they put poison in the breakfast and killed all but two family members, who were saved only because they overslept. After an investigation, the two slaves were hanged from an oak tree on Ashley Avenue.[74] For six months, beginning Christmas Eve 1825, a fire was set every night in Charleston, intensifying white fears. More than one hundred thousand dollars' worth of property was destroyed in just one of these fires. But only one person was arrested for arson in the six months, a slave woman named Winnie, who was arrested in June 1826 for attempting to burn her master's home to the ground.[75]

The anger that fueled blacks' acts of retaliation against bondage and whites' acts of cruelty took many turns in the prewar years and would reemerge during Reconstruction. In July 1849, a slave named Nicholas defied the workhouse master and threatened to strike him with a hammer. The white man escaped through a door, but half a dozen black prisoners gave chase and threw themselves against the locked entrance. One of them shouted that he was Santa Anna, the Mexican leader who had become a hero to American slaves because he was a person of color who opposed the institution of slavery and the importation of slaves to Texas. The following day, after Nicholas was captured and tried in what was no more than a charade of a trial, a mob of whites threatened to retaliate by demolishing the nearby "nigger" Calvary Episcopal Church.[76] The historical record is full of such cases of black violence against whites, leaving no question that black Charlestonians were not contented with their lot and were willing to strike blows for freedom, regardless of the consequences.

Life for free blacks in antebellum Charleston was not much better than it was for slaves. Only the wealthy elite, who made up less than 20 percent of free blacks, lived in a measure of comfort and relative security.[77] The few rights free blacks enjoyed in the early decades of the nineteenth century were steadily eroded under the weight of legislation to restrict their freedom. Fear of all blacks, free or enslaved, intensified after the quelling of the Vesey insurrection plot, and the status of the free black increasingly began to resemble that of the slave. Laws were passed, for example, that required every free black to have a certificate of freedom in his or her possession at all times. Without the certificate a free black risked being claimed as a slave.[78]

Furthermore, Charleston and other local jurisdictions required all free blacks to register with the police or court authorities. By the 1830s, migration to another Southern state was either restricted or prohibited. In South Carolina and most other Southern states, free blacks did not have the right to vote, and their right of assembly was proscribed. South Carolina law also prohibited free blacks from serving on juries or testifying against whites. Free blacks convicted of crimes routinely received harsher punishments than did whites convicted of comparable crimes. Often, convicted free blacks were whipped prior to imprisonment or even sold into bondage.[79]

In addition, a curfew was imposed on the evening activities of free blacks, and the presence of a "respectable" white person was required at the meetings of black churches or benevolent societies. Because free blacks were seen as potential insurrectionists, they were discouraged from mingling with the slave population and they were required to apply for a special license in order to legally possess either a gun or a dog, since the motives for such ownership were always questioned by whites. It was not unusual for free blacks to be identified as vagrants and sold into servitude.[80]

Despite the efforts by whites to keep free blacks and enslaved blacks apart, an urban center like Charleston necessarily brought them into close contact with one another. There was little social distinction made between the masses of free blacks and the slaves. They were often engaged in the same kinds of trades; they gathered and socialized in the same taverns and regularly attended church services together,[81] and they intermarried. Entire neighborhoods developed where slaves who had been granted permission to "live out" lived side by side with free blacks. A classic example of this could be found in Charleston Neck, the northern part of the city. Here slaves and free blacks were able to establish a close-knit community.[82] Accordingly, when South Carolina seceded from the Union and the Civil War fighting began, it was natural for free blacks and slaves to participate together in the war to ensure a Union victory. Likewise, during Reconstruction when white Charlestonians sought to deny the former slaves the freedoms entitled them as a result of the Union victory, blacks who had been free before the war also felt threatened and joined with former slaves to counter such moves by the white authorities.

Charleston's free black elite stood apart from the free black masses, distinguished by wealth and by color. In 1860, the elite group numbered no more than 500 out of 3,237 free blacks, and the vast majority were mulattoes.[83] Most owned both slaves and real estate.[84] The Kinlock family, for example, were wealthy millwrights and plantation owners. The Holloway family ran a successful carpentry business and supplemented their wealth with heavy investments in land. Similarly, Thomas Small was a carpenter and real estate speculator. Charleston's best-known hotelier was Jehu Jones, who also held title to several valuable sites in the center of the city's business district on Broad Street.[85] This free black elite held themselves aloof from the masses of free blacks and slaves, choosing to interact socially[86] and to marry among themselves.

Although members of Charleston's free black elite were sometimes subjected to the same restrictions as were the masses of free blacks and slaves, they were usually able to escape the full impact because they had personal relationships with powerful whites in the city who shielded them from persecution. They developed these relationships at work, in church, and in their neighborhoods. Prominent Southern white men were often the legal guardians, and sometimes the blood relatives, of free blacks; it was fairly common practice for the white and free black aristocracies to mix. The free black elite could not have built their substantial social and economic accommodations during the antebellum years without this informal, personal connection with influential whites.[87]

As the white South moved toward secession, beginning in the late 1850s, the black elite's social position grew more and more tenuous and tilted ever more steeply toward that of the slaves. There was no solid middle ground for free blacks in the South. Most whites saw mulattoes as light-skinned blacks, not as a separate racial group, and so, on the belief that anyone with a trace of black blood should be considered a slave, pushed them toward the status of slave. White friends of the elite refused to defend them during the enslavement crisis of the 1850s when white South Carolinians sought to enslave all free blacks, including the free black aristocracy. The situation became so bad that some of the free black elite made up their minds that to survive they would have to leave the city.[88]

Hundreds of Charleston's free blacks did leave the city in the midst of this crisis,[89] but most of the free black aristocracy chose to remain. They felt unable to walk away from their accomplishments and soon became trapped by the depreciated value of their property. After 1861, they were also hampered by the business standstill brought on by secession, as well as by the increasing difficulty in getting safe passage out of the state. More important, they remained with the hope of reestablishing their old personal connections with powerful whites once the opportunity presented itself.[90]

Many of Charleston's free black elite actually supported the Confederate war effort, for they were deeply entrenched in the economic order of the South. Barely one month after South Carolina seceded from the Union, eighty-two black Charlestonians offered their services in a petition to the state through the mayor. The petition proclaimed:

> We are by birth citizens of South Carolina, in our veins is the blood of the white race in some half, in the others much more, our attachments

> are with you, our hopes of safety and protection is in South Carolina, our allegiance is due alone to her, in her defense we are willing to offer up our lives and all that is dear to us, we therefore take the liberty of asking the privilege of volunteering our services to the State at this time, where she needs the services of all her true and devoted citizens. We are willing to be assigned to any service where we can be made useful.[91]

However, the free black signatories to this petition volunteered their services only if the community would promise to take care of their families, an obligation the Confederacy did not fulfill for whites until well into the war.

Wealthy free blacks did provide nonmilitary forms of support to the Confederate cause. Francis Sasportas, a butcher, sold meat to the Confederate government to feed soldiers.[92] Others contributed money. The *Charleston Mercury* for September 5, 1861, for example, reports that the "Free Colored Men . . . contributed $450 to sustain the cause of the South."[93] The elite Brown Fellowship Society voted to donate $50 toward medical expenses for sick and injured Confederate soldiers.[94] Not to be outdone, a group of free black women collected $450 and presented it to the YMCA for the Confederacy.[95] A measure of the trust white Charleston had in the free black elite was the decision by the city council in 1862 to enroll them in the city's fire-fighting companies.

Self-interest, both economic and social, was clearly behind black support of the Confederacy. Those who owned slaves and other property stood to lose everything should the Union triumph. By aligning themselves with the Confederacy, the free black elite sought to clearly separate themselves from the social status of the free black masses and the slaves and to strengthen the ties to white elites that had been weakened during the enslavement crisis. Indeed, as a consequence of the close ties with aristocratic whites, some free blacks made huge profits during the war.[96]

While the free black elite attempted to ingratiate itself with and profit from the Confederacy, all other blacks in Charleston, free and enslaved, looked to the Union forces for support of their resistance and retaliation and their attempts to escape to freedom. In a visit to Charleston before secession, the Northern abolitionist James Redpath noted the aggressive tendencies of the city's blacks but concluded that blacks dreaded the power of the slaveholders and might well have attempted an insurrection had they not been kept in check by the strictly enforced city ordinances and the fear of potential traitors among them. Redpath also believed, because of conversations he had with slaves, that things could change drastically.

> If the guards who now keep nightly watch were to be otherwise employed—if the roar of hostile cannon was to be heard by the slaves, or

a hostile fleet was seen sailing up the bay of Charleston—then, as surely as God lives, would the sewers of the city be instantly filled with the blood of the slavemasters.[97]

Redpath's vision was never realized, but with the outbreak of war and the proximity of the federal forces occupying the South Carolina Sea Islands by the fall of 1861, blacks in Charleston began with some confidence to strike continuous blows for freedom. A federal fleet had swept into Port Royal Sound, fifty miles south of Charleston, on August 21 and captured Hilton Head Island, Port Royal, and Beaufort. The Union forces thus had coaling stations for the blockading fleet, huge stores of cotton, and most significant, a base from which to attack Charleston and Savannah.[98]

The occupation of the Sea Islands alarmed whites living in the vicinity of Charleston. There were constant rumors that Union soldiers and gunboats were being rushed to Charleston, stoking the very real fear that the city itself would soon be attacked. In early November, John Berkley Grimball observed "great panic" and noted that "many men have removed their families to the interior."[99] James Petigru heard people talking incessantly about "setting fire to the city if they cannot defend it."[100]

Fears of a slave insurrection intensified when planters from the Sea Islands, fleeing from the occupying federal troops, took refuge in Charleston. Those who were able to "save" some of their slaves brought them to Charleston, increasing the size of the already large urban slave population and aggravating fears among whites of the influence that federal forces in the area could exert on this huge and dangerous black population.[101] Many of the planters had watched alarming numbers of their slaves fleeing to enemy lines, and some felt betrayed. For example, one wealthy planter, Louis Manigault, maintained that "this war has taught the perfect impossibility of placing the least confidence in any negro."[102]

The pressures of the war changed the relationship of master to slave in and around Charleston. Emboldened by the presence of federal troops, many slaves escaped. Those who remained gained the confidence to release their pent-up bitterness toward whites.[103] Some owners tried to prevent slaves from escaping to Union lines by increasing the frequency and brutality of whippings, and others simply shot their slaves. Slaves retaliated by helping Union soldiers capture their owners and asked the soldiers for arms as protection against vindictive owners.

Throughout the war, slaveholders left Charleston and moved their families and their slaves to the interior for safety.[104] But many slaves refused to go. They wanted to stay close to Union lines, where their opportunities to escape would be greater. All around the city slaves watched constantly for the arrival of Union boats. And fear among the whites intensified. Emma Holmes, a wealthy white Charlestonian, writes that her friend Maria "feared the Negroes might not go to the upcountry, as Willie [her husband] could not be there to make them."[105] One slave, William Summerson, prevented his wife's master from carrying her to the interior by hiding her, with the aid of friends, until they could escape together.[106] When slaves such as Benjamin Holmes refused to go to the interior, their owners sold them to a slave trader.[107]

Every report or rumor of an escape inspired other slaves. In one week forty-eight slaves escaped from a single plantation near the Charleston and Savannah Railroad. Forty slaves owned by Evans Elding ran away in a group that also included two prized male house servants belonging to another master; they had almost three days' head start before a search party of whites was sent after them.[108]

Probably the most spectacular slave escape of all time was Robert Smalls's commandeering of the Confederate steamer *Planter* in May 1862. As the hired-out slave pilot of the ship, Smalls convinced the enslaved sailors to use the ship to escape to freedom. While the ship was anchored in Charleston Harbor and the captain was on shore, the black sailors secretly guided their families on board. They stayed overnight at anchor, and on the following day Smalls maneuvered the ship beyond the Confederate's heavily fortified lines in the harbor to the safety of the federal blockade lines. For this heroic feat, Smalls was commissioned second lieutenant in the Union army and given control of the *Planter.* He used his knowledge of Charleston Harbor to help the Union forces break the Confederate supply lines and remove the torpedoes he had helped to lay while still in servitude.[109]

Smalls's military intelligence supported the first attempt to capture Charleston. When federal troops were landed on James Island, southeast of the city, on June 2, 1862, people in Charleston, fearing attack, began loading carts with their belongings and removing them to safety. The bells of St. Michael's Church were taken down and sent to Columbia for safekeeping.[110]

The first attack against Charleston came at 4 A.M. on June 15, 1862, near Secessionville on James Island. Roughly five hundred Confederate troops confronted over six thousand Union troops. After three assaults and nearly three hours of bloody hand-to-hand fighting, the Union troops retreated. Despite the failure of the first attempt to take Charleston, slaves continued to run away to the enemy, encouraged by the presence of the Yankee blockade of Charleston Harbor, the success of Robert Smalls and other slaves who escaped to Union lines, and President Lincoln's Preliminary Emancipation Proclamation of September 22, 1862.[111] The Preliminary Emancipation Proclamation amounted to a warning to the Confederacy that if they did not surrender by January 1, 1863, all their slaves would be freed. The final proclamation turned this warning into reality.

For the Union cause, the immediate effect of the proclamation was to help fulfill the spiraling demands of the army for manpower. The Emancipation Proclamation stipulated that henceforth freed slaves would be accepted by the Union military "to garrison forts, positions, stations, and other places, and to man vessels of all sorts in said service."[112] The Militia Act of July 1862 gave the president discretion to enlist black soldiers as he saw fit, but black recruitment did not begin in earnest until May 1863, when the War Department established the Bureau of Colored Troops.[113]

For slaves, the Emancipation Proclamation meant freedom. Slaves were so elated by the announcement of the proclamation that "one old man," Benjamin Holmes noted, "held a prayer meeting right there in the mart."[114] Shortly after the Emancipation Proclamation was issued, Robert Smalls noted that black Charlestonians were anxious to fight for their liberty and needed only the opportunity. In his view, if the United States Army had a headquarters in Charleston, as many as ten or fifteen black regiments could be raised there.[115] He was right, for when Martin Delany was sent to Charleston to recruit blacks in the waning weeks of the war, they flocked to join the federal ranks as soldiers.

Charleston slaves were seizing opportunities to steal away to freedom in such alarming numbers that city officials felt compelled to put more restrictions on their movement. Slaves could no longer fish in certain parts of the harbor. The evening curfew was enforced more rigorously, and passports were required for traveling into or out of the city.[116] Slaveholders became embittered. Having always assumed that there was some personal bond between them and their slaves, like the Sea Island planters, slave owers in the city felt betrayed when their slaves ran away to join the Yankees. Some even preferred to pay Confederate government fines rather than allow their slaves to work on fortifications,[117] where they might find opportunities to flee to Union lines. Masters such as William Middleton became so angry over the loss of their property that they sought retaliation. When one of his slaves escaped, Middleton wished only, he said, "to see him hang."[118]

The slaves who remained in Charleston did what they could to support the Union cause, often risking their lives to help prisoners of war. On October 5, 1862, some Union officers escaped from imprisonment in Charleston's Roper Hospital by dressing as Confederates. Knowing no one in the city, they sought help from blacks. Thomas Brown, a black barber, obliged the men by placing his son in charge of their safety. Brown's son found a place for them to hide among some blacks for nearly a month. They moved around in the city for two months, "relying all that time on the negroes for safety."[119]

Mack Duff Williams, the Charleston slave who hired himself out as a farm laborer, kept about half a dozen Union prisoners at his house for two days, giving them vegetables grown in his garden and three pairs of pantaloons so they could disguise themselves and escape. Like other blacks who helped Union soldiers, he did not ask for or receive anything from the soldiers for his help.[120] When Lieutenant James M. Fales and other Union officers broke out of a Charleston prison on the night of November 9, 1864, they sought and received the aid of slaves, who guided them to an abandoned barn where they could sleep without fear. "Whole Negro families stood guard while we slept," Fales reported.[121]

Domestic slaves who hoped for a Union victory and watched for the opportunity to escape assured their masters and mistresses regularly of their confidence that the Yankees would be "whipped," but "all the while they prayed and believed otherwise."[122] Mary Boykin Chesnut was unnerved by the calm of her slaves during the bombardment of Fort Sumter. "Not by one word or look," she wrote, "can we detect any change in the demeanor of these negro servants. Lawrence sits at our door, sleepy and respectful, and profoundly indifferent." Lawrence's demeanor reflected that of the other servants, and Chesnut wondered whether they had even heard the awful roar going on in the bay, just as she wondered whether they ever heard the conversations of whites who tended to talk in front of the slaves as if they were mere furniture incapable of hearing. They made no sign, but she considered, "Are they stolidly stupid or wiser than we are, silent and strong, biding their time?"[123]

Slaves who were less fearful of white retaliation prayed publicly for a Union victory. One slave preacher led such noisy meetings of blacks praying for Union success that Confederate officials, suspecting that the participants were speaking in support of the Yankees, forbade them to hold further meetings. Unmoved, blacks continued to meet. On one occasion, Confederate soldiers locked a slave preacher and his congregation in their meeting house for several hours. Afterwards, the preacher made no denial of having prayed for the Union cause.[124]

By late summer 1863 blacks had reason to believe that their prayers were being answered: the war took a disastrous turn for white Charleston when Union forces launched a powerful bombardment of the city that would last for 587 days. Those who could afford to, took carts, carriages, and trains to safer communities such as Camden, Columbia, and Flat Rock; others were forced to seek refuge on the race course or other open squares. More and more Charlestonians could not afford to feed, clothe, or house themselves, as Confederate money continued to depreciate while prices in the city soared. Banks, hospitals, and the city post office were moved north of Calhoun Street, out of the line of fire, and the city's orphans were evacuated to Orangeburg. Meanwhile, the blockade steadily tightened and Union land forces grew in number, inching ever closer to the city.[125] Seeing the devastation done to the city by the bombardment and the increased number of federal military personnel in and around Charleston, and hearing news of the escalating Southern military losses in the field, slaves, in astonishing numbers, continued to seek refuge in Union lines. Jacob Schirmer's diary entry for August 31, 1863, nine days after the bombardment began, best epitomizes the feelings of white Charlestonians: "Our prospects are darker and darker every day."[126]

As the war progressed, the United States government continued to actively recruit black troops for combat duty. To most white Charlestonians, slaves in arms as Union soldiers were still slaves and were engaged in insurrection. Therefore, they had no right to be captured and treated as ordinary prisoners of war, and they should be given no chance to surrender; instead they should be shot.[127] Confederate soldiers inflicted heavy casualties on black soldiers during fighting on Morris Island, though thirteen black soldiers were captured and imprisoned in Castle Pinckney with thirty-three other black Union soldiers and sailors.[128] In fighting on James Island, however, Confederate soldiers made no effort to take prisoners. They pursued and fired on black troops, killing most. Only the intervention of one of the Confederate officers prevented the soldiers' gunning down all of the black troops; the officer preferred to capture some and hang them as an example. But the sixteen black prisoners taken for this purpose were never hanged for fear the Yankees would retaliate on Confederate prisoners. Instead, they were brought to the city hatless, coatless, and barefooted and tied in a gang like a coffle of runaway slaves.[129]

Confederate officials in Charleston and throughout the South routinely refused to treat captured black Union troops as prisoners of war. For example, forty-six blacks, mostly from the Fifty-fourth Massachusetts, spent several days in December 1864 in a Charleston civilian jail, contrary to the established rules of war and under deplorable conditions, before being turned over to the Confederate military. But their situation only worsened when they were sent to the military prison stockade at Florence, South Carolina, as miserable a place as Andersonville. Disease spread through the prison, killing some of the prisoners.[130]

Despite the disproportionately heavy casualties that Confederates inflicted on black Union soldiers, Charleston blacks continued to enroll in the United States Army in huge numbers. Freedom was precious enough to fight for under any circumstances, and most blacks felt they could not be truly free unless they contributed directly to the fight for their emancipation. As Solomon Bradley, a Charleston slave who enlisted in the Twenty-first United States Colored Troops at Hilton Head, put it, "In Secesh [slavery] times I used to pray the Lord for this opportunity to be released from bondage and to fight for my liberty, and I could not feel right so long as I was not in the regiment."[131] By serving in the Union forces blacks hoped to demonstrate that they were loyal Americans. Like Bradley, most Charleston blacks who joined the United States Army did so before the waning days of the war when Union forces finally captured Charleston and began recruiting in the city. Some were runaways who officially enlisted at other localities. Others were free blacks who had worked as laborers and farmers. Among them were Gustavus Perryman, William E. Gordon, Moses Billingsley, Thomas Cleveland, David Holms, Barry Holms, Alfred Wooley, Benny Smith, and Willie McElmore.[132] Black soldiers, including many from the Charleston area, would play an important role in toppling the Confederacy. In the last days of 1864, they, along with the black community in Charleston and civilian blacks throughout the South, could sense that a Union victory and their ultimate freedom was near at hand.

THANK GOD WE ARE A FREE PEOPLE

Emancipation Arrives in Charleston

By early 1865, most whites could sense that these were the last days of Confederate Charleston. The city had been under siege by federal forces for nearly two years. The unrelenting Union bombardment had done almost irreparable damage, and the numbers of Union soldiers in the area had reached alarming proportions. General William T. Sherman's huge army, marching north from Savannah in the conduct of a policy of total war, had sent the homes and fields of the well-to-do low country planters up in flames. Churches, and even entire villages, continued to smolder as this army stood poised and ready to capture Charleston. By the middle of February, General William J. Hardee had decided that it was not militarily feasible to defend the city; and so, during the night of February 17, affluent townspeople and the remaining ten thousand Confederate troops evacuated Charleston.[1] The fall of Charleston to Union forces was a sweet victory. Most federal officials had regarded Charleston, site of the first shots in the war, as the hotbed of the rebellion. Furthermore, it had been the most important city in the territory of the Carolinas and Georgia for nearly two centuries.[2] With Charleston's defenses broken, on February 18, 1865, the mayor surrendered the city to Lieutenant Colonel A. G. Bennett, white commander of the Twenty-first United States Colored Troops.[3]

Shortly thereafter, the Twenty-first United States Colored Troops entered Charleston, followed closely by a detachment of two companies of the all-black Fifty-fourth Massachusetts and the Third and Fourth South Carolina regiments, many of whom had been slaves in Charleston just before the war.[4] It is one of the ironies of American history that former slaves were the first to march victoriously into the cradle of secession. Charles Coffin captured the drama for the *Boston Journal.* These black soldiers, he observed, proved their courage and heroism on the battle-field, "and on this ever memorable day they made manifest to the World their superiority in honor and humanity." Here were former slaves "with the Old Flag above them, keeping step to Freedom's drum beat, up the grass-grown street, past the slave shambles, laying aside their arms, work-ing the fire-engines to extinguish the Flames, and in the Spirit of the Redeemer of men, saving that which was lost."[5]

Fear and hopelessness overcame most of the white population of Charleston on the first day of Union occupation. With rumors spreading that Union troops would take over all occupied houses, women and children hastily barricaded themselves in. The second day of federal rule brought no relief, as soldiers of the Twenty-first United States Colored Troops began a tour of liberation. They roamed the streets of the city, breaking into houses and grabbing whatever they could carry, all the while intensifying the horror by cursing and raving at the inhabitants.[6] Former slaves, savoring their freedom, also roamed the city. Many had been held as slaves until the surrender, despite the Emancipation Procla-mation. When a reporter for the *New York Tribune* discovered a black family in the office of the *Mercury,* one of Charleston's leading newspa-pers, he told one of the women that she ought to break the bust of John C. Calhoun that adorned the front room since he had so vehemently supported the institution of slavery. She made no reply, but when the reporter went to retrieve the bust as a trophy for the *Tribune*'s office, he found that she had "done gone and broke it."[7]

The Fifty-fifth Massachusetts, a second black regiment recruited un-der the auspices of Governor John A. Andrew, entered Charleston three days after the surrender, setting off a wave of jubilation among the for-mer slave population.[8] "The black people turned out en masse," reported one contemporary observer. Their "shouts, prayers, and blessings" were heard around the city. One black soldier, holding aloft a banner an-nouncing "Liberty," rode a mule down Meeting Street at the head of an advancing column. He was nearly knocked off the animal when a black woman shouting "Thank God! Thank God!" dashed over to hug him but missed her mark and hugged the mule instead. Several other blacks present at this scene were so overcome with emotion that they wept.[9] In another part of the city, an elderly black woman rushed up to two news-paper reporters, grabbed their hands, and, dancing about, chanted:

> Ye's long been a-comin',
> Ye's long been a-comin',
> Ye's long been a-comin',
> For to take de land.
> And now ye's a-comin',
> And now ye's a-comin',
> And now ye's a-comin',
> For to rule de land.

"You are glad the Yankees are come, then?" asked one of the reporters. "O Chile," she said, "I can't bless de Lord enough. But I doesn't call you 'Jesus' aid. And I call your head man de Messiah."[10] "Bress de Lord," said another, gray-haired woman, pointing toward heaven and expressing the feelings of most people of color in Charleston. "I's waited for ye, and prayed for ye, long time, and I knowed you'd come, and ye has done come at last."[11]

Civil War. The Fifty-fifth Massachusetts Colored Regiment enters Charleston on February 21, 1865. Black Charleston Photographic Collection, College of Charleston Library.

Reconstruction. Scenes from Emancipation Day in Charleston, January 8, 1877. Black Charleston Photographic Collection, College of Charleston Library.

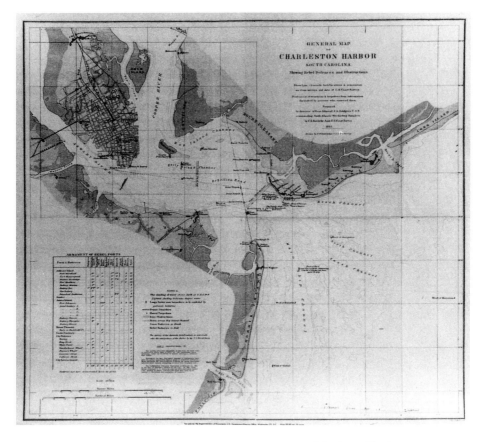

Charleston Harbor in 1865. South Carolina Historical Society, Charleston.

The remaining companies of the Massachusetts Fifty-fourth entered Charleston on the morning of February 27, 1865, and they too were given a hearty welcome by the black population.[12] When Brigadier General Alexander Schimmelfennig, one of the Union commanders there, left the city, the scene of his departure at the wharf, according to a contemporary observer, "was perfectly indescribable; the band played Dixie and the Negroes were perfectly wild, shouting, dancing, beside themselves with excitement."[13]

As Union troops advanced toward Charleston, former slaves had begun seizing property on the plantations outside the city. By the time Charleston had been evacuated, former slaves had taken total control of Gabriel Manigault's two rice plantations. They broke into the well-furnished houses on these plantations and seized or destroyed what they wished. A black woman named Peggy took Mrs. Manigault's large mahogany bed for her own use and some pink ribbons to dress her daughter's hair. None of the former slaves who remained on these plantations interfered or attempted to save anything for the owners.[14]

Because the arrival of Union troops ensured emancipation, the former slaves looked upon the soldiers as their liberators. Most significantly, these troops who had fought for their liberation and led the occupation of the city were black. Having endured slavery, and in doing so having always had to mask their feelings in order to survive, the former slaves greeted their liberators with unchecked emotion. They sang and danced; they shouted for joy; they proclaimed prayers of thanksgiving. They also destroyed property and seized what they believed rightfully belonged to them. Soon, however, the spontaneous outbursts were replaced by more orderly, planned celebrations.

Members of the black community in Charleston began taking charge of the new situation and asserting themselves as the hosts of these troops who were now honored guests in their city. They staged parades, made presentations to the Union forces, passed resolutions thanking the Union army for their liberation, and organized other celebrations to express their joy and gratitude.

Blacks seemed especially interested in lavishing praise on the black federal troops and made presentations honoring black troops' role in the war before honoring the white troops in similar ways. The former slave status of some of the soldiers added to their stature and was enhanced by the bond of race.

Within two weeks of the Union occupation of Charleston, the black women of the city organized a ceremony for the three black regiments. They presented flags to the troops and gave the officers flowers as well as a white swan fan designated for President Abraham Lincoln. Then the three regiments staged an exhibition drill to conclude the ceremony.[15] By making these presentations the black women were demonstrating their independence in two respects. As former slaves they were now able to perform whatever services they chose to render, and as women they were operating independently of men in a male-dominated society.

The excitement of the Confederate retreat and the Union occupation of Charleston was still fresh in the minds of most blacks when Major Martin R. Delany arrived. A free black born in West Virginia, Delany had come to recruit and organize black troops from the city's population.[16] He arrived on a Sunday when most people were attending church services, but news of his arrival quickly traveled throughout the city. For about six or seven hours, blacks of all ages and all social and economic levels came to his residence to greet him. Most Charleston blacks were impressed by this well-educated man, and his popularity grew rapidly in the black community.[17] As the highest-ranking black Union army officer, he was a model of what these newly freed slaves might aspire to, someone they could look to for guidance. His presence among them was the crowning glory of their liberation. Many of the well-schooled blacks saw in Delany a potential leader for the black community.

In only a few days, Delany was officially welcomed at the all-black Zion Presbyterian Church by an enthusiastic crowd of nearly three thousand people that spilled out of the church and onto its surrounding yard and the adjacent street.[18] Freedmen came from miles away to greet Delany, whose presence seemed to verify their freedom. The church, established before the war to accommodate black members, had a seating capacity of two thousand. Because of its size, from the time it was built it had been a focal point of organized activity in the black community.[19]

At this church, Charleston blacks met on March 29, 1865, to draft resolutions thanking the Union forces and President Lincoln for their liberation.[20] Most of the blacks in attendance had been free before the war and represented some of the most educated blacks in the state of South Carolina. Some of them would go on to become important political figures in the state, including Robert C. DeLarge, the secretary of this group.

Shortly after the resolutions were passed, a huge emancipation parade was staged, organized by the black leaders of the community. The four thousand marchers assembled at noon and formed a two-and-a-half-mile-long procession, led by two black horsemen wearing blue sashes and red, white, and blue rosettes. Then followed the Twenty-first United States Colored Troops with their splendid band; next came the butchers, then a company of schoolboys carrying a sign that read, "We know no masters but ourselves." The "car of liberty" followed, carrying thirteen young girls dressed to represent the original thirteen states. Next came the preachers, elders, and Sunday school teachers of the numerous black congregations of Charleston, each bearing a Bible and a hymnal. Next in the procession were schoolchildren carrying several banners, one of which read: "No caste, or color."

The trades were represented in this parade by tailors, barbers, coopers, painters, carpenters, blacksmiths, wheelwrights, and others. Also in the procession was a cart bearing a mock auction block. Behind it came a hearse with the "body of slavery," followed by mourners all dressed in black. On the hearse were the following inscriptions: "Slavery is dead," "Who owns him? No one," and "Sumter dug his grave on the 13th of April, 1861." Impressed by the spectacle, by the organizational skill that went into it, and by the community pride it expressed, the crowd, made up of freedmen from both Charleston and its rural environs, loudly applauded its approval.[21] White Charlestonians thought somewhat less of the spectacle, "but they had enough good sense to keep their thoughts to themselves."[22]

Black leaders in Charleston were not content with passing resolutions or staging celebrations to thank the Union army for their emancipation. A few weeks after the emancipation parade, two organizations of the historically free black community, the Friends of the Martyrs and the Patriotic Association of Colored Men, in collaboration with Northern whites, prepared a burial ground for the federal forces, laying out the ground, raising the burial mounds, and erecting an elegant fence to enclose the area. The *Charleston Courier* printed a favorable report of the moving dedication ceremony. Opening speeches were followed by ten minutes of silence in commemoration of the slain Union soldiers. Then, in closing, more than two thousand black schoolchildren led the crowd through the graveyard to lay flowers on the graves.[23] Out of this ceremony grew the current observance of Memorial Day. James Redpath, who had been appointed superintendent of schools in Charleston in March 1865, established the custom of decorating the graves of American soldiers on May 1. By 1868, the United States Army had changed the date of observance to May 30, and shortly thereafter, the various legislatures of the Northern states set aside this day to honor the nation's war dead.[24]

Free black community organizations that had been in existence in Charleston since before the war were well able to put together the various celebrations and commemorations of the Union occupation. The leaders of these organizations were educated and organized. Furthermore, most free blacks felt a sense of community with the former slaves because of close ties through family, marriage, church affiliation, and even work milieu, and so they greeted the emancipation of the remaining slaves with as much enthusiasm as did those who were emancipated.[25] Thus, it was natural that the free black middle class of Charleston would assume leadership in the postwar festivities.

Members of the free black middle class dominated the political gatherings of Charlestonian blacks staged in the first months of emancipation. In the political gatherings in September and November 1865, not one of the fifteen wealthiest black men of the community was present. One might think their experience, background, and socioeconomic standing would have induced them to step forward and assume political leadership. But the black elite remained aloof. Their prewar social and economic ties to the white community were still strong and created a great gulf between them and the rest of the black community.[26] However, as Ira Berlin points out, most free blacks in Charleston did not belong to the black elite and felt little sense of community with them.[27] After the war the economic interests of most free blacks and the former slaves were similar, and the economic standing of the black middle class was often threatened along with that of the lower classes of blacks, just as some of the proscriptions of the Black Code, passed months after emancipation, hurt the black middle class almost as much as it hurt other blacks.

The free black middle class may have taken responsibility for organizing the postwar celebrations and commemorations, but freed slaves turned out in huge numbers at all the events and were enthusiastic participants. Being able to congregate in large crowds was a new fruit of liberty they rushed to enjoy. This was true particularly for freedmen from the rural areas, where gathering in large groups without the presence of whites had been proscribed by the conspiracy-conscious white community.

Black racial consciousness was also a powerful driving force behind the freedmen's participation in these communal celebrations. As Joel Williamson notes, these events were important for more than their symbolic assertions of freedom: they gave the black population a sense of unity and an awareness of their power[28] that must have been intensified by their identity with the leaders. Such prestigious figures as Delany, DeLarge, and M. G. Camplin had organized the celebrations, and they too were black.

Both urban and rural freedmen revealed the intensity of their feelings over emancipation by gathering in huge numbers outside Charleston to witness the ceremonial restoration of the American flag over Fort Sumter. Since there were no boats to carry them to the island, according to the correspondence of Elizabeth Botume, a contemporary observer, they used whatever means were available. Hundreds of enthusiastic celebrants climbed into dugouts or embarked on flats, hoping to acquire safer passage to the ruined fort aboard larger ships.[29]

The city of Charleston was left nearly deserted on April 14, 1865, while out on a little harbor island thousands of blacks and whites shouted and prayed as the stars and stripes of the Union flag were returned to their rightful place atop Fort Sumter.[30] The ceremony included hours of speeches, but more impressive than any speech was the presence of such people as William Lloyd Garrison, the Northern white abolitionist, and Robert Smalls, the black war hero who had daringly delivered a Confederate steamer to Union forces. Smalls, himself a former slave, used this same steamer to transport three thousand blacks to Fort Sumter for the ceremonies, while on the quarterdeck stood Martin Delany, and flanking him was the son of Denmark Vesey, the man who had been hanged forty-three years earlier for plotting a slave insurrection in Charleston.[31] By thrusting these black men into the limelight, emancipation helped to nourish racial pride among Southern blacks. These men were not just heroes, but black heroes, people like themselves.

The former slaves extended their admiration and respect also to white abolitionists and honored those in attendance at the flag-raising with a huge parade later that day in Charleston. Besides Garrison, this group included Joshua Leavitt, Theodore Tilton, George Thompson, Rev.

Henry Ward Beecher, Judge Kellogg, and others. Black schoolchildren, marshaled by their superintendent and his assistants and led by stirring band music, paraded the streets of Charleston to honor these visitors. The children were flanked by thousands of cheering adults. Speakers stood on stands erected in the Citadel Square, where the crowds were densely packed, and at Zion Church, where the crowds spilled out into the street. The people "swayed to and fro like a rolling sea,"[32] shouting and cheering for the Union, the army, President Lincoln, General Saxton, Major Delany, and above all, for their freedom, the freedom that gave them the right to assemble like this in public to speak and to celebrate.[33]

At the conclusion of the celebration on the following morning, crowds of blacks followed the departing visitors to the wharf, where they presented bouquets and called over and over again for more words. Thompson, Tilton, and then Garrison obliged them with further speeches.[34] In the crowds at the celebrations of the Union victory were both rural and urban freedmen. Although the experiences under slavery in Charleston bore few similarities to the experiences on plantations, the freedmen all responded to emancipation with the same enthusiasm and the same readiness to join any celebration.

The great celebrations honoring the Union victory would be upstaged by a traumatic event, however, as the assassination of Lincoln in Washington occurred on the very day the American flag was raised again over Fort Sumter. Lincoln was a hero to blacks, who hailed him everywhere he went.[35] Blacks in Charleston had hoped that he would visit the city so that they might honor him. In a speech in Zion Church on the day Charleston blacks staged a parade for the abolitionists, Garrison asked a gathering of one thousand black children if he should send the president, on their behalf, an invitation to come to Charleston so they might fete him as they had other heroes of the war. There was unanimous assent to this suggestion, but the visit was not to be.[36]

The assassination was a devastating blow to the freed blacks and the federal troops in Charleston. Even many whites in the city mourned his death. Flags were hung at half-mast, minute guns were fired, bells were tolled, and army headquarters buildings were draped in black. Officers pinned black crepe to their uniforms. Nearly all blacks who were observed on the streets displayed in some form or other the badge of mourning. The words of a well-dressed elderly servant woman overheard speaking to a crowd of her acquaintances conveyed the sentiments of these blacks: "'Pears like we all ought to put on black for him, for he was a mighty good father to us."[37]

Blacks in Charleston actively took part in the national mourning for Lincoln. Zion's Church was draped in black for a year. Freedmen nailed black flags against the fronts of their dwellings or let the flags float from the roof.[38] Yet, even these attempts at mourning seemed feeble against the enormity of the loss of so great a figure.[39]

Charleston was in chaos for days after the announcement of the assassination. Major Delany was besieged by black people demanding advice about what to do next, and most whites, fearing for their lives, avoided all intercourse with blacks. Their fears may well have been justified, by the estimates of one contemporary. Blacks were determined to avenge the death of their president—and their friend. They believed that Lincoln was the one most responsible for their emancipation, and many feared that because of his death they would be returned to slavery.[40] This prospect triggered panic among the former slaves. Had it not been for the influence of Major Delany, whom the black population greatly respected, violent confrontations between blacks and whites might well have ensued.

Freedmen responded with enthusiasm and in large numbers to Delany's recruitment efforts, so when the need for their services was curtailed by General Robert E. Lee's surrender at Appomattox on April 2, many of the new recruits were distressed. It is difficult to guess who hated news of the surrender most, Charleston's blacks or Charleston's whites. The new black battalion being trained for war were extremely disappointed. When Major Delany gave them news of the surrender, no cheers rose from the ranks. Instead, the soldiers clung to the hope that their camp would continue training them for battle, refusing to believe that the war was truly over.[41] The Union army had delivered them their freedom, and they had wished to preserve that freedom by serving in the Union forces and defeating the Confederacy. The opportunity to fulfill this wish had been snatched away from them by the Confederate surrender. The surrender signaled the complete end of slavery, however, and blacks in the vicinity of Charleston continued to stage celebrations of emancipation into 1866.

After the initial wave of rejoicing sparked by the fall of Charleston and the arrival of Union troops, by the arrival of Delany to recruit for the Union army, and by Lee's surrender at Appomattox, blacks in Charleston found other opportunities to celebrate their emancipation. On the first New Year's Day and the second Fourth of July following their emancipation, former slaves from the city and its surrounding rural area staged massive commemorations. The New Year's celebration involved over ten thousand people gathered at the race track to sing emancipation songs and hear Unionist whites advise them about how to conduct themselves in their changed circumstances in order to be successful in American society.[42]

Southern whites were often annoyed by these celebrations. To blacks the festivities were opportunities to assert their newfound freedom; to whites they were opportunities for blacks to act saucy and obnoxious. Whites felt blacks had forgotten their "appropriate place" in the Southern social order. Describing the 1866 Independence Day celebration, one elderly white Charlestonian wrote, "The Fourth was a dreadful day for us on South Battery." Charleston blacks and those from the rural hinterland, he complained, kept this loud, annoying celebration going until two o'clock in the morning. "The whole affair was an outrage which would not have been permitted in a civilized community."[43] By "civilized community" this Southern aristocrat meant the white social order as it existed before the war. At least temporarily, that order was a thing of the past; blacks were determined to celebrate their freedom as loudly, as publicly, and as frequently as opportunity allowed.

Blacks also took every opportunity to exercise their new status, which to all freedmen meant the right to ignore the infinite catalogue of minor formal and informal regulations they had been obliged to abide by as slaves. Now they traveled without passes, owned dogs and guns, chose their own forms of dress, refused to yield the sidewalks to whites, rode horses and mules in the presence of white pedestrians, and refused to display any of the deference previously required of them by whites. They conversed both in public and in private with whomever they chose and entered into a variety of voluntary associations.[44] As early as summer 1865, Charleston freedmen were living in "some of the best residences," while black schoolchildren sang "John Brown's Body" "within ear-shot of Calhoun's tomb."[45]

Expressions of outrage over the assertiveness of the freedmen fill the letters, diaries, and journals of contemporary whites. An Irish woman visiting Charleston remarked that "the colored persons are awful sassy in Charleston. They take the inside of the walk of a white person, and they insult you as quick as they see you, and if you say a word they make faces at you."[46] Mrs. Aiken, a wealthy white Charlestonian, visited the Freedmen's Bureau to complain of being insulted by freedmen. Daniel Heyward expressed chagrin that many freedmen he spoke to did not accord him the respect he felt entitled to by his race. Instead, they remained seated and did not remove their hats in his presence.[47] Another Charleston aristocrat stopped taking his meals at the Charleston Hotel because the black waiters seemed to shun him during his visits there.[48]

Freedman missed few opportunities to ignore their old masters or to ridicule any remaining symbols of slavery. Ellison Capers, a white visitor who had been born in Charleston, wrote, "Rosetta Lizzie's maid, passed me today when I was coming from church without speaking to me, she was really elegantly dressed, in King Street Style."[49] Laura Towne visited Charleston to witness the ceremonial raising of the flag at Fort Sumter and took a tour of the city. Upon sighting what she believed to be the place where slaves were publicly whipped, she asked an old black woman if, indeed, that was the place. "Dat's it," came the reply, "but it's all played out now."[50]

Henry W. Ravenel, whose comments about the conduct of the freedmen are generally favorable, observed on one of his many trips to postwar Charleston, "It is impossible to describe the condition of the city—it is so much unlike anything we could imagine." He saw whites being shoved off the sidewalks by blacks, and black women in fancy dress with veils and parasols riding in carriages and on horseback alongside black soldiers. His own servant, when exposed to the city, became "excessively insolent." Ravenel became so disgusted with blacks that he desired some day, he said, to "be in a land that is purged of them."[51]

Southern whites misinterpreted the actions of the freedmen. What whites called insolence, sauciness, and "putting on airs" were to the freedmen simply demonstrations of their freedom and their social equality with whites. Their refusal to touch their hats to whites, their failure to yield sidewalks to whites, their determination to remain seated while speaking with whites, and their tendency to ignore their former masters and mistresses in public were not necessarily intended as provocations or discourtesies. They were positive assertions of the blacks' new status as free men and women.[52] The deference that whites had once required of them had marked the social distance between whites and blacks under slavery. That social distance, blacks felt, was no longer appropriate and neither, therefore, was the deference.

While most former slaves seized any opportunity to display their liberty, there were some who continued to show the same respect and cordiality toward whites they had shown before emancipation.[53] Scattered sparsely through contemporary accounts of the times are comments about this unusual and unexpected behavior. A young planter visiting Charleston wrote to his wife, "I have been agreeably disappointed in the behavior of the Negroes. They are as civil and humble as ever. All I met greeted me enthusiastically as 'Mass Gus'."[54] To Ellison Capers, "the Negroes behave admirably when you consider the ordeal of temptation and teaching they have passed through."[55] An elderly Charlestonian also noted that "blacks treat the whites with the utmost of respect and goodwill."[56] Carl Schurz contended that the first Southern men whom he met in Charleston in 1865 "designated the general conduct of the emancipated slaves as surprisingly good. Some went so far as to call it admirable."[57]

Blacks' unwillingness to bow to whites signaled their determination to lay claim to more personal autonomy within American society than urban slaves had ever had. White families whose former slaves stayed on as paid domestic servants had only to observe what was taking place in their own households to note the transformation emancipation had wrought. Many servants were striking blows for freedom in the homes where they worked.[58] Some did this by redefining the rules under which they would work and by refusing to be treated as they had been under the old order; others simply would not work for their former owners.

Many of the former slaves who became paid domestics vented years of anger and resentment through words and actions that shocked and angered their white employers. Responding to this dramatic change in attitude, one white South Carolinian woman advised other white women to be very prudent in dealing with black domestics because, she warned, "colored domestics give back word for word, and even follow up words with blows, if reprimanded too cuttingly!"[59] When, for example, a Charleston woman demanded that her servant scour some pots and kettles, the servant shot back, "You better do it yourself. Ain't you smarter an me? You, think you is—Why you no scour fo you-self?"[60] In the Jacob Schirmer household, the servant Cornelia contended that because she now had her freedom she had as much right as whites did to sit at the family table during meals and use their glassware. When the Schirmers refused to accord her these liberties, she left.[61]

Some of the freedmen who stayed on to work for former owners seem to have done so out of genuine loyalty and contentment;[62] others made clear that they felt free to leave at any time. One former slave owner returned after the war to his large and elegant town house in Charleston and found it still occupied by his former servants. Nothing appeared to have changed since their emancipation. The house had been kept as he would have expected it to be, and the servants were as humble, attentive, and respectful as they had ever been.[63] This was unusual, and the man might well have been extremely grateful. The experience of the De-Saussure family of Charleston was probably more common. They lost every servant except the nurse, and she agreed to stay only "as a favor until they hire white servants."[64] In such circumstances, white masters and mistresses may well have believed that, in agreeing to remain, the freed blacks were fulfilling obligations learned under slavery. The freed blacks, however, probably understood their own actions in a different light. By agreeing to stay on only temporarily, with the option to leave whenever they chose, they would have felt that they were invoking their freedom of choice, as well as displaying the dignity and self-respect befitting their new status.[65]

In another case, when the Reverend A. T. Porter returned to Charleston after the Union occupation, he found his house stripped of furniture, supposedly requisitioned by the United States government. He had no money and would have starved, he wrote, "if it had not been for the old black woman whom [he] had left in charge of the premises." A family servant for nearly thirty-five years before the war, she furnished him with both supper and breakfast.[66] Another white Charlestonian wrote in September 1866 that his coachman and the coachman's wife continued to serve him faithfully after the war ended.[67] Such instances were rare, however, and became increasingly so as Reconstruction progressed.[68]

Most former slaves chose not to remain in the employ of former owners. Their work had not been so arduous as that of rural field slaves, and their relations with owners had been relatively intimate,[69] but nonetheless defection by the domestic class was almost universal. Furthermore, having once left their former owners, Charleston domestics tended to move regularly from household to household, to the point where one newspaper referred to them as "perfect nomads."[70] Jacob Schirmer reported hiring eighteen different servants in the first year following emancipation.[71] When all seven former slaves left the household of the wealthy rice planter Gabriel Manigault at the time of emancipation, he complained that they were all ungrateful. In the first two years of Reconstruction, he found he could not retain a servant for more than a few weeks before he or she moved on.[72]

Many whites thought that the freedmen who deserted their former owners were foolish. They assumed that former owners could better provide for their former slaves than the former slaves could provide for themselves.[73] But, like other freed slaves, the domestic servants were apparently motivated by the constant longing to assert and test their freedom. One black cook, for example, who was satisfied in her position, resigned nonetheless because "it look like old time to stay too long in one place."[74] Pringle Smith's servants did not stay long at all but left with packed bags within hours of the Yankee seizure of Charleston.[75]

The mass defections of domestics threw many white households into disarray, unaccustomed as the whites were to performing domestic chores for themselves.[76] "We are literally our own servants except for cooking," one wealthy white Charlestonian remarked. Whites were forced to make up their own rooms and to tackle the dreaded washtub sometimes for two or three weeks in a row. Washing clothes was such an arduous task that when one white Charleston woman's mother had to perform it, the woman remarked that it almost made her cry to see her mother in such a predicament.[77] Jacob Schirmer wrote that it was discouraging to him and his family to have been without servants for several months.[78] Gabriel Manigault complained that after a year or two of constantly changing servants in his household, his sisters now had to do the cooking and the washing.[79]

The huge number of black servant defections puts to rest the stereotype of the "faithful old family retainer" who held steadfast to his or her former owner and pulled the owner through the rough spots of Reconstruction. It has been well documented that those so-called faithful few were often bound to certain individuals by specific family arrangements or that they were unable to relocate with any ease because they were too old, too young, or too infirm.[80]

The value that the newly freed slaves put on freedom is made clear over and over in the diaries, letters, journals, newspapers, travelers' accounts, and other forms of correspondence of the time. Sidney Andrews, a Northern white correspondent who traveled throughout the South, asked more than one hundred Charleston blacks in the early years of freedom whether they preferred to return to their former master's employ and whether they knew of any former slave who might harbor that preference. Not a single one answered yes to either question.[81] The institution of slavery had stifled the slaves' pursuit of personal autonomy within American society, and so, when emancipation arrived, blacks took action to seize the autonomy formerly denied them under slavery—to be free, and to shout, "Thank God, we are a free people!"

WE ONLY ASK FOR A CHANCE

The Struggle of Charleston's Freedmen for Economic Independence

3

In the immediate aftermath of the Civil War, Charleston, once the watering place of rich cotton and rice planters in the summer months, was the picture of desolation.[1] The business district and the handsome residences in the lower half of the city were entirely uninhabited. To one white native, "Charleston seemed more like a city of the dead than anything else with its silent and deserted streets." It was difficult to find a roof that had not been shattered by a shell. In addition, a great fire in 1862 had burned a swath one-half-mile wide through the center of the city, leaving only a forest of chimneys in its path. The post office and the customhouse were both riddled with shell holes and totally dilapidated. Other public and private buildings were also demolished.[2]

General William T. Sherman visited the city in May 1865 and, after seeing the destruction, said, "Anyone who is not satisfied with war should go and see Charleston, and he will pray louder and deeper than ever that the country may in the long future be spared any more war."[3]

Along with the physical destruction was almost total economic destruction at war's end. Every bank in Charleston had lost its capital assets,
many industries had been destroyed, and much of the Southern railroad
system was ruined.[4] Charleston's economy was so depressed that only a
small number of people were able to secure work to support themselves.[5]
The vast majority of both black and white Charlestonians were unemployed and suffering. In this labor market, where demand had so drastically decreased, whites whose wealth had disappeared with the war
competed with blacks for jobs they would previously have disdained,[6] or
else they survived on government rations.[7] The increased labor supply,
coupled with decreased demand, reduced the job opportunities for
blacks. As late as 1867, some formerly wealthy and prominent whites
shared the hunger of the masses,[8] and one formerly wealthy white had
to be buried with the contributions of friends.[9] Despite the efforts of
aid societies and the Freedmen's Bureau, destitution among the white
and the black masses of Charleston and the rest of South Carolina
continued.[10]

Aggravating the burden on the reduced urban economy in the early
Reconstruction era was the continuing flow of rural black freedmen to
Charleston and other Southern cities.[11] They came expecting access to
the freedmen's schools, to black churches and benevolent societies, and,
above all, to expanded economic and political opportunities. Some came
to the cities seeking lost family members. Many came looking for the
protection of the Freedmen's Bureau against violence at the hands of
Southern whites who refused to acknowledge their new status.[12] The city
epitomized freedom and protection. To many rural blacks, "freedom
could only be found down country" in the vicinity of Charleston and in
the presence of the army, as far away as possible from their former
masters.

After emancipation rural blacks began moving in large numbers toward coastal South Carolina. When asked where they were headed, most
answered simply, "Goin' to Char'ston." When asked what they hoped to
do there, most answered, "Dun know."[13] But they apparently planned to
stay, for they took with them all their belongings in sacks, boxes, baskets,
and in barrels, tied up in blankets. They brought beds, tubs, pails, pots
and kettles, and even hens, pigs, and starving dogs.[14]

As more and more freedmen abandoned the plantations, whites used
violence to try to stop them. On a Clarendon district plantation, for
example, blacks refused to continue working, and six fled for Charleston.
But they were caught by whites with dogs; one was shot trying to escape
and the others were immediately hanged by the roadside. For a month
after the incident no freedmen attempted to leave that plantation, but
the desire to get away was so great that eventually many took the risk and

escaped to Charleston.[15] Shortly after the surrender of Charleston, a detachment of Union troops surveying areas surrounding the city visited Benjamin Whaley's plantation, where they came upon fifty blacks. When the soldiers returned to Charleston, they had fifty delighted blacks in tow.[16]

Despite the often violent resistance by whites, the black migration to Charleston continued. Even blacks whom whites considered loyal eventually left for Charleston to take advantage of all the opportunities they assumed they would find in the city. Chloe, for example, the servant of Emma Holmes, agreed to remain in her employ; but she expressed the desire to go to the city once the railroad to Charleston was finished in autumn.[17] And Henry W. Ravenel's servant Peter professed attachment to the Ravenels but nonetheless moved himself and his family to Charleston because he felt he could do better in the city.[18]

Whites saw no promise in the black migration to Charleston, and to those in the city it was an invasion. Henry W. Ravenel claimed that blacks from Aiken, South Carolina, were leaving in large numbers for Augusta, Georgia, and Charleston, and he mused that perhaps the fields were no longer attractive to blacks.[19] A visitor to the city in 1865 found it literally "full of country negroes,"[20] and a native complained that the city was "overrun with Negroes of all sorts and conditions."[21] Many whites were of the opinion that exposure to urban life corrupted the average rural black. According to one South Carolina planter, whose former slave had gone to Charleston, "Bob is somewhere about the City, going to ruin."[22] Despite the steady flow of rural migrants to the cities and despite the worries of white planters who depended on rural black labor, a large majority of blacks remained in the rural areas.[23]

Nevertheless, the black migration had a significant effect on the population of Charleston, which increased from 40,467 in 1860 to 48,956 by 1870. Rural black migrants accounted for nearly all the increase, transforming Charleston's black population into a clear majority. There had been only 17,146 blacks in the city in 1860, but their numbers had grown to 26,173 by 1870.[24] While the black population spiraled upward, the white population actually declined, from 23,321 in 1860 to 22,749 in 1870.[25] (See Appendix, table 7.)

The spatial distribution of the races in Charleston changed as well in the years following the war. In the decade between 1860 and 1870, the black population of Charleston underwent a gradual shift northward. Seven of the city's eight wards experienced increased black populations from 1860 to 1870. In 1860, 9,728 of all Charleston's blacks lived in the four southern wards (one through four), while just 6,932 lived in the four northern wards (five through eight). In 1870, 12,864 of the city's blacks lived in the four southern wards, and 13,309 now lived in the four northern wards. Thus, though the black population significantly increased during this ten-year period, it expanded much more rapidly in the northern wards, where the increase varied between 82 and 119 percent, whereas the largest growth rate registered by any of the lower wards was 56 percent. In fact, ward two experienced an 8 percent decline in the black population.

While the black population made a gradual shift northward from 1860 to 1870, there was no such trend for whites. In 1860, there were 12,942 whites in the lower four wards and 10,224 in the upper four wards. But by 1870, there were 12,790 in the lower four wards and only 9,959 in the upper four wards. Just four of the city's eight wards experienced increased white populations, and this growth was relatively modest, varying between 3 percent and 8 percent.

The huge increase in the number of blacks in Charleston had little effect on the overall residential structure of the city. In 1870, the black and white pattern of residences was similar to what it had been ten years earlier. In 1860, most black slaves lived in buildings on the same lots as their white owners. Besides being convenient, this arrangement that interspersed blacks with whites was considered useful in preventing a slave revolt. By 1870, despite the upheavals of the Civil War and early years of Reconstruction, there was no fully segregated black area in the built-up sections of Charleston, though some blacks continued to live along back alleys rather than on streets. Also, in 1870, Charleston was predominantly female. Among whites, women outnumbered men in seven of the city's eight wards, and among blacks women outnumbered men in all eight wards (see table 8).

The increase in population and the stability of the residential pattern notwithstanding, most black migrants to Charleston found that freedom did not confer the economic progress they had anticipated in the initial phase of emancipation. In the early years of Reconstruction, destitution and disease characterized the lot of Charleston's freedmen.[26] Similar hardships plagued blacks throughout the Reconstruction South.[27] Charleston's freedmen were fortunate, however, that there were services available to alleviate some of the suffering. The Freedmen's Bureau could provide rations, clothing, and some medical attention, and the Charleston Hospital maintained an extension dispensary to serve the poor.[28] The Freedmen's Bureau established an Orphans' Home for the numbers of black children left without parents and an Old Folks' Home for aged and infirm blacks. At war's end, many of the Freedmen's Aid Societies provided relief to white refugees as well as black.

Black organizations began complementing the work of the Freedmen's Bureau. The Colored Women's Relief Association solicited cloth from the Freedmen's Bureau, which the women sewed into clothing for the poor. The black congregation of Zion Presbyterian Church collected and distributed clothing for the children of destitute freedmen, and the Mutual Aid Association and the Patriotic Association of Colored People distributed essential supplies and provided burials.[29] Even so, the array of services was insufficient to reach the masses of suffering freedmen in a city desolated by war.[30]

As the urban migration continued, the conditions of Charleston's blacks worsened. Forced to live in crowded, unsanitary conditions and lacking wholesome food, many died—of starvation, of disease, of inertia and ignorance. Medical care was hard to find, and many freedmen, having had no experience fending for themselves, had difficulty following the doctor's advice when they did find care. In these desperate conditions, the death rate among blacks rose to one hundred a week in early 1866.[31] Maj. James M. Johnston, a Freedmen's Bureau official, was appalled by the living conditions of Charleston's freedmen: "Much suffering prevails among the old and infirm freedmen. They have been suffered in some circumstances to congregate in abandoned buildings, where they are dragging out a miserable existence, suffering extremely from lack of food, clothing, fuel, proper quarters and medical attendance."[32] Many destitute freedmen were housed in army camps around Charleston, where, according to the description of a Freedmen's Bureau agent who toured one of the camps, conditions were no better than in the worst sections of the city:

> I have inspected the negro Camp and find it in a filthy and dirty condition; the Negroes are crowded together as closely as they can be— both under the street and around the wharf; obstructing the passage way; pigs, chickens, and children of all ages are in one promiscuous huddle; old clothes and bedding, which is very dirty and filthy is heaped up in different places—vermin can be seen crawling over the inmates of this camp. They build fires under the street and around the wharf to keep themselves warm, and to cook their scanty rations.[33]

In emancipation's initial stages, poverty, disease, and starvation stuck to freedmen in Charleston and throughout the South as lint sticks to cotton. Their fates were made worse by the actions and policies of the Freedmen's Bureau.

The presence of federal troops and the Freedmen's Bureau office drew many blacks to the city, but once there, blacks found that the federal authorities provided little or no protection. Most Union officials advised the migrants to return to work for their former masters, who, according to these officials, knew what was best for them. Federal officials were nearly as anxious as were the planters to return the freed slaves to plantation labor, and, when necessary, used force to accomplish this goal. Freedmen were mistreated by those whose protection they had sought.

Some were arbitrarily arrested and brutalized by occupation troops; others had their food rations suspended by the Freedmen's Bureau.[34] In June 1865, the commander of Charleston's occupation force, Colonel William Gurney, issued a warning to the large number of freedmen who had congregated in the city. He told them they must return to the farms, and when they failed to take this advice, "he asked ward committees to report the names of all able-bodied idle-persons so that they might be put to work on the streets."[35] Any unemployed freedmen whom Bureau officials found on the street were designated as vagrants, denied food rations, and removed from Charleston. In this way, the Bureau hoped to stem the tide of black migration to the city.[36]

In order to promote the return of freed slaves to the plantations, the Freedmen's Bureau did try to find them farming jobs and offered transportation to these jobs. J. T. Trowbridge, a Northern white correspondent, on a visit to Charleston in the first months of emancipation, observed at least fifteen hundred freedmen waiting for transportation either to their former places of servitude or to other plantations where they might be hired.[37] Many Union officials believed this policy was necessary given Charleston's economic depression, which had worsened with the influx of indigent rural black migrants.

The federal government felt it should not and could not provide the services necessary to sustain the masses of freedmen in the city. Sometimes the Freedmen's Bureau, assisted by Northern aid societies, sent young black orphans or the aged and the infirm to homes they found for them in the North. Sometimes the Bureau provided government-sponsored transportation to help freedmen get to jobs they had secured in the North.[38]

In general, only aged, infirm, or orphaned freedmen were granted government rations,[39] while those who could work were forced to do so. Federal authorities did not view the obvious lack of available employment in Charleston as a sufficient reason to give rations to able-bodied freedmen. The testimony of one woman, who had been waiting two weeks for transportation back to Colleton District, underscores this point: "De jew and de air hackles we more'n anything. De rain beat on we, and de sun shines we out. My Chil'n so hungry dey can't hole up. De Gov'ment, he han't gib we nottin. Said dey would put we on board Saturday. Some libs and some dies."[40] With the slavery system defeated, the capitalist system now required that Southern blacks be quickly socialized to the free-market work ethic. That is to say, blacks were free to work, if they could find work, and free to starve if they could not. The whip of slavery was being replaced with the lash of hunger in an economy that could provide few subsistence-level jobs.

Belying the assumptions of many white people, most freedmen seemed honestly embarrassed to need government aid, disdaining such handouts in favor of providing for themselves whenever possible. As slaves, they had had to take such food and clothing as the masters "gave" them. Having to accept assistance from whites after emancipation may well have reminded them too much of their status under slavery. Reflecting the thinking of many, one freedman remarked that now "we wants to git away to work on our own hook. It's not a good time at all here. We does nothing but suffer from smoke and ketch cold. We wants to begin de planting business."[41]

One thing the new urban migrants could do "on their own hook" was to take over urban estates and houses abandoned by whites during the general evacuation before the surrender of Charleston. Many freedmen believed that since the Southern whites had lost the war, they had to relinquish all their property, not just their property in slaves, and that the freedmen were the logical beneficiaries of this imagined policy. The Freedmen's Bureau was besieged by whites complaining of such take-overs, creating yet another thorny problem for the Bureau to resolve. Freedmen occupied the houses of Mrs. Bainbridge, the widow of former Governor Austin, the Widow Pettigrew, Francis Porcher, Benjamin Huger, and Mrs. Judge Huger. Unfortunately for the freedmen, the Bureau generally sided with the Southern white complainants and removed freedmen from white-owned estates, using force when necessary.[42]

Because of the problems associated with the black urban migration, Freedmen's Bureau agents embarked on a campaign to dissuade or prevent other blacks from coming to Charleston.[43] Explaining this problem to Ralph Ely, a Freedmen's Bureau agent in upcountry South Carolina, O. D. Kinsman of the Charleston Bureau urged in January 1866, "Please by all means in your power, keep the coloured people from coming to Charleston." There were no jobs available for blacks who wished to come to the city, he pointed out, and once they did come, the government had no means of transporting them to other areas. In the meantime, as a result, many blacks were living along the city docks, with no shelter and often with nothing to eat. Moreover, smallpox was running rampant because of the crowded conditions of the city and was taking a devastating toll on the black population. Kinsman urged Bureau officials to make blacks in the interior aware of these problems and to encourage freedmen to contract with the planters in the interior instead of coming to Charleston.[44]

In a determined effort to stem the unrelenting tide of black urban migration, to force unwilling blacks to seek plantation work, and to regiment the freedmen to their new status, the white legislature of South Carolina in November 1865 enacted four separate laws known as the "Black Code."[45] The laws stipulated that black children could be bound out as apprentices at the age of two and that men could be released from apprenticeship only when they reached age twenty-one and women only when they reached age eighteen. Employers could legally inflict moderate punishment on black workers, and the legal relationship between a contract worker and the employer was, by definition, a master-servant relationship. Little had changed as a result of emancipation.[46]

Although the Code granted a freedman the right to marry, to hold and sell property, and to sue and be sued, as Leon F. Litwack notes, "[T]he key provisions were those which defined him as an agricultural laborer, barred or circumscribed any alternative occupations, and compelled him to work." If a freedman or freedwoman was found to be unemployed, he or she could be jailed and fined as a common vagrant. Black men or women unable to pay such fines would be hired out to an employer who would pay the fine in return for labor.[47]

In enacting these laws, Southern whites sought to curtail the movement of freedmen to the cities and to ensure that they remained a landless agricultural labor force. As such, these laws threatened the livelihood of many blacks who desired to become or already were artisans, mechanics, or shopkeepers. Blacks who wished to pursue a trade had to obtain special licenses and certificates from a local judge, who would verify the applicant's skill, fitness, and good moral character. Then these mechanics and artisans had to pay an annual fee of ten dollars just to maintain their certificates. Black shopkeepers and peddlers had to pay one hundred dollars a year for the privilege of doing business. As William C. Hine points out, "This was a drastic departure from the antebellum era when no such requirement existed."[48]

Up to the moment of emancipation, many skilled trades in Charleston had been dominated by free blacks.[49] The postwar Code now effectively proscribed such employment by making it almost impossible to obtain licenses to practice certain trades. It was difficult for a black person to prove to a Southern white judge who might prefer to believe otherwise that he or she was a skilled tradesperson, a competent business person, and in possession of a good moral character. Furthermore, cash was scarce in the economically depressed city, and it would have been difficult for many black artisans to pay the fees. Thus the effect of the Code was to restrict or eliminate black competition in the trades and the business community of South Carolina. Previously free blacks already in business were unable to continue their trades, and aspiring freedmen were unable to pursue their aspirations.[50] The cumulative effect of the Code was to drive the free black middle-class artisans closer to the economic and social status of the recently freed slaves.

Thus the black community of Charleston was largely unified in opposition to the Black Code. Only the free black elite appeared to be unconcerned about the potential effects of the new laws on their lives. Many had supported the Confederate cause in the war and maintained ties of kin and support with aristocratic whites who could vouch for them.

Furthermore, the free black elite were already well entrenched in the city's economy and able to use their money, power, and connections to counter the harsher effects of the Black Code on their own lives and to maintain the huge gulf that existed between them and the black masses.[51]

Within days of the passage of the Black Code, Charleston's black community, without the support of the elite, registered its opposition by organizing the Colored People's Convention of South Carolina, held at Zion Presbyterian Church in Charleston. The members from Charleston constituted twenty-two of the forty-five delegates present, and most were men who had been free, middle-class artisans before the war and whose livelihoods were threatened by the Black Code. The convention delegates passed a resolution denouncing the Black Code as class legislation. Addressing themselves to the white South Carolina legislature, the delegates asked "very firmly that the laws enacted that apply to us on account of our color, be repealed."[52]

Individual blacks wrote letters to the Freedmen's Bureau to complain about the Code's implications for their lives. For one thing, they pointed out, it constituted a serious impediment to the signing of labor contracts between black workers and the planters. Most blacks did not understand the exact provisions of the Code, but they did understand that it made distinctions between black and white laborers under the contract system. They also understood that the Code legalized harsher punishments for black workers committing an offense than it did for white workers who committed the same offense.[53] "Blacks have anxious fears," Rev. T. Willard Lewis noted, "that class legislation will be allowed" under the Black Code.[54] More than any other event in the first year of emancipation, the passage of the Black Code increased blacks' distrust of whites by reintroducing the concept of master and servant that the freedmen had hoped would be banished under emancipation. Many blacks believed that the Code would jeopardize their chance to receive equal justice in nearly every realm of life. They correctly understood that the laws were passed to keep them in as near a state of slavery as would be permitted.[55] Black opposition to the Code was so intense that many whites feared an insurrection in the wake of its passage.[56]

But no insurrection ever occurred. In the black community, it was felt that an insurrection against the Code would be suicidal. One black observed: "If we did not rise when our emancipation hung on the long doubtful issues of the late war; for what should we rise now?—If not to subject ourselves to the sharp edge of military extermination."[57] Charleston's black community also felt that an uprising would greatly endanger the lives of rural blacks by giving whites in the countryside the excuse they needed to brutalize them. It was also suggested that by rising up and taking up arms against the Code, blacks would be proving to their enemies that emancipation was exactly the disastrous idea that Southern whites had claimed it to be.[58]

The black community did not need to rise up violently against the Black Code because very soon all these laws were either repealed or revised. In the first place, the Code was not passed as easily as historians have previously maintained; the South Carolina legislature seethed with dissension on this issue.[59] Moreover, passage of the Black Code proved to be a careless move by the legislature. The intransigence and lack of repentance these laws indicated on the part of the defeated former Confederates almost guaranteed federal intervention. Indeed, federal officials did see these laws as too discriminatory and repressive and therefore ordered many of them suspended on the grounds that freedmen should be subject to the same regulations, penalties, punishments, and protections as whites were. In response, the South Carolina legislature revised the Code in September 1866, leaving intact several social restrictions pertaining to interracial marriages, domestic relations, and vagrancy laws. But General Daniel Sickles, the military commander of South Carolina, believed that all laws should be applied equally to both blacks and whites and therefore regarded even the modified Code as blatantly discriminatory. Thus, in October 1866 he nullified the entire Black Code.[60] Given the short duration of the harsher provisions of the Code in South Carolina, which lasted only eleven months, and the threat of force against a violent insurrection, the majority of blacks chose only to verbally protest the Code.

Meanwhile, Charleston's whites circulated rumors that blacks refused to provide for themselves through work[61] and that they preferred government aid instead. The *Charleston Courier* of April 25, 1865, published these rumors as editorial sentiments. The *Courier* noted that the city of Charleston contained thousands of blacks who were infatuated with the notion that they were under no obligation to help themselves, despite the fact that they were now free. This attitude, the paper said, was all wrong, and local whites certainly were not going to help a lazy and shiftless group of blacks. Whites wanted to see freedmen go to work and help themselves and not rely on the government, which whites believed had done enough for blacks by giving them freedom.[62] Contrary to what whites preferred to believe about black dependency on government aid,[63] most blacks wanted only to provide for themselves; they were not using freedom as a cloak for licentiousness.[64] Having labored hard under slavery, freedmen were prepared to work under emancipation. They argued that if any class could be considered lazy, it would be the planters, who had lived in idleness on stolen labor all their lives. One scholar argues that "blacks brought out of slavery a conception of themselves as a 'Working Class of People' who had been unjustly deprived of the fruits of their labor."[65]

The efforts undertaken by blacks in Charleston and throughout the South to secure work during the Reconstruction era lend credence to their claim of being a working class of people.[66] Blacks could be found working in all areas of Charleston.[67] William Middleton and Robert Small

Reconstruction.
Street vendors,
Charleston, 1879.
Black Charleston
Photographic
Collection, College of
Charleston Library.

Reconstruction.
Postcard dated
March 26, 1875.
Old Maumer selling
groundnut candy
in the streets of
Charleston.
Black Charleston
Photographic
Collection, College of
Charleston Library.

Reconstruction. Watermelon market at Charleston. Black Charleston
Photographic Collection, College of Charleston Library.

Alex Knox's Plantation,
Mt. Pleasant, S.C., 1870.
South Carolina Historical
Society, Charleston.

The Orphan House, 160
Calhoun Street, Charleston,
Reconstruction period.
South Carolina Historical
Society, Charleston.

Charleston in 1869–1870. South Carolina Historical Society, Charleston.

found employment as section hands for the Savannah and Charleston Railroad.[68] Isaac Allen was employed as a fisherman.[69] Charles Hamilton[70] and Mingo Adams worked at Hudgin's Saw Mill.[71] Other blacks worked packing bone dust at the Etiwon Phosphate Company.[72] Joe Simons worked as a hack driver,[73] Peter Miller was a janitor at the Military Hall,[74] and Eddie Poinsett was a porter in Fitzgibbon's Store.[75] Still other blacks sewed clothes, washed clothes, hawked vegetables, and worked in the gardens near Charleston to support themselves.[76] Outside the city, freedmen also worked as farm hands. Many hoped to secure homesteads to be able to live as independent farmers.[77] One contemporary observer wrote of these black farmers that "their perseverance and earnestness in working their crops and securing means of comfort were unprecedented."[78]

In fact, blacks in the Charleston area were determined to support themselves and avoid government or private aid,[79] but the economic dislocation created by the Civil War made finding work difficult for both blacks and whites. As a result, some Northern white observers developed the impression that many of Charleston's whites, because of their need to provide for themselves and their families, were prone to thievery—an impression similar to the Southern white stereotype of blacks.[80]

Nevertheless, blacks worked as steadily as conditions permitted. Caroline Gilman reported in 1865 that many servants had deserted their former owners but could be seen looking for work.[81] When rural migrants left jobs, they usually did so to take employment in other places, not to become idle. Contemporary records are full of examples. Rebecca and Andrew, two freed slaves in their former master's employ, resigned their positions with him in order to attend to their own planting.[82] One woman resigned a servant's job to return to work under her former master.[83] Sidney Andrews spoke to many whites and was told repeatedly that blacks could not lead productive lives as free people. But all of the examples he collected were to the contrary. A plantation owner living in Charleston told Andrews that he had lost sixteen black workers, but he did not care because they were a nuisance. When asked what they were doing now, the planter said that he knew that two or three of the men had joined the army, one of the women was employed as a cook in the North, another woman had become a chambermaid on a steamer, and three of the men had found work on the wharf.[84] Another planter complained to Andrews that blacks were lazy and governed only by the whip. He had treated his slaves well, he said, but they were all ungrateful and had left him when the federal troops reached Charleston. Contradicting his own expressed opinion of his former slaves, he indicated that he believed them all to be working, with the exception of two who had since died.[85]

Not only were freedmen working where it was possible to obtain employment, but it was argued that they were good workers when well paid.[86] A labor survey of 761 black men eighteen years of age or older, based on the 1870 Census, reveals that nearly 88 percent of them were employed at some capacity despite the slack demand for labor and restrictions on the occupations they could enter. (See table 9.) Blacks proved to be such industrious workers that the movement to recruit Asian or European immigrants never came to fruition. Replacing black workers with Asian and European immigrants was considered in large part because of the view held by many whites that blacks were lazy and either would not work or would not work as efficiently as white men and women. One planter told John W. Alvord, the superintendent of education for the Freedmen's Bureau, "We don't want China-men." Pointing to the cabins of his black workers, and voicing the view of countless planters, he said, "These people are used to our work, and we are used to them."[87]

Despite the zeal with which freedmen tried to obtain work, the economic decline and the overabundance of labor in Charleston made acquiring steady work difficult. A white visitor touring the city in 1868 was "struck by the number of men who appear to have no employment."[88] In late 1869, when the city inspector's office, the office responsible for the maintenance of municipal property, announced its intention to hire fifty new street hands, nearly six hundred men—the vast majority of whom were skilled black workers—massed at the office to apply for the jobs. The crowd blocked the pavement around city hall, raising fear that "the street cars would be interrupted in their trips," and finally became so unruly that the police were called to maintain order.

Responding to the overwhelming demand for jobs, the Charleston city government adopted a policy that would provide employment to the largest possible number of laborers by filling a single job with a series of men, each of whom worked two days a week. Some of Charleston's black workers went outside the city to work on the railroads; some went as far as Aiken to help build a Roman Catholic church.[89] Although workers complained about their meager incomes, most were happy to be able to work at all. One Charlestonian noted that "the negroes are very thankful for work at even the very scanty wages our friends can now afford."[90]

Not only did economic and demographic circumstances make obtaining and keeping work difficult for Charleston's blacks, but also Southern politics stood in their way. Many had to either work for Southern Democrats or rely on them as customers, and those who showed sympathy with or had any ties to the Republican party frequently suffered either blatant or subtle forms of political discrimination. Some black workers were fired for revealing Republican party preferences.[91] Edward P. Wall, a Charleston tailor, sought work as a Freedmen's Bureau agent when his ties to the Republican party became known and prevented his acquiring enough business to support his family.[92] When Charleston's black butchers publicly supported the Republican party, the *Charleston News and Courier* urged whites to boycott black butchers, arguing it was time to "withdraw our patronage, custom and employment from those who would make war upon us."[93] This strategy was widely applied. W. G. Marts wrote from Charleston in 1877 that many blacks had been refused work for months because they lacked the piece of paper verifying that they had voted the Democratic ticket.[94] Despite these obstacles, freedmen continued to find work and continued to try to become productive free citizens of American society.

For many freedmen in Charleston and throughout the South, moreover, the ownership of land was of paramount importance.[95] They seemed to see in it, as Martin Abbott points out, "the symbolic and actual fulfillment of freedom's promise." The slogan "forty acres and a mule" epitomized the longing of former slaves to acquire land and, through it, economic independence.[96] Writing to General Charles Devens, a Freedmen's Bureau agent, Rev. T. Willard Lewis noted that "the freedmen regard the ownership of land as a question of almost life or death with them and their children."[97]

In the early years of Reconstruction, many former slaves were confident that, having set them free, the federal government would now provide them with forty-acre plots taken from the plantations on which they had previously been enslaved. Admiral Dahlgren, a visitor from the North, noted that former slaves in Charleston were asking what good it had done them to be made free if they were not to have the land to which their own labor had given value.[98] Captain Bradford of the Charleston Freedmen's Bureau reported that he had been asked a similar question again and again by former slaves in that city. "Gib us our land," they said to him, "and we take care orselves; but widout land, de ole massas can hire us or starve us, as they please."[99]

Early government policies convinced former slaves that a policy to grant land to all freedmen would be carried out. As early as January 1865, General Sherman responded to the large numbers of freedmen who flocked to his troop lines by designating all the Sea Islands south of Charleston, and all abandoned rice fields along rivers up to thirty feet deep, as land available for black settlement. Black families were to be settled on forty-acre plots and given "temporary title" to the land. Once assured of the correctness of General Sherman's Special Field Orders No. 15, General Rufus B. Saxton, an assistant commissioner of the Freedmen's Bureau, proceeded to execute the Freedmen's Bureau program of land redistribution.[100] But the program never took effect. President Andrew Johnson's Amnesty Proclamation of May 1865 pardoned former Confederates and restored all their property rights to them, except the right to own slaves.[101]

Reconstruction did not resolve the land issue for freedmen. The policy of granting land to former slaves had no strong political advocates. By June 1867, Radical Republicans had wrested control of most Southern state governments from conservative whites, and the issue of land grants to freedmen was seen as sufficiently inflammatory to jeopardize that control. Instead, Radical Republicans concentrated more on the issue of voting rights for blacks and on demonstrating Southern recalcitrance in the wake of the South's rejection of the Fourteenth Amendment. When Representative Thaddeus Stevens proposed Southern land confiscation to the United States Congress, he could not obtain the support of the Republican party. Congress was not persuaded that the former slaves needed economic independence from their former masters in order to be free.[102] Furthermore, Northern and Southern white Republicans refused to vote to redistribute Southern white-owned property to blacks because the right to own property in America had been considered a sacred right since the founding of the country and abrogation of that right for any reason would set a dangerous precedent.

Even black politicians in South Carolina opposed land redistribution. W. E. B. Du Bois argued that most black politicians believed in the petty bourgeois values of the accumulation of wealth and the exploitation of labor on which United States capitalism is based and as a consequence did not wholeheartedly support a program of land redistribution designed to benefit the masses of former slaves.[103] These men, who had been among the free black elite before the war, had little in common with the former slaves. They tended to have light complexions and some education. They tended to own property and to have a trade or profession.[104] Thus it fell to the insufficient ranks of former-slave politicians to support issues specifically of interest to freedmen, such as land reform and redistribution.

Although some of the freeborn black politicians apparently were farmers, others were real estate speculators, engaging in one of the few capital ventures that had been available to them in prewar South Carolina.[105] This interest, and the fact that many owned their own property, may help to explain their lack of support for any legislated land reform. Furthermore, they aspired to become part of the emerging capitalist class of postwar South Carolina.[106] As a result, they voted their own best interests, which did not always coincide with those of former slaves. The huge social and cultural distance between the black elite and the emerging black working class resulted in legislative behavior that followed class rather than racial lines, with mulatto legislators abandoning the causes of former slaves despite their own dependence on the political support of these constituents.[107]

The freedmen of Charleston were disappointed by the government's failure to make good the perceived promise of land and embarked on their own campaigns to secure this "right." Believing they were entitled to some portion of former owners' estates and believing their new citizenship solidified that right, some freedmen simply occupied white-owned estates and refused to release them to the former owners.[108] When the rice planter Gabriel Manigault, a former slave owner, returned to his farm on the outskirts of Charleston, he found that he was a victim of one of these takeovers and that his life was in danger. The freedmen occupying his farm were assertive and well armed. Moses, one of his principal hands, warned Manigault that if he ever threatened to move the former slave off the place, Moses would shoot him on the spot.[109] What was worse, Frederick, the driver, was the ringleader of the group and had encouraged all the freedmen on the farm to believe that not only the land but everything on it belonged to them. Furthermore, he had convinced the freedmen that their former owners had no rights there at all. As a consequence, many freedmen planted small gardens on Manigault's land and held steadfast to the plantation under Frederick's leadership.[110]

Similarly, a group of freedmen from Charleston who were also pursuing control over their lives and labor through land ownership seized several acres of land on James Island. One freedman, who had a large family, explained his intentions to John Trowbridge. He had been working on a small farm when he "heard there was a chance of we being our own driver here, that's why we come." Even though he could work the land better with a horse, as long as he could "git de land," he would take a chance on working it without a horse. When the owner, aided by the white journalist Trowbridge, attempted to persuade the freedman to give up the land and work on contract for him instead, this freedman steadfastly refused.[111] Few Charleston freedmen, however, were able to maintain control over property seized in this manner.

Another strategy freedmen used to try to achieve economic independence was to deposit their meager savings in the Freedmen's Savings Bank until they had enough to purchase land individually or collectively. Branches of the bank were opened in most major Southern cities in the first few years following the war, and the enterprise was almost immediately successful.[112] All in one day in 1868, seventeen freedmen withdrew their savings from the Charleston branch to pay individually for farms of forty to fifty acres at ten dollars an acre. In another case, ten Charleston freedmen combined cash saved from the sale of cotton to buy a seven-hundred-acre Sea Island plantation that was being sold at the cotton merchant's auction.[113]

There were other instances of economic cooperation among freedmen. Two hundred Charleston freedmen, for example, established a society whose sole purpose was to obtain land and homes for former slaves. In 1868, they made a down payment on a six-hundred-acre plantation on Rewly's Point near the city, agreeing to pay the balance of sixteen thousand dollars in eighteen months. In the first year they planted 150 acres of cotton, but what was not destroyed by cotton worms was almost all stolen, and they yielded only one bale. The next year, determined to have a successful harvest, they planted thirty acres in Sea Island cotton and about the same acreage in corn, and this time guarded their crops day and night.[114] Rural freedmen were probably most interested in acquiring land to produce crops for consumption and sale. But the data available on this topic, though sparse, seem to suggest that former slaves from Charleston usually wanted land, not for farming, but for building houses, schools, churches, and businesses. Indeed, black Charlestonians, like other blacks, had developed a belief in hard work that was predicated on the ownership of some form of property, a belief that grew out of their slave experience.[115] Their efforts to acquire property after emancipation underscore this point.

Efforts to acquire property began with saving money. Many contemporary observers comment on the seriousness with which Charleston's freedmen saved money.[116] Robert Somers, for example, notes that "the Negro begins to deposit in the Freedmen's Bank usually with some special object in view." That object may have been to purchase land, a house, a shop, or mules and carts, or to provide a fund against death, sickness, or accident. And the freedman or -woman, Somers emphasizes, would pursue his or her object until it was accomplished.[117] More important than the size of each bank deposit "was the idea of saving towards a better life." A savings account symbolized freedom and advancement, a chance for "getting on in the world."[118]

Despite the many barriers placed in their way, some of Charleston's freedmen were getting on in the world by making intelligent investments. Two groups of freedmen purchased steamboats. The larger of the two steamers, acquired by a group of discharged soldiers, had a black captain. It provided first-class service and ran from Charleston to Florida. The smaller steamer provided a similar service for blacks traveling from Charleston to Edisto Island. The Charleston branch of the Freedmen's Bank contained forty thousand dollars in deposits from former soldiers alone. Hundreds of these depositors used their savings to begin businesses, including grocery stores, cotton and wool stores, and other small businesses in the Charleston Market. At this market, black women rented stalls and sold cakes, fruit, candy, and lemonade.[119]

Some of Charleston's freedmen formed labor unions as yet another means to obtain their share of the economic pie. Once organized, they could use their collective strength in certain trades to force concessions from employers. Even before the longshoremen organized officially in late 1868, they had already engaged in two successful strikes and were on their way to becoming the most powerful black union in Charleston. The longshoremen first went on strike in January 1867 for a wage increase from $1.75 a day to $2.00 a day.[120] This strike was notable for the assertiveness with which these freedmen pursued their goal. Strikers gathered on the steps of the post office and, according to the *Charleston Daily News*, threatened violence against anyone willing to continue working.[121] One striker, however, wrote to the *Charleston Mercury* pleading for understanding of their position: "We hope that the Community won't think that we done the act for an offense or for injury to commerce, but our condition compelled us further."[122] The strike was successfully concluded in four days when the demand for a two-dollar day was granted.[123] It has been argued that the strikers won because no whites were willing to do the strenuous and demeaning work that the black longshoremen did, and the shippers had therefore been unable to recruit enough "scabs" to break the strike.[124] The solidarity of black workers, who would not break the strike at a time when many blacks were unemployed, contributed to the success.

Inspired by this success, the longshoremen initiated a second strike one year later, with two to three hundred black longshoremen walking off the job and demanding a pay hike to $2.50 a day[125] to keep pace with the cost of living and to counteract the instability of this seasonal work. The strike turned violent, and the acting military mayor, General W. W. Burns, had two strikers arrested.[126] Once again, the shippers' efforts to replace black longshoremen with scabs failed, and after four days, the wage demands were granted.[127]

In September 1869, several months after Charleston's black longshoremen organized themselves into a union, the city's journeymen tailors formed a union. A month later, one hundred tailors, including many whites, went on strike for higher wages. This union was notable because, unlike many of the other predominantly black labor organizations, it had both black and white members and they were skilled craftsmen. Many of the black tailors had probably been free before the Civil War. The strike was precipitated by the tailors' learning that their wages were significantly lower than wages of tailors in many other cities. To settle the strike quickly, the merchants who employed the tailors proposed a schedule of task rates that, they argued, would allow the average tailor to make between twenty-five and thirty-five dollars a week. The strikers rejected the offer at first but then a day later they accepted it, and the strike ended without violence.[128]

Not all strikes by black labor organizations in Reconstruction Charleston succeeded. Nearly two weeks after the tailors' strike, black and white journeymen painters walked off their jobs in separate but related strikes. The main objective of the black painters was to increase their wages. First-class black painters earned $1.75 a day while white painters of equal skill earned $2.50 a day. Second-class black painters earned $1.25 a day while second-class white painters earned $2.00 a day. The white painters were not bothered by the pay differentials by race. They were upset that they did not receive as many labor contracts as the black painters did, and this issue became central to their strike. Employers used race, however, as a means to keep the painters divided and to win the strike. After the strike had gone on for two weeks, employers offered a uniform $2.50 a day to white painters but refused a similar wage hike to black painters. This offer pacified the white painters, and the strike crumbled, forcing black painters back to work at their original wages.[129] If the white painters had united with the black painters for a uniform wage for all, it would have solved the problem of their not getting enough labor contracts. Instead, this lack of solidarity must ultimately have worsened their chances to compete with black painters for work contracts. This strike is a good illustration of both the necessity of labor solidarity between races and the failure to achieve interracial labor solidarity in Reconstruction Charleston.

Organized labor in Reconstruction South Carolina reached its high point in Charleston in late 1869 with the successes of two more strikes by the Longshoremen's Protective Union Association (LPUA).[130] In September the longshoremen went on strike demanding a wage raise to $2.50 a day and changes in the mandated workday. They wanted an $8\frac{1}{2}$-hour day from October 1 to May 1 and a 9-hour day from May 2 to September 30. Work done past the mandated workday was to be paid an additional $.40 an hour in overtime. The strike ended in less than a week, with most demands met.[131] According to the agreement, wages were increased to $2.50 for a $9\frac{1}{2}$-hour day, from 7:30 A.M. to 6 P.M., with 1 hour off for lunch. Work done after 6 P.M. would earn the additional $.40 an hour overtime wage. The agreement also recognized a closed shop, and so while the LPUA did not get its shorter workday, all other demands were met, and the union was guaranteed that its members would not have to work alongside nonunion labor.[132] Like the tailors' strike a year earlier, this strike was notable for the participation of whites who had joined the union.[133]

Only one month later, the LPUA went on strike again, but this time for political reasons, to protest the firing of G. B. Stoddard, a white member of the LPUA who lost his job for being involved with the Republican party.[134] The strike continued until the shippers were forced to rehire Stoddard.[135] The LPUA's showing of a united front in this matter made clear that it was a union and as such it would stand behind its brothers regardless of race.

As labor union activities intensified and achieved some success, Republican leaders, both blacks and whites, tried to gain the support of union blocs to advance their own political careers.[136] In October 1869, for example, three Republican leaders in Columbia called for a state labor convention. The convention passed a few mild resolutions, which were forwarded to the state legislature, but the key purpose for the gathering was to garner support for Republican leaders.

Like land reform and confiscation, labor issues were of primary importance to freedmen but were of little concern to black politicians. Approximately 40 percent of Charleston's black politicians were skilled tradesmen, and half of these had been free before the war. They enjoyed a higher social standing in the community and were better educated and more economically secure than the city's black labor force, a major part of their constituency, which consisted largely of unskilled workers, most of whom were freedmen.[137]

By the early 1870s, in part because of the Republican party's lack of support for labor issues and the Democratic party's success in using race to divide black and white labor,[138] any solidarity that had existed between black and white workers had all but evaporated. The unions of black bricklayers and of black mechanics had each promoted solidarity between black and white laborers,[139] but their pleas for labor unity had fallen on deaf ears.[140] Aggravating the situation, white longshoremen and other white workers began to organize segregated unions.[141]

While thus crippled, the labor movement of the 1870s continued to be active. When the Panic of 1873 and the subsequent depression caused the wages of longshoremen to drop from $2.50 a day to $1.75, the union went on strike. The sole intent of this strike was to restore the $2.50-a-day wage. The few longshoremen who stayed on the job despite the meager wage were attacked by the strikers.[142] The economic panic ushered in an era of particularly violent strikes, and this one was no exception. Aggravating the economic situation were the frustrations of black workers, increased tensions between black workers and white workers, and the growing assertiveness of Charleston's black community.

The longshoremen's strike in the fall of 1873 became the catalyst for further strikes. Workers at Chisolm's Rice Mill and at Steinmeyer's Lumber Mill walked out, followed closely by workers at West Point Rice Mill and at Hudgin's Lumber Mill. Like the strikes that occurred at other times throughout the nineteenth century, these strikes were extremely violent. Furthermore, they took on a racial character as white workers refused to join striking black workers, and blacks made no effort to recruit them.[143] Roaming bands of strikers, demanding a minimum wage of $2.50 for all black mill workers, attacked a store near Hudgin's Mill and later assaulted two white men. The mill owners and the *Charleston News and Courier* bitterly assailed the police for failing to restore order.[144]

Walkouts spread to the phosphate works north of town, where employees of the Stono, Pacific, Atlantic, and Etiwon phosphate companies went on strike.[145] In an effort to justify the action, phosphate workers, signing themselves as "Many Laborers," sent a letter to the *Charleston News and Courier*. The letter explained that five to six dollars a week in wages was insufficient for workers whose jobs required increased expenses for work clothing and shoes, and that they had gone on strike for a wage that would cover these expenses as well as their subsistence needs.[146]

The strikes closed most of the phosphate, rice, and saw mills in the Charleston area. A week after the strikes had begun, however, most of the workers returned to Steinmeyer's and Chisolm's mills while the other mills remained closed.[147] Undoubtedly many of the black strikers were forced back to work by economic necessity. The depression following the Panic of 1873 made job competition fierce. No matter how small the wages, almost any job was better than no job. As a result, strikebreaking became an attractive occupation and fewer and fewer strikes were successful.

While labor union activity in Charleston waned in the mid- to late 1870s, continuing efforts were made to improve the economic position of freedmen. Black labor leaders were locked in an ongoing though losing battle with industry managers and owners. The defeat of the longshoremen's strike of 1874 by black strikebreakers protected by the police was indicative of the trend after 1873.[148] The LPUA experienced one defeat after another, as strikebreakers of both races were protected by the police against the hostile and sometimes violent union members. The labor strife on the wharves in 1877, just two months before the removal of federal troops from Charleston, marked the last such defeat in Reconstruction Charleston.[149] Management's power over labor steadily increased, and both black workers and white workers were constantly confronted by escalating bouts of economic depression and high unemployment rates. These difficulties to some extent overshadowed the accomplishments made by black workers during the Reconstruction era. Black workers' hopes and aspirations had been raised, then dashed. Nevertheless, the LPUA emerged from the era continuing to do battle on behalf of black labor, albeit significantly weakened.[150]

Throughout the Reconstruction period, both black and white politicians and civic and religious leaders warned freedmen not to become worthless idlers and vagabonds but instead to be thrifty, to save and invest wisely, and to purchase homesteads for themselves and their families.[151] It is not clear whether instruction on becoming productive free citizens was needed, but freedmen did strive to make themselves independent. Most former slaves were determined to make good this opportunity. Their perseverance to achieve their goals against tremendous obstacles is one of the most remarkable features of the Reconstruction period.

WE GOTTA GET US SOME BOOK LERNIN'

The Role of Black Charlestonians in Freedmen's Literacy

4

Freedmen in Charleston, South Carolina, and throughout the South during the Reconstruction era made determined efforts to educate themselves and their children, despite their meager incomes, their lack of economic resources, and their lack of political power. Most freedmen were living at a subsistence level, but nevertheless they managed to pay school tuition, purchase books, build and maintain school buildings, and hire and provide for school teachers, all the while confronting other costly and sometimes dangerous challenges to provide education for their children.[1] These efforts were part of the historical quest for education by blacks, which W. E. B. Du Bois described as "one of the marvelous occurrences of the modern world; almost without parallel in the history of civilization."[2] What the former slaves did to try to acquire and provide education during the Reconstruction era is amply documented. However, many scholars have chosen to emphasize, instead, the energy that Northern whites expended in providing education for Southern freedmen, but in so doing they give only part of the story.[3]

The quest for education by freedmen in Charleston should be understood as a continuation of extensive, clandestine efforts under slavery. Miss "L" of Charleston, for example, for many years successfully used the guise of a sewing school to teach black children to read and write. Whites doubted the authenticity of her "sewing school," and from time to time the police would investigate it. But the school always survived these investigations. It was protected by blacks who guarded it from suspicious whites and by the students themselves, who always kept a piece of sewing at hand, "hiding their books before a white could make a successful entrance to the school."[4]

Many domestic slaves were able to use the circumstances of their servitude to acquire an education. For example, Mamie Garvin Field's great-great-uncle Thomas, a valet for the sons of a wealthy white Charlestonian family, attended some of the young white men's classes with them; and when they were sent overseas to Oxford University to study, Thomas accompanied them. While at Oxford, he became proficient in Hebrew and Greek and later taught his skills to his sons. Those sons, Abram and James B., taught their sisters, who subsequently taught other slaves. One person who benefited from this slave-generated literacy campaign, Anna Berry, later organized her own clandestine school for slaves in Charleston.[5]

Much of the importance that freedpeople attached to education was derived from its having been both formally and informally prohibited to slaves. The freedpeople never wavered in their pursuit of literacy. As slaves, they had observed through their daily interactions with whites the advantages that went with being educated. They did not assume that education would provide easy riches or equality, but they recognized that basic literacy might, for example, protect them against fraud in transactions such as the formal written contracts the Freedmen's Bureau insisted on between planters and former slaves in the Reconstruction era. As Ronald Butchart suggests, many former slaves perceived education as "a means to economic protection" and an important part of their strategy to prevent racist exploitation. It was one way that freedpeople could give substance to their liberty.[6]

The leaders of these freedpeople heartily endorsed public schooling for blacks as a goal for the postwar period in South Carolina. Black delegates at the Zion Church Colored People's Convention in Charleston in November 1865 passed one resolution declaring that "knowledge is power." They passed a second solemnly urging "by the sad recollection of our forced ignorance and degradation in the past and by the bright and inspiring hopes of the future" that schools be established in every neighborhood and that children be "kept in regular attendance at school." Once blacks gained some political power, they maneuvered expeditiously to put these resolutions into effect and to establish a uniform system of common schools. At the first state convention of the Republican party, in March 1867 in Charleston, representatives declared that a uniform system of common schools should be open to all "without distinction of race, color or previous condition," and should be supported by a general tax on all kinds of property. Similar declarations were made by black delegates to a second state convention that met in Columbia in July 1867 and a constitutional convention that convened in Charleston in January 1868 and lasted until March of that year.

Black leaders all agreed on the importance of attaining an education but disagreed over the goals and uses of education. Most of the black elite of South Carolina, who had been free before the war, believed in encouraging literacy among the black masses by requiring that black men pass a literacy test and pay a poll tax in order to vote. The poll taxes would help pay the cost of providing education. Black political leaders of slave origins saw the issue differently. "A literacy requirement," they believed, "would be political suicide for a largely illiterate black electorate," and, fearing that such a requirement would be enforced, they demanded public education for blacks immediately. Despite these differences, when a new constitution was approved at the Constitutional Convention of 1868, it included two provisions that supported the establishment of a system of public schools that were to be attended by all children, regardless of race. Thus, poor white children would presumably be forced to attend public schools with blacks.[7]

But state financial support for the education of blacks fell far below need. The Freedmen's Bureau provided no federal monies for the education of freedmen until summer 1866, when it allocated only five hundred thousand dollars.[8] Nevertheless, Northern benevolent societies and the Bureau provided valuable support for the education of freedmen, particularly in the early stages of Reconstruction. The benevolent societies donated books and thousands of dollars to build schools and pay teachers' salaries. Through them, more than a thousand people were sent to the South to teach freedmen. But these efforts were insufficient, and federal government support continuously lagged behind the actual need. Consequently, the twin burdens of financing and operating the freedmen's schools fell in some part on the shoulders of the former slaves themselves.[9] By 1870, blacks had spent more than one million dollars on education.

In this endeavor, freedmen were sometimes assisted by freeborn blacks. Countless black Charlestonians who had been free before the war came to the aid of freedmen by volunteering as teachers. Only five days after the Charleston schools opened in March 1865 under the direction of James Redpath, blacks accounted for twenty-five of the forty-two teachers employed, with the majority being native Charlestonians. Most of the teachers were members of Charleston's black aristocracy and had light complexions. Many had been educated in Charleston and had operated private schools for blacks before the war. One such teacher was Mary F. Weston, who had been jailed for operating an illegal school.[10] When the American Missionary Association (AMA) sent Thomas W. Cardozo to Charleston in April 1865 to organize the Lewis Tappan Night School for freedmen, Cardozo hired Mary Weston along with other freeborn black Charlestonians, including William O. Weston, Amelia Shrewsbury, Francis Rollin, Henry S. Spencer, and Margaret Sasportas, as teachers.[11] Six months later, when Francis L. Cardozo, a freeborn Charlestonian and preeminent educator also assigned by the AMA, succeeded his brother and organized Saxton School, he retained all these teachers and hired in addition Richard Holloway, Rosabella Fields, Harriet Holloway, Catherine Winslow, and Charlotte Johnson.[12]

The black educators who came from the North included several female graduates of the Philadelphia Institute for Colored Youth, who taught at the Zion Church School in Charleston;[13] Jonathan C. Gibbs, a Presbyterian minister from Philadelphia, who founded the Wallingford Academy for blacks in Charleston; and Benjamin Franklin Randolph, a Methodist minister educated in Ohio, who became assistant state superintendent of education. While serving in this capacity, Randolph played a leading role in securing teachers for the freedmen's schools and also established schools for freedmen on plantations outside Charleston.[14]

Randolph's application for employment by the Freedmen's Bureau illustrates a strong racial consciousness, common among the black teachers in Charleston, which translated into a firm commitment to freedmen's education.[15] "I don't ask position," Randolph wrote. "But I ask a place where I can be most useful to my race. My learning, my experience as a Teacher [in the] North, and my faithful service as a Chaplain demand that I seek such a place among my race."[16] Similarly, Richard Cain, a black minister from Brooklyn, New York, who had moved his pastorship to Charleston and organized a freedmen's school there, wrote: "We must take into our hands the education of our race. Honest, dignified whites may teach ever so well, it has not the effect to exalt the black man's opinion of his own race."[17] The AMA teacher William Weston stood so firmly behind education for freedmen that he expressed the opinion that it would be a sin in the sight of God for an educated black person to refuse to come to the aid of his or her black brethren seeking literacy.[18] Helping to prepare the newly freed slaves for their new position in society reflected a long-standing tradition of racial self-help among North American blacks. The phenomenon of blacks, both freeborn and freedmen, invoking the principle of racial self-help in support of education suggests that Charleston's black community was united in its belief in education. This unity on the issue of education may well have been used to ease existing tensions within the black community and to bridge the gap between groups of blacks on other important issues.

Freedmen made willing sacrifices in the pursuit of education. For many, attaining an education was yet another way to break free of their shackles and assume a degree of autonomy denied to them under slavery. One Northern white teacher wrote home from Charleston, "With few exceptions, I find the parents hardworking, very poor, and exceedingly anxious that the children should get lernin', and willing to make any sacrifice to that end."[19] Another white teacher, from the Charleston area, wrote, "I find a general pressure for money, but in the lowest cabins, they all show the same thanksgiving for freedom and are ready to sacrifice much that their children may learn to read and write." When the Union soldiers took Charleston, many freedmen lost their savings in now worthless Confederate money, but one woman intimated that she did not care because she had received, in exchange, freedom and the possibility for her children to become educated. This attitude was common among freedmen.[20]

There is too little evidence on record to differentiate between the factors that drove rural freedmen and those that drove urban freedmen to seek education, but it appears that rural freedmen may have been even more highly motivated to pursue literacy than were their urban counterparts. One possible explanation may be that since the laws against education for blacks were much more strictly enforced in the rural areas before emancipation, slaves in Charleston had had more opportunities to receive some education. Another explanation might be that rural freedmen perceived themselves as less sophisticated than urban freedmen and, identifying education as the factor that made this so, pursued education more diligently in order to fill this void. To clarify these issues, studies are called for that compare the factors that drove rural freedmen with those that drove urban freedmen to pursue education. Until these studies are done, it can only be said that all freedmen in the Charleston area struggled mightily to attain education.

Charleston public schools were tuition-free, but the task of providing books and supplies usually fell to the pupils and their families. This was a major hardship for poor families, especially because of the steadily worsening economic conditions in Charleston during Reconstruction. To help alleviate the problem, teachers would sometimes lend books to a few of their pupils, and the Northern benevolent societies would sometimes provide slates and books. But these efforts fell far short of filling the need. Many young black pupils, ill-clad, worked at odd jobs to help pay for their supplies.[21] Their efforts did not go unnoticed. Readers of the *New York Times,* for example, were told, "Most students find it necessary to work at odd jobs early and late, when out of school and often go barefooted and hatless saving their pennies for the purchase of some necessary volume."[22]

Even at the Avery Normal Institute, a private school whose student body consisted mostly of children from the families of Charleston's black elite, poverty caused hardship. To avoid having to leave school when economic hardship made it impossible for their families to pay their expenses, three of the school's best pupils agreed to work as janitors in exchange for their board, tuition, and clothing.[23] Until 1870 when the AMA changed its policy, some students at Avery supplemented the costs of their education by washing their teachers' clothes.[24] Others were not so fortunate in securing employment. "William D.," for example, a gifted black orphan, was willing to work his way through school but could not find work. He was forced to live with an aunt who had such difficulty feeding her own children that she often could not provide his meals.[25]

Indeed, some of the sacrifices freedpeople made to obtain literacy after emancipation are unprecedented in American history. Mary Brown, a ten-year-old from the Charleston area, and her younger brother lived with their grandmother, who was barely able to afford hominy to feed them. These children were so distressed over not being able to pay the school tax that their grandmother offered them the choice of paying the tax or eating dinner. They chose to pay the tax. When Mary's teacher asked her how she could get along without her dinner, she said, "O, we don't mind, for we go to bed soon and then we forget all about it."[26]

The records of the AMA for the Reconstruction era are full of stories of hardship among schoolchildren that accompany reports of impressive academic achievement despite adversity and requests by teachers for help for these children from the national headquarters. Many children, especially those on the rural plantations, walked several miles a day to attend school in Charleston, often ragged and barefoot and sometimes hungry. One AMA teacher wrote that "Alonzo T." had to get up before sunrise and walk a long distance to get to school. Then he worked in the evenings to support his family because he had no father and his mother was sick. Nevertheless, his teacher wrote, "in a little more than a year he has made his way through two classes, is now further advanced than the highest, is studying Latin, and lately brought a Greek book begging for instruction in that, and with a hope of going to college." Alonzo's teacher asked for financial aid from the national headquarters so that Alonzo might not be "prematurely broken down by hard work, night study, poor food and scant sleep."[27]

Another AMA teacher wrote to the headquarters requesting aid so that "Paul M." could continue his studies. The boy's father, the letter explained, was a "drunkard" and unemployed, his mother had been an invalid for three years, and there were three younger children in the family to be provided for. Paul barely had clothes on his back and most of these had been donated by the AMA. Despite his hardships, Paul excelled in school and during winter evenings taught five adults what he had learned. But Paul was seriously considering leaving school to work full time to support his family, and the teacher hoped that with help from the AMA Paul could stay in school.[28]

It should be recognized that most freedmen, despite the need for aid in order to continue their educations, did not expect handouts. Through the daily struggle to survive under slavery, blacks had gained the mental and spiritual strength needed to deal with the economic hardships of the Reconstruction era. As slaves they had fended for themselves, neither expecting nor receiving much in the way of handouts from whites. Carrying this expectation of self-reliance into the Reconstruction period, they were appreciative of the services provided by various benevolent agencies, but their actions indicated that they did not expect acts of charity or regard them as crucial.

Freedmen contributed what they could to the teachers as in-kind payments of school expenses and as an indication of their appreciation. These offerings might be cakes, candy, apples, oranges, groundnuts, or even chickens. Phebe Alcott, an AMA teacher at Charleston's Saxton School, wrote that one man, who had previously given her a pair of fowls as a form of school tax payment for his son, came by the school later and offered the superintendent some chickens as a token of his appreciation to "the people who provides school for us."[29] In the same letter, Alcott reported that the children of other freedmen had brought her gifts of fancy mugs and cups. "No less than five adorn my shelf," she said before going on to describe them in detail: "This one reminds me of the long and patient drill before Patsy became interested in her lessons, that of the brief but hard struggle before Phebe yielded and became one of my best girls. So with each one." To this teacher, the gifts were a source of pleasure and an encouragement to work harder at inspiring and instructing her pupils.[30]

Under the leadership of the white Episcopal minister Rev. A. Toomer Porter, Southern white Episcopalians in Charleston who feared that blacks were becoming contaminated by Yankee education founded the Franklin Street School in 1866 to "properly educate freedmen."[31] The school was financed largely from the contributions of Northern philanthropists and the Protestant Episcopal Freedmen's Commission, and the building was designed by Porter. The efforts by whites to keep blacks out of the schools that were led by Northerners and to enroll them instead at Franklin gave freedmen an opportunity to get their children good educations. And so when the facilities at Franklin proved inadequate to the need, some freedmen voluntarily took reduced wages to work at renovating them.[32]

According to the records of John W. Alvord, the general superintendent for the Freedmen's Bureau schools, freedmen often took it upon themselves to organize or build schools. When Charleston's schools became overcrowded in 1867, for example, a group of blacks proposed to donate a suitable lot for another freedmen's school if the Freedmen's Bureau could appropriate funds to build a school large enough for two hundred students.[33] Another group of Charleston's blacks applied to the

Freedmen's Bureau for three thousand dollars to supplement the one thousand dollars they had already raised to build a school. Although they expected to raise more money themselves, they estimated they would need the additional three thousand dollars to complete the building.[34]

There were many disappointments. "Father" Haynes, described by Alvord as "a colored man of the genuine African type," tried doggedly but unsuccessfully for several months to have a teacher assigned to the Charleston area. He finally established his own school for the children of freedmen in the outlying areas of Charleston but could sustain it for only a week. For days after the school closed, however, some children continued to attend, walking as far as seven miles in the hope that they would find a teacher present. But no teacher ever arrived and the school remained closed, forcing the children to seek education elsewhere.[35]

Disappointments such as this did not break the will of freedmen. They only strengthened the conviction that racial self-help alone could ensure that education would be available to all freedmen. As a consequence, countless freedmen pooled their meager resources to establish schools.[36] Throughout the South, they organized "pay schools" where the teachers' salaries were drawn from the fees charged to the students.[37] Because many of the schools organized by Northern benevolent societies were overcrowded or inaccessibly distant, pay schools provided educational opportunities for freedmen who otherwise would have had none.[38] Alvord was impressed with a pay school he saw in Charleston. In a letter sent back north, he wrote: "The Freedmen's Pay School (150 pupils), with colored teachers is a landmark, showing the progress of these people. All its expenses are met by the freedmen."[39]

Freedmen donated money to establish the Shaw Memorial School in March 1865, the same month the Charleston public schools opened. Significantly, black soldiers and residents of the Sea Islands of South Carolina, none of whom had children who would attend the school, contributed thirty-five hundred dollars to this mission, and, with additional monies raised by Northern philanthropists, the school was built.[40] Cooperative efforts like this one, as Herbert Gutman points out, illustrate how "reciprocal obligations operated beyond the immediate family and bound together former slaves living in rural and urban communities."[41]

In the immediate aftermath of the Civil War, black churches, working on the principle of racial self-help, were in the vanguard of the freedmen's educational movement. These churches had been the focus of black self-help activities since the time when, under slavery, blacks had sometimes been allowed to have their own churches. One Northern traveler, after visiting a black church in Charleston, described watching nearly all the parishioners, regardless of their poverty, put some money into the collection plate being passed to fund education. "Five dollar notes were plentifully handed in, and everybody present gave something.

The people are keen for education, which they see to be necessary to their children in the future of equal rights."[42]

In spring 1865, a representative of the AMA found a freedmen's school already organized and in operation at Plymouth Church in Charleston. All the teachers and the superintendent were black.[43] Later that year, Richard Cain, a black minister, organized Cain's Institute, a school for freedmen located in Liberty Hall on Morris Street,[44] and Jonathan Gibbs, a black minister, founded Wallingford Academy, located in the basement of Charleston's Zion Church. Like the Plymouth Church school, these schools were staffed entirely by blacks and their main source of financial support came from former slaves.[45] In Charleston, black Baptists and African Methodists and the members of the Methodist Episcopal Church each maintained freedmen's schools.[46] The families of the students worked valiantly to provide the schools with the necessary support.

Black self-help became increasingly necessary as Northern benevolent societies and the Freedmen's Bureau cut back the support they provided for education. As early as March 1865, James Redpath, the superintendent of the Charleston public schools, insisted, "I will make them pay for their own school books."[47] By summer 1866, benevolent societies had decreased their contributions and had begun to insist that freedmen shoulder even more of the burden of educational support for their children.[48] And so, despite their poverty, freedmen paid for tuition as well as books and supplies.

When aid societies opened freedmen's schools, the freedmen contributed what they could to maintain these schools. One such school was Wallingford Academy, founded by Rev. Jonathan Gibbs in 1865. It was funded by the Committee of Missions for Freedmen of the Presbyterian Church and the Freedmen's Bureau, with each organization donating equally to the $13,500 required to open the school.[49] Economic hardship, however, caused dramatic fluctuations in the tax payments, which are documented in numerous Teachers Monthly School Reports for Charleston. In October 1868, for example, J. H. Bates, Wallingford's principal, tried to collect the 25¢ tax from each pupil, but of the 267 enrolled, none paid that month.[50] The succeeding months were better. Eighty students paid in November, and 85 out of 348 enrolled paid in December.[51] In January 1869, enrollment was 306, but again no students could pay. By February, 68 out of an enrollment of 298 paid, and in May 64 out of 335 paid. By January of the following year, 107 students out of an enrollment of 323 were able to pay the school tax.[52]

For the Shaw School, 218 students out of 333 enrolled in November 1867 paid the 25¢ tax. The following month, the percentage was much higher, with 271 students out of 306, or 89 percent, paying the tax.[53] In a six-month period during 1868 and a five-month period during 1869, an average of 57 percent of the enrolled students paid the tax each month.[54] Reports for 1870 and 1871 are incomplete, but they suggest that freedmen continued to pay school taxes to support Shaw School. In January 1871, incredibly, all 339 enrolled students not only paid the tax but paid an additional sum of $9.60.[55] To most freedmen, the monthly tax of 25¢ a student was a substantial sum, and payments to all schools fluctuated considerably. In January 1868, for example, 164 students out of 525 enrolled at the Zion School paid the tax,[56] and in June 1868, 150 students out of 260 enrolled paid the tax at the Cain Institute.[57] The struggle to obtain cash to pay the schools should not be underrated. Because currency was scarce and low-income workers often did not receive their wages in cash, these tuition payments underscore the freedmen's conviction that education was crucial to their success in American society.

Freedmen's payments to the Franklin Street School, like the payments to Shaw, continued with some regularity despite economic hardship (see Appendix, table 10). This is the school that had been initially funded, in 1866, by Northern philanthropists and the Protestant Episcopal Freedmen's Commission and later renovated by freedmen.[58] Freedmen continued to play a leading role in its maintenance. The school's principal, Kate B. Savage, reported in June 1870 that "the tuition for pupils during the year has amounted to $223.05, which has paid the Janitor's wages; supplied fuel, stationery and defrayed some other incidental expenses of the school." The teachers' salaries, however, amounting to $2,200 a year, were paid "by the Protestant Episcopal Home Missions to Colored People."[59] Clearly, freedmen were determined to pay something whenever they could.

Despite the difficulty in raising funds, the new schools achieved considerable success. Much of the success of Saxton School, considered from its inception in 1865 to be a first-rate institution, was due to the efficient organizational and administrative efforts of its founder and principal, Francis Cardozo, the preeminent educator who was extremely popular in the city's black community.[60] But the quality of the school can also be attributed to the active efforts of its students and the black community to ensure its success. As early as 1866, the students at Saxton, three-quarters of whom were former slaves, paid for their own books.[61] Furthermore, in August 1866, Cardozo reported that "the scholars contributed $35.00 to the incidental expenses of the school during July." He expressed confidence that the students would continue in this practice, proposing to ask them "for another contribution during August, which I think they will give cheerfully."[62] While no record of contributions could be found for the months of August, September, and October, Cardozo did report in November 1866 that students had contributed $105 toward their tuition.[63]

Contributions to the maintenance of Saxton School persisted in 1867 and 1868. In January 1867, parents paid $95 toward the school "tax" and contributed $77 for books and supplies. Some students could not afford to pay the 25¢ a month and needed to have the tax waived. Some students also found it difficult to afford books, and teachers usually provided books for them. At least half of the students paid the tax every month,[64] and so Cardozo collected $105 in February 1867.[65] According to Teachers Monthly School Reports for 1868, contributions to Saxton School continued to be stable. For example, in March 1868, Ellen W. Pierce, a teacher employed by the AMA, reported that 46 students in her class had contributed $11.25, Lizzie F. Pratt reported collecting $11.60 from 48 students, and Jennie M. Paimelert reported collecting $12 from 54 students.[66] By the time all of the teachers had reported to Cardozo, the total amount of school taxes collected for March 1868 was $97.50. Of 407 students enrolled, 390 paid the 25¢ monthly tax.[67]

Freedmen continued to support the school after it was converted to a normal school, renamed Avery Normal Institute, and after it eventually moved to a new, large building on Bull Street on May 1, 1868.[68] The building had been built the preceding fall by two local white contractors at a cost of $17,000.[69] It was built specifically to be a school for freedmen. Each month the number of students enrolled and the percentage who paid changed. In October 1868, for example, 190 of the 325 students enrolled paid the school tax, in November 160 out of 354 paid, and in December 157 out of 318 paid.[70] Payments toward the 25¢ monthly school tax continued in 1869. Ellen Pierce reported that 240 freedmen had paid a small tax in January.[71] Mortimer A. Warren, Avery's principal, reported that all 334 enrolled students had either paid or worked for their February 1869 school tax, with 264 students having paid in cash; 273 of the 332 enrolled paid in April 1869; 238 of the 292 enrolled paid in June; and 285 paid in October.[72]

Warren reported receiving overwhelming economic support from freedmen for Avery Institute in 1870 as well, with enrollment and school tax contributions continuing to rise. In January, 273 students paid the school tax,[73] and by February Warren could report, "My school is continuing to increase almost against my will, and receipts from taxes for tuition [are] increasing also."[74] In March, 244 students out of 338 enrolled paid the monthly 25¢ tax, with some apparently contributing more than was required, for a total of $75.29.[75] Avery continued to flourish, and despite great economic distress in the spring and summer months, payments of school contributions did not taper off.

Avery Institute went through the ultimate test of its durability when, in fall 1870, the federal government withdrew its financial support, requiring a school tax increase to $1.25 a month, payable in advance. In October 1870, the *Charleston Daily Republican* reported that "the parents (to their great honor be it said) accept the situation, and one and all

Reconstruction period. Zion School for freedmen located in the basement of Zion Presbyterian Church. Avery Research Center for African-American History and Culture, College of Charleston.

Avery Normal Institute. Avery Research Center for African-American History and Culture, College of Charleston.

SHAW MEMORIAL SCHOOL,

Charleston, *November 26, 1876.*

AWARDED TO *Whithers Houston*

in the *Eleventh* Class for regular and punctual attendance,

perfect Lessons, and correct deportment during the past week.

E. J. Adams

PRINCIPAL

This is my first.
I got the first week I went to school

Certificate of exemplary attendance from Shaw Memorial School issued by
Rev. Ennals J. Adams. Avery Research Center for African-American
History and Culture, College of Charleston.

Francis L. Cardozo,
a prominent educator and
politician. Avery Research
Center for African-Ameri-
can History and Culture,
College of Charleston.

seem to accede to the justice and propriety of the increase."[76] While Avery served students from Charleston's mulatto elite, who could more easily afford this increase, it should be noted that from 1868 to 1870, at least half of Avery's students came from families of former slaves, many of whom were nearly penniless.[77]

The black community of Charleston reinforced its support for education by staging public examinations to demonstrate the outstanding academic progress of black schoolchildren and to acknowledge the excellent performance of black teachers as well. These examinations were attended by parents, relatives, and friends of the students as well as interested community members. At an examination staged in June 1867 at Zion School in the basement of Zion Presbyterian Church, students ranging in age from six to seventeen demonstrated proficiency in grammar, mental and written arithmetic, and other subjects. Those who excelled in each class received a medal.[78] Shaw Memorial School staged a similar examination, where students impressed the audience with their skill as well as the skill of their teachers with high-speed responses to questions in grammar, spelling, and arithmetic.[79]

Charleston's black community also held meetings to promote education and occasionally petitioned to have schools established or maintained. Several freed black families attended the Zion Church Colored People's Convention in November 1865, where resolutions were passed emphasizing the importance of education.[80] A mass meeting of Charleston's freedmen was held a year later, with the same objective of promoting education as a means of elevating the black race.[81]

Although Freedmen's Bureau officials often voiced the fear that this intense desire for education would wane once the initial enthusiasm wore off, freedmen continued their unrelenting pursuit of education throughout the Reconstruction period. For many, this relentlessness yielded impressive results. In the closing years of Reconstruction, black pupils were found to be advancing as rapidly in their studies as were many of their white counterparts.[82] Indeed, the principal of one of Charleston's public schools, the Morris Street School, declared that black children learned as readily as whites and that their thirst for knowledge was actually much greater than that of whites.[83] A reporter for the *New York Times* remarked upon seeing black students in Charleston working algebra problems, answering questions in ancient and modern history, and reading literature with good comprehension.[84]

Letters to the AMA national headquarters written by Francis Cardozo in late 1865 and early 1866 detail the favorable impressions freedmen's schools in Charleston made on prominent white visitors from Europe and from the North, including a correspondent from *The Nation*. These letters also reiterate the freedmen's zeal for education and their steady progress in achieving it. In late October 1865, leaders from the national headquarters and the South Carolina offices of the Freedmen's Bureau—including General Oliver Otis Howard, commissioner of the Freedmen's Bureau; General Rufus Saxton, assistant commissioner of the Bureau; John W. Alvord, general superintendent of the Freedmen's Bureau schools; and Reuben Tomlinson, the state superintendent of education for the Bureau; accompanied by Howard's brother, a local minister—toured Saxton School and addressed the seven hundred students of the school at an assembly. Howard commended the students on their appearance and their academic progress. Later in the same week, another visitor, the Reverend Mr. Kennedy, told them that they represented one of the finest schools in the nation.[85] A couple from Boston, identified as Mr. and Mrs. Bird, were so enthusiastic over the progress of the students at Saxton School that as soon as they returned home they pledged a substantial donation to the AMA to help it continue its efforts to educate blacks.[86]

In 1870, Alvord, in his capacity as general superintendent, toured eight schools in Charleston serving roughly twenty-five hundred students and reported that he found the schools in good condition, with one or two possible exceptions. He noted that Morris Street School had some shortcomings but that nevertheless its eight hundred pupils and staff were an honor to the city. He ranked Shaw Memorial School and Avery Institute very high, declaring, in fact, that Avery was the best school in the entire state.[87] Avery students enrolled in and excelled in such courses as botany, geometry, rhetoric, bookkeeping, general history, civil government, and political economy. On a typical day there, the school's advanced students would transpose, analyze, and parse passages from Milton's *L'Allegro*.[88]

Black Charlestonians were so successful in their educational endeavors that some of their Southern white critics had to acknowledge this achievement,[89] although sometimes with reluctance. Many whites argued that the achievements of students at Saxton School, before it became Avery Institute, did not constitute a true representation of the educational progress of Charleston's blacks because the mulatto elite sent their children there.[90] This was a class-based argument that did not hold up under scrutiny. Francis Cardozo, as the school's principal, "found no difference in the intellectual capacity of freemen and freedmen." Freeborn blacks ranked above freedmen in their class status only because of their earlier legal and educational advantages,[91] not because of superior intellect. On at least two occasions several distinguished Southern whites visited Saxton School. Among them were George A. Trenholm, the former secretary of the treasury for the Confederacy; his daughter and a female acquaintance; and three prominent and influential Episcopalian ministers, A. T. Porter, C. P. Gadsden, and C. C. Pinckney. They witnessed classes performing regular exercises and some special exercises. Not only were they pleased with the school's methods of teaching but also they were favorably impressed with the efficiency and behavior of the students.[92]

As is true for the students in any school system, not all black children in the Charleston schools exhibited good conduct and not all learned rapidly. A few at Shaw School appeared not to understand the difference between right and wrong.[93] Some students at other schools, having had no preparation for school life, found it extremely difficult to sit still and focus on schoolwork. They wanted to talk or to get up and walk around the room. Sometimes students fell asleep in their seats and might even be seen crashing to the floor. Sometimes students got into fights. Elizabeth Rice, a white teacher from the North, reported that on her first day of teaching at a freedmen's school, two big boys started fighting, and before the sentinel at the door could interfere, one viciously cut the other in the face with a knife.[94] Even Avery Institute had a few unruly children. Hattie Foote became so upset with her students that she wrote to the national headquarters of the AMA requesting a transfer to another field because she felt that the children in her classes "have no proper idea of order or study, and are deficient in studies."[95]

Educators in the black schools sometimes made distinctions between the freeborn and the freedmen pupils. These distinctions were usually expressed in terms of color since, historically, lighter color often correlated with free status. But as Mortimer Warren, principal of Avery Institute, seemed to be gratified to point out, lighter color did not necessarily equate with better performance. Describing an event so rare that it had not been equaled in any similar school in the entire South, he noted that a mathematics class at Avery was far enough advanced that its students would probably finish algebra the next term. "Some of them," he noted, "are very black and some very white, but the blacker are the smarter."[96] The darker-skinned students may well have been freedmen, and as such, had more motivation to strive because their families had fewer advantages than the freeborn elite and more disadvantages to make up for. Arthur Sumner, principal of the Morris Street School, observed that 20 percent of the students in the highest classes were freeborn. He found it especially interesting that students who had been slaves before the war were equal in terms of intellect and scholastic achievement to those who had been free and who had received instruction before and during the war. He took care to note that "the jewel and pride of the school is a perfectly black girl, 16 years of age."[97]

Relations between freemen and freedmen at the various schools in Charleston were usually cordial during the Reconstruction period, but occasionally animosity flared up between the two groups that recalled their sometimes negative prewar relations. The actions of some AMA teachers and of Francis Cardozo, Charleston's leading educator, who had been a relatively privileged free black before the war, illustrate this point. When economic conditions made it virtually impossible for many of the freedmen attending Saxton School to pay the monthly school tuition, Cardozo sent them home. At one point, the pupils sent home for nonpayment numbered as many as four hundred. When Sarah W. Stansbury, an AMA teacher at Saxton, launched a protest on behalf of these students, Cardozo fired her. With the help of others, Stansbury responded by organizing a small school outside of Charleston to educate former slaves who were poor.[98] A concerned and chastened Cardozo, recognizing the need to maintain the support of both freemen and freedmen to sustain Saxton and fearing that rumors of racial prejudice would spread to the larger black community, reversed his decision. To halt the drop in enrollment at Saxton, he sent his teachers to the students' homes to invite them to return and tried to alleviate their financial burden by providing books at below cost or free of charge to orphans and those without fathers.[99]

Another incident also reflects badly on Cardozo's impartiality. When containers of clothing sent by some Northern benevolent societies for destitute freedmen arrived at Saxton School's Mission House, Cardozo asked a teacher to tell prospective recipients to come for the clothing on the following Saturday. But when one concerned teacher looked into the clothing barrels that Saturday, she was distressed to find them nearly empty. She suspected that Cardozo and other AMA teachers had distributed the best of these items to freeborn students, some of whom were from former slave-owning families themselves. She may well have been correct, because when she complained to Cardozo, he fired her.[100] Whatever the truth of the story, it appears that Cardozo did not take the best interests of freedmen into account when handling these charitable contributions.

This was not the only example of a problem between freemen and freedmen in the Charleston schools. Another incident involved some students at Avery Institute. Of students enrolled at Avery, the high percentage from the light-skinned black elite of Charleston for the most part occupied the advanced courses, while most freedmen were concentrated in the lower grades.[101] When a dark-skinned woman identified as Mrs. Shaw arrived at the Mission House in April 1875 to begin teaching at Avery, several of the lighter-skinned students protested her appointment and insisted that they would leave Avery rather than be taught by a "black" teacher. Some believed that because of her skin color she would be an inferior teacher. Others argued that black teachers should not be brought from outside the Charleston area but instead should be chosen from Avery's graduates.[102]

James Ford, the principal of Avery at that time, encountered so much difficulty over the appointment of Mrs. Shaw that he expressed regret over the decision. He had had the impression, he said, that "Mrs. Shaw was a light-colored woman like most of our school," and he would not have hired her if he had known her true skin color. His stance was based on his understanding that the "light-colored people in the City of Charleston were just as prejudiced against blacks as were [numerous] whites." Mrs. Shaw was allowed to stay at Avery Institute, however, and no student actually left the school because of her color.[103]

Tension between freeborn and freed people of African descent continued throughout the Reconstruction period, and sometimes it resulted in the two social groups attending different schools. One Northern visitor to Charleston was "told that the free blacks, as distinguished from the freed people, still cultivate a feeling of exclusiveness, and among other modes of displaying it, still send their children to private schools."[104]

Despite this tension within the black community, a more serious threat to the freedmen's schools in Charleston was the white opposition to their existence. Countless white South Carolinians perceived the education of blacks as detrimental to Southern society because it would allow blacks to believe that they could be equal with whites. Such an idea would not be easily tolerated by a society that had been built on the myths of white superiority and black inferiority.

White opposition to the education of blacks was exacerbated by the Freedmen's Bureau's practice of commandeering schools previously used by whites to create schools for freedmen.[105] One white Charlestonian, voicing the feelings of many others, complained that blacks would keep these schoolhouses "until the little nigger race shall be prepared to enter college, whilst our poorer white children are growing up in Ignorance and vice."[106] White Charlestonians also tended to blame Northern white teachers for spreading education to Southern blacks. The hostility was strong enough that some of these AMA teachers, Phebe Alcott among them, worried that white Charlestonians might some night set fire to the Rhett House, where they lived.[107]

Despite these fears, open confrontations with whites over the freedmen's schools were rare. Whites who were angered by the existence of these schools tended to avoid them. Francis Cardozo wrote that, of all the white visitors to his school, none of them had been "Rebels." Speaking of white opponents, he said, "They pass by on the opposite side, and mutter curses as they hear the children sing."[108] Some, however, were more intrusive. Cardozo wrote that one "woman, very finely dressed, and apparently quite lady like, stopped at the door the other day while the children were singing, and said, 'oh, I wish, I could put a torch to that building. The Niggers!'"[109] On another occasion a prominent white man briskly approached the school door while the children were singing a patriotic song. When Cardozo asked what he wanted, the man simply grumbled that "the school was a damned nuisance." "Why are you making all this noise disturbing the neighbors?" he went on. "Didn't you know there is a lady sick next door?" Caught off guard by Cardozo's politely assuring him that the singing was part of the school's exercises but that if anyone was sick, the children would certainly stop singing for that person's sake, the man walked off muttering "damned nuisance."[110]

In addition to divisiveness within the black community and white opposition to the education of blacks, a serious obstacle to freedmen's education remained the lack of sufficient funds for schools. Freedmen's schools fell on hard times in the late 1860s and suffered throughout the rest of the Reconstruction era as the Freedmen's Bureau and benevolent societies gradually withdrew their financial support.[111] The support freedmen continued struggling to provide was not enough to fill the need.

Schools organized by the freedmen themselves were the first to be affected by dwindling funds. Of these, the Cain Institute, which was self-supporting, was particularly vulnerable to the increasing poverty of freedmen. The principal, W. D. Harris, wrote that many blacks had been thrown out of work because of their affiliation with the Republican party and, as a result, "the school does not sustain itself and we have not the necessary facilities and means to make the school what we desire it to be—for instance we have only one Room—and four teachers beside myself."[112] Finally he was forced to close because of the insufficient funds.

Regular attendance was another obstacle to keeping schools open. Many black children were compelled to work rather than attend school. Seeing this happen at Shaw School, Arthur Sumner wrote, "One great trouble in these schools is, that the children are often taken away just when they are getting a good ground work laid."[113] At Avery Institute, Mortimer Warren was equally frustrated: "Our school opens fairly successfully but there is the constant tendency, year by year and term by term for our older pupils one by one to drop out. If we do not watch for them, they are gone before we know it. Despite our patient and hard work, we find we have been educating children to become barbers and shoemakers."[114]

The poverty of their pupils forced the staffs of some freedmen's schools to make their own sacrifices to maintain the schools and the children's access to education. At one point, Warren decided to forego hiring a janitor at Avery. He did part of the work himself and delegated the sweeping to two young men at reduced wages. One teacher there agreed to waive her salary until the school was faring better with tuition collection.[115] Poverty was rampant in Charleston in the last months of 1871, and Warren noted that with more than twelve thousand people unemployed in the city and no relief in sight, Avery's tuition payments "are going to come by hard grinding—they come in slowly, just now, at any rate."[116]

Throughout the 1870s, school payments would continue to come in slowly, reaching an all-time low by 1876, the year that marked the end of Radical Reconstruction in South Carolina. Most freedmen were Republicans, and because of the political climate they lost whatever poorly paid jobs they had held. Commenting on the gravity of the situation, Amos W. Farnham, principal of Avery Institute at the time, wrote, "With regard to the small number in school, I think the prevailing poverty of the colored people in Charleston, is the prime cause. Owing to political differences many lost their jobs last fall, though they received meager wages at best from them. Some families are not properly fed." Poverty made it virtually impossible for some families to clothe children, buy their books, or pay their tuition. Farnham observed that the largest number of pupils whose families could not pay school tuition were from the lower grades.[117]

Nevertheless, the available data suggest that despite increased poverty and economic instability the school attendance rates of freedmen remained steady as the Reconstruction years wore on, and not just in Charleston. James Anderson has shown that blacks throughout the South maintained remarkable school attendance rates during Reconstruction.[118] Data differentiating attendance rates for rural and urban freedmen enrolled in Charleston's schools are not available, but it seems possible that, as economic hardships increased, a smaller percentage of the rural freedmen were able to maintain their school attendance. Many of these rural children would have been needed to supplement their parents' incomes by working with them on the plantations.

Teachers Monthly School Reports for Shaw School, Avery Institute, Franklin Street School, and Zion School for the years 1867 through 1871 reveal consistently high attendance rates for enrolled freedmen. In October 1867, for example, average attendance at both Franklin Street School and Zion School was 80 percent of those enrolled.[119] Attendance at Shaw School in November and December of 1867 ranged from 81 to 83 percent.[120] Attendance at Shaw School was 88 percent for a six-month period in 1868, 91 percent for five months in 1869, and 88 percent and 90 percent in January 1870 and January 1871, respectively.[121] Attendance at Avery Institute averaged 80 percent for part of 1869 and increased to 81 percent in January 1870 and 86 percent in March 1870.[122] Franklin Street School averaged 87 percent attendance for a four-month period in 1869, and 85 and 88 percent for January 1870 and January 1871, respectively.[123]

Attendance at Wallingford Academy, however, according to the monthly reports, fluctuated a great deal more, with the rate dropping from 80 percent to a dismal 50 percent in only three months of 1868.[124] In 1869, Wallingford's attendance rate fluctuated from 65 percent to 85 percent in three months, averaging roughly 77 percent a month.[125] Few records survive for the school in 1870, but we do know that attendance in January of that year was 70 percent.[126]

Enrollment figures for the city at large constitute a further indicator of the strength of the drive among freedmen to get an education (see table 11). The number of blacks enrolled in schools throughout the city of Charleston compared favorably with that of whites. Of the 7,888 students enrolled in 1870, 48.8 percent were black. This figure corresponds closely with the racial composition of the city. In seven of the city's eight wards, more than 40 percent of eligible white students were enrolled. Black enrollment did not lag far behind. In five of the eight wards, enrollment of eligible blacks was more than 40 percent. Blacks were also enrolled in large numbers in schools in Charleston County in 1870. They constituted 54 percent of the 9,680 students enrolled that year. Whereas the number of white male students was nearly equal to the number of white female students, black female students held a sizable numerical advantage over black male students, outnumbering them 2,828 to 2,447.[127]

The comments of travelers to Charleston add meaning to these attendance figures. A woman visiting from the North near the end of Reconstruction wrote, "Education is doing its work slowly but surely; there are schools everywhere, where they [blacks] receive exactly the same training as the whites, and consequently the colored population of today is a great advance on the enslaved race of twenty years ago."[128] This is a fitting tribute to the countless black Charlestonians whose great sacrifices to acquire an education caused another visitor to characterize Charleston as "a city of idle ragged Negroes who with no visible means of support, nevertheless send an astonishing multitude to school."[129]

Literacy figures for 1870, 1880, 1890, and 1900 point out the effectiveness of Southern blacks' strong efforts to become educated. In these years the United States Census Bureau defined illiteracy as inability to write. According to this criterion, 12,093 of the 22,150 blacks in Charleston in 1870, aged ten or older, were illiterate, and thus the illiteracy rate for blacks in that year was 54.6 percent.[130] In each decade between 1880 and 1900, the black population increased, but the number of illiterates decreased significantly. In 1890, the total number of Charleston blacks aged ten or older had reached 24,190, but the number of illiterates had dropped to 8,400, for a black illiteracy rate of 34.7 percent.[131] By 1900, the total number of Charleston blacks aged ten or older had increased to 25,110, while the number of illiterates had dropped to 7,462, causing the illiteracy rate for blacks to plummet to 29.7 percent.[132]

Charleston blacks were thus steadily becoming literate in the first few decades after their liberation. A comparison of the illiteracy rates for blacks in the fourteen Southern cities with total populations over twenty-five thousand in 1890 and 1900 makes the educational achievement of Charleston blacks seem all the more remarkable (see table 12). In 1890, blacks in Charleston had the lowest illiteracy rate of these fourteen cities, and in 1900, blacks in only three of these cities had illiteracy rates lower than that of Charleston.

The decreasing rate of illiteracy among black Charlestonians in the nineteenth century put them in the vanguard of a state and national trend. The illiteracy rate of South Carolina blacks aged ten or older was 78.5 percent in 1880, but it dropped to 64 percent by 1890 and to 52.8 percent by 1900.[133] At the same time, the national black illiteracy rate was also dropping, from 70 percent in 1880 to about 30 percent in 1910.[134] Compared to the thirteen other Southern cities examined, Charleston had the smallest percentage-point change in its black illiteracy rate between 1890 and 1900, but this figure can be understood as normal for a city that had already eradicated much of its illiteracy. By 1900, blacks in other Southern cities were beginning to make the great strides toward total literacy that had already been achieved in Charleston.

The drive and determination of Charleston blacks to acquire an education is dramatized by the stories of some of the graduates of the city's schools. Although records for the graduates of most Charleston schools during the Reconstruction period are sparse, a significant number of records do exist for those of Avery Institute. This school is unusual for having had a disproportionate number of graduates who had been free before the war, but an examination of the achievements of some of its graduates is illuminating nevertheless. Eighty-six students were graduated from Avery between 1872 and 1877. A large majority of them pursued additional studies or became teachers. More than half went on to teach in public schools. A few, including Martha C. Gadsen and Sallie O. Cruikshank, taught at Shaw in Charleston, but others had to leave the city to find teaching jobs because Shaw was the only one of the two black municipal public schools to hire black teachers. Those who left the city to pursue additional studies amassed an impressive record of academic achievement. As the school superintendent, Francis Cardozo helped procure college scholarships for Joseph Wilkinson, Walter Jones, Arthur O. Hear, Thomas McCants Stewart, and Joseph W. Morris. Hear attended Oberlin College in Ohio and received his degree at Howard University in Washington, D.C. Stewart transferred from Howard to the University of South Carolina at Columbia, where he earned two degrees. Cardozo persuaded several other Avery graduates to transfer from Howard to the University of South Carolina at Columbia, where they too earned degrees before embarking on distinguished careers.[135] Theirs was the ultimate achievement, which had begun with the same understanding most Charleston blacks had, that "they must get them some book lernin'."

WE ARE ALL BROTHERS AND SISTERS

Black Family and Community Life in Charleston during Reconstruction

5

Many words have been expended by scholars on the crippling effect of the legacy of slavery on black families, particularly in the first half of the twentieth century.[1] The system of slavery made it almost impossible for most black families to maintain stability. Slave families were often broken up at the discretion of slaveowners; slaves were sometimes severely punished, and often black women were sexually molested by white men. Furthermore, the legal and social definition of slaveowners as the head of the slave families seriously compromised the influence of black parents, particularly black fathers, on their families.

But despite all the hardships, some degree of stability did exist in the slave family and carried over into the Reconstruction period. Many slaves viewed the twin institutions of marriage and family as sacred.[2] And some slaveowners actually encouraged and acknowledged slave marriages, although they did so within the limits of the institution.[3] A large number of rural slaves ran away to join family members who had been sold to other planters, while others refused to take flight from slavery in order to remain near family members. Slaves in the cities and on plantations often lived in family units with their owner's blessing. By allowing slaves to live in family or quasi-family units, owners were able to reduce the cost of their upkeep. Within these units, slave men supplemented meager rations by hunting and fishing, while slave women made clothing and tended to family illnesses. Extended family members helped with child care and maintained ties by exchanging small gifts. Out of this, some sense of family could and did emerge. Within the family, the slave found love, companionship, sexual gratification, and sympathetic understanding of suffering. Strengthened by being part of this unit, the slave learned to cooperate with other blacks and to maintain his or her self-esteem, and, drawing on the experience of older family members, the slave also found ways to avoid punishment. Even though the family had no legal existence in slavery, it provided many enslaved blacks with insulation against the hardships of bondage.[4] Indeed, blacks revealed their strong attachment to blood kin by often naming children after grandparents or other relatives.[5] By the early years of emancipation, two-parent households were common among blacks.[6]

The strong sense of family among slaves was accompanied by a sense of community as well. Whenever possible, blacks organized benevolent societies to aid one another. Some organizations provided food and shelter for runaway slaves. Literate free blacks and slaves sometimes secretly taught others how to read and write, and some free blacks purchased the freedom of relatives and friends. Although limited, familial and communal ties grew even under bondage in Charleston, and after emancipation, black Charlestonians sought to make these ties stronger.

As soon as emancipation became effective, the most pressing and immediate task for former slaves was to find family members who had been sold or taken away during slavery. The work of emancipation, they believed, was incomplete until the family members who had been dispersed by slavery were reunited.[7] For example, after an extensive letter-writing campaign, Maria Robinson learned through the Freedmen's Bureau that her mother, Jane Watson, whom she had not seen for thirty-one years, was living in Gainstown, Alabama. She asked the Freedmen's Bureau to provide transportation to return her mother to Charleston.[8] Similarly, Charlestonian Mary Gibbs found her mother, Martha Gibbs, in New Orleans, Louisiana, through the help of the Freedmen's Bureau. Martha Gibbs had been sold to a gulf port planter before the Civil War. This reunion, like many others, was particularly poignant because the mother had nearly lost all hope of finding her daughter.[9] Nothing better illustrates the remarkable resiliency of black family ties than the efforts of former slaves to reunite with family members.[10]

Sometimes black Charlestonians asked the Freedmen's Bureau to provide transportation for them to visit family members who, they claimed, could not survive without their care. Many, however, after visiting relatives and friends and becoming assured of their well-being, asked that the Bureau then return them home. According to one Freedmen's Bureau agent:

> A woman would obtain transportation of me on the plea that she wanted to rejoin a child in Charleston whom she had not seen for ten years and who was suffering for her care; then having enjoyed a sufficient amount of family gossip in the city, she would apply to the Bureau officer there to save her from starvation by returning her to Greenville.

This Bureau agent became so accustomed to these actions that on occasion he would casually ask the freedman applicant, "When do you want to come back?"[11]

Those who did not solicit the aid of the Freedmen's Bureau sometimes saved money to try one day to locate family members themselves. One such man hoped soon to "haf money enough to go back and look fo my old woman and babies."[12] As a slave in Charleston fifteen years before, he had been sold to a man in Alabama and had neither seen nor heard from his wife or child since that time. During the bombardment of Charleston, another slave, whose wife and children belonged to a different owner, had assented to his family's being taken away to the country for their safety.[13] It is most likely that this family was reunited after emancipation.

Black soldiers sometimes risked military punishment to seek out or assist their families.[14] William Emory, a sergeant in the 128th South Carolina Colored Troops Regiment, left his regiment without authorization to help his sick mother and family. Upon his return, he was charged with desertion and threatened with imprisonment. Hoping to be exonerated, Emory asked General R. K. Scott to intervene on his behalf.[15]

The first concern of any black soldier who was incarcerated was how he would provide for his family. Milton Ford, a private also in the 128th, was arrested in Charleston in May 1866. The charges against him are not clearly recorded, but it is clear that he was sentenced to three years in prison and a dishonorable discharge. Fearing for the survival of his family without his army pay, Ford wrote from prison, "My wife and children have no means of support but me and now I am situated so I can do nothing at this time." He requested from army officials the sixty-one months of back pay due to him so that he could provide for his family. He also requested that his sentence be remitted so that he could return to his family in Charleston.[16] Similarly, John Bennett, a corporal in the Thirty-fifth United States Colored Troops in Charleston who was charged with murder in July 1866, feared for how his family, already suffering from his absence, would fare if he were convicted.[17]

The United States Congress legalized slave marriages in March 1865, and several months later the South Carolina legislature did the same. In response, freedmen flocked to provost courts, army camps, churches, and Freedmen's Bureau offices to legalize their marriages.[18] "Among the newly freed Blacks," a contemporary noted, "each party to a marital union was usually satisfied with one partner, and seldom was it heard that the one or the other had a lover on the side."[19] But for many former slaves the opportunity to legitimize a union posed a dilemma. Those who had been forcibly separated from their spouses in many instances had since taken other partners. The question then arose of who was to be regarded as whose husband or wife and who should have custody of the children.[20]

Countless Charleston freedmen and freedwomen, like former slaves throughout the South, experienced legal and emotional complications in reuniting with spouses and children. For example, when Robert Washington, who had escaped to the North before the war, returned to Charleston in 1870 to reclaim his wife, Lucretia, and their child, he was dismayed to discover that Lucretia had already taken another husband. The magistrate who heard the case, T. J. Mackey, ruled against Washington. In Mackey's opinion, Washington should have had enough interest in Lucretia to have returned to Charleston sooner than he did.[21] Another magistrate agreed in 1875 to hear the case of two Charleston freedmen who were threatening to get into a physical fight over a woman whom each claimed as his legal wife.[22] The stories of Charleston freedmen and freedwomen who chose to return to their original spouses suggest that many initial marriages were based on genuine affection or strong respect for family obligations.[23] Jane Ferguson of Charleston left no doubt where her loyalty lay. Initially, she married Martin Barnwell and had a child by him. Shortly thereafter, Barnwell was sold away from her and the infant. Being alone now, and not expecting the sickly Barnwell ever to return, she married a man named Ferguson. She made it clear to Ferguson that if Barnwell returned, he would be welcomed as her husband, and Ferguson assented. But when Charleston fell to the Union army in February 1865 and news reached Jane Ferguson that Barnwell was still alive and anxious to reunite with her, Ferguson was not quite so ready to give her up. From Florida, where he was stationed with the Union army, he wrote, "Martin has not seen you for a long time. He cannot think of you as I do. O Jane! Do not go to Charleston. Come to Jacksonville: I will get a house and we will live here. Never mine [sic] what the people say. Come to me Jane." Despite this plea, Jane Ferguson and her child reunited with Barnwell.[24]

A close reading of the Freedmen's Savings Bank records for the Charleston branch for the years 1865–1874 reveals that, even though the slave family was not protected by law, a large number of former-slave couples in Charleston had lived together for a long time. An indication that these unions were probably long lasting is that a good many of the married depositors, according to the records, were elderly and usually had several adult children. Furthermore, these records also reveal that many Charleston freedmen lived in two-parent families within just a few years of emancipation. Approximately 85 percent of the two thousand depositors of adult age at the Charleston branch of the Freedmen's Savings Bank were married during the early years of emancipation, and their spouses and children lived in the same households.[25]

Although contemporary observers frequently commented on what they perceived as instability in marriages between blacks, census statistics suggest that the black family in Charleston had achieved a degree of stability by 1870. Of black adults living in all-black households, the percentage of those who were married was in fact strikingly close to the percentage of married white adults living in all-white households. Percentages were calculated from a random sampling of 9,334 inhabitants taken from Charleston's eight wards. The sample group was selected from the manuscript census returns of 1870 and constitutes slightly less than 19 percent of the city's population that year. Residents of the eight wards were divided into three categories: all-black households, all-white households, and mixed-race households. Although there were many mixed-race households, most households were either all black or all white.

In 1870, in seven of the eight wards, more than 50 percent of the adult residents of both all-white households and all-black households were married. For the whole city, nearly 58 percent of the adult residents of all-white households were married, while slightly over 56 percent of the adult residents of all-black households were married (see Appendix, table 13). Significantly, these percentages are nearly equal, and though these figures are entirely static and do not reveal how long couples remained married, they testify to the inner strength of blacks as a people and reflect their commitment to marriage and family.

A very different pattern emerges, however, among the minority of blacks residing in mixed-race households. Although some blacks who lived in such households constituted families, most were unrelated to one another. A large majority were children and women who worked as domestic servants. Not surprisingly, these circumstances did not give rise to normal family relationships. Sample census statistics for 1870 reveal that in six of the eight wards in Charleston, fewer than 50 percent of the black adults living in mixed-race households were married. Overall, only 42 percent of these black adult residents of mixed-race households in Charleston were married. Whites living in mixed-race households, however, were more likely to have normal family relationships. In five of the eight wards, more than 50 percent of white adult residents of mixed-race households were married, and overall, the proportion was close to 53 percent (see table 13).

It was not unusual in the Reconstruction years for both all-white and all-black households to contain more than one nuclear family or one nuclear family plus additional relatives or boarders. Economic and war-time dislocations may have contributed to the somewhat larger-than-usual households. It was only five years after a war during which housing had been destroyed and in a city to which war refugees and migrating freedmen had flocked. Some households contained two or more families, but more typical were households of one or two single people living either with a family or with other single people. Sometimes several generations of one family lived together; it was not unusual for one family to include grandparents, aunts, uncles, and cousins. The sample census statistics suggest that on average the number of residents in a household was larger for blacks than whites (see table 14).

If we consider the average nuclear family to be the average number of children for a couple plus the married couple itself, then among all-black households, the average nuclear family had four to five members, while the average household had seven to eight members. Among all-white households, the average nuclear family had five members while the aver-age household had six members. In both all-black and all-white house-holds these additional residents were likely to be extra relatives or board-ers.

Unfortunately, some Charleston freedmen husbands and fathers failed to fulfill the socially dictated family role of provider by not support-ing their families financially. Ready Simons, for example, was forced to file charges against her husband for his refusal to support her and their four young children. Some men committed crimes against their families; there were even cases of wife and child abuse that sometimes resulted in murder. Joe Richardson stabbed his wife, Emma, to death; James Robert-son beat his wife nearly to death; and Smart Chisolm drowned his two-year-old stepdaughter, Cornelia Verdier.[26]

Such individual transgressions, however, were not the norm during Reconstruction in the South. Most black families demonstrated a re-markable degree of stability.[27] The acts of irresponsibility and of violence can in many instances be linked to the particular problems of overcom-ing the legacy of slavery and of trying to make a living in a crowded city where jobs were scarce and poverty was widespread. Under slavery, the labor of enslaved blacks helped to enrich the slaveowner, but it also provided the slaves' own subsistence. With emancipation, the ravaged economy of the postwar South left the former slaves with the difficult burden of providing their subsistence under the new conditions. Unfortunately, some were ill-prepared to undertake this task all on their own, and they became idlers or vagabonds.

With emancipation also came the lifting of legal sanctions against relationships between blacks and whites. To a few black men this meant that they now had the right to cohabit with white women if they so desired. One such relationship incensed white Charlestonians. Sergeant Major Overton, a member of the Thirty-fifth Massachusetts Regiment of Colored Troops and a wheelwright by trade, eloped with the wife of a white grocer who lived on Calhoun Street. Prior to the elopement, the two exchanged several love letters. Overton in his letters promised the woman that she would never want for anything if she gave him her love and came to live with him.[28] The scandal of this elopement appeared to confirm one of whites' worst fears about the aftermath of emancipation: that black men in great numbers would take white women as sexual mates. Their fears were unfounded, however, for such unions were rare during the Reconstruction period.

Blacks asserted their new rights in other ways. Black men, for example, were no longer compelled by slavery to stand by and watch while white men committed acts of violence against black women and girls. Some white men believed that emancipation had changed nothing and that they could take any liberties they chose.[29] But when Hughey Kern, a white man, stabbed and attempted to rape a nine-year-old black girl near Happoldt's farm in the suburbs of the city, the girl's father and the police together pursued and captured Kern.[30] Responses like this heralded a new social order in which black people asserted rights that had previously not existed.

During Reconstruction, black women also asserted their new rights. Almost immediately after the war, many began to resist working as domestic servants in white homes as they had under slavery. Those who did accept domestic employment frequently refused to live in their employer's residence.[31] They wanted to reduce their risk of sexual harassment by white male household members and avoid the hardship of living away from their families. Most black women objected to being employed as domestic servants because they believed that working in a home as a domestic servant was not consistent with their new freedom.[32] They hoped for a role in the family more in line with the role they had seen white women enjoying.

Black women's withdrawal from waged domestic service presaged a rewriting of the black woman's as well as the black man's role in the family. The black community of Charleston as a whole supported the withdrawal of women from wage labor. Men equated with freedom their right to choose whether their wives would work at wage labor. As the head of the family under emancipation, black men hoped to be able to provide for their families so their wives could remain at home to care for the

family, and they sought to protect black women from the sexual exploitation that had existed under slavery. Black men felt that ending this
exploitation was imperative, and they were determined to do so.[33] Moreover, as one contemporary scholar suggests, "Many Black women independently desired to devote more time than had been possible under
slavery to caring for their children and to domestic responsibilities like
cooking, sewing, and laundering."[34] White Charlestonians were incensed
over the withdrawal of black women and children from wage labor. This
move upset the smooth operation of many white households, and worse,
there was an implication of social equality in blacks' having the same
roles and expectations for their family members that white families had.[35]

These fears, however, were unwarranted, for the shift in the locus of
black women's labor from the homes of whites to their own homes
proved to be a temporary phenomenon. When the depression of the
1870s pushed up the cost of rent and in every way intensified the poverty
of most black families, all family members, men, women, and children,
had to work at wage labor to contribute to the family's income.[36] Moreover, given the widespread attitude of independence among black
women, some undoubtedly preferred to work, whether or not their
incomes were needed to help support the family. A *New York Tribune*
correspondent in Charleston in the 1870s commented on the large
number of black women who washed and sewed and worked in the
gardens near the city.[37]

Throughout this period, despite the trend of black women's staying at
home as housewives, a much higher percentage of black women and
children than of white women and children in Charleston worked for
wages. The 1870 manuscript census of 9,334 residents reveals that over 50
percent of adult black women worked for wages, while only 14 percent of
adult white women did so (see table 15). The percentage of male children working outside the home was about 14 percent for both blacks and
whites, while the percentage of black female children who worked outside the home was considerably higher (nearly 16 percent) than that of
white female children (5 percent) (see tables 16 and 17). Although emancipation did not eliminate wage labor by black women and children, it
fundamentally altered the locus of control. Now the decision about
where and when black women and children would work was made by the
family itself, headed by the black man, rather than by the white owner or
overseer. As a consequence, blacks were able to liberate their families to
some extent from the authority of whites. To most blacks, this was a
crucial element of freedom.[38]

The yoke of slavery had been lifted from black men, but freedom
meant they bore all the responsibility of providing for their families and
for themselves. Most met the challenge by caring for their children at the
time and also providing for their futures. Some went as far as opening

bank accounts for the future security of their offspring. For example, Daniel Matthias opened an account for his one-week-old son, and James Hardy opened accounts for his six-month-old daughter and his four-year-old son. Bank records also show that black men opened accounts for their adult daughters, even those who were married and employed. Once daughters reached maturity and remained unmarried, fathers appeared to be particularly interested in their welfare, perhaps mirroring the view of the dependent female held by most white men at the time, and they tended to open bank accounts for these daughters, regardless of their employment status. William Peronneau opened an account for his adopted daughter, Lena Bullwinkle, even though she was self-employed as a mantua maker, sewing dresses for women. These two even had a joint account on which either could draw, and "in case of death, to one of us we desire the living one to draw all the money."[39]

Former slave women, whether married or single, also demonstrated a strong determination to support their children. But fulfilling that responsibility was more difficult for black women than for black men, and their record of achievement is therefore more impressive because employment opportunities were scarcer for black women than for black men, and what jobs there were for black women usually paid less than did jobs for black men. Women's efforts to provide, like those of men, also show up in bank records. Anna Oakes was a married, self-employed mantua maker who started accounts for her nine-year-old son, Erasmus, and for her five daughters: nine-month-old Lilla, three-year-old Catherine, six-year-old Josephine, eleven-year-old Harriet, and thirteen-year-old Mary. Mary Whaley took responsibility for the third generation by contributing money to accounts for her three granddaughters, probably because the father of the older two did not live with them and their mother. Among blacks in Charleston, the task of managing household money seems most often to have fallen to women. This responsibility sometimes extended to their assisting older children in dealings with the bank. The institution of slavery had required all blacks, regardless of age, to labor in some capacity and contribute materially to the survival of the family. When emancipation occurred, most black children, having never experienced the freedom of a traditional childhood as it was known to white children, accepted the need to work and contribute toward the family income. These children were encouraged by their parents or guardians to save what they could, and most often their mothers went with them to open savings accounts.[40]

All of these dealings with the bank attest to the interdependence of the black family and suggest that the earnings of grown children may have been considered not their private earnings but part of the material base of the household. These dealings are also examples of how black women were performing family roles denied them during slavery.

Some married black women displayed a remarkable degree of independence by opening bank accounts for themselves, refusing, it would seem, at least in the financial realm, to placidly accept the increasingly patriarchal quality of black family life. Records of the Freedmen's Savings Bank reveal also, however, that some black women started accounts for their husbands, some married black men started accounts for themselves, some started accounts for their wives, and couples started joint accounts. A deposit slip for Frederick and Matilda Elliott, for example, states that "either the husband or wife could draw the money." Joseph Berthune, a seventy-two-year-old waiter, shared a bank account with his wife, Silvia. The money was to be drawn by either Joseph or Silvia, and in the event of their death, "it was to be paid to their daughter, Sophia Berthune." As one contemporary scholar notes, "These patterns had little obvious connection to work or wage earning roles within the family." Instead, how married people set up their bank accounts more likely reflects the elusive elements of their relationship, that is, the implicit and shifting balance of power and sharing in the relationship.[41]

The interdependence of the black family, including the extended family, and the sense of responsibility for one another shows up in records of children helping their parents with bank accounts, of spouses and siblings helping one another, of uncles helping nieces and nephews, and even of in-laws and cousins helping one another when other familial relationships were absent. Children opened accounts for their parents, and offspring sometimes made provisions for the parent to draw money from the son's or daughter's account in the event of the child's death. In many instances, children offered support to their elderly parents when the parents were still able to care for themselves. Abraham Smith, for example, opened an account for his father while the father was still self-employed as a shoemaker, and Rebecca Gibbs opened one for her mother, Rose Johnson, while the mother was still working regularly as a cook; James Chisolm's elderly mother was unemployed when he opened an account for her.[42]

When a family was facing an economic crisis caused by the loss of a job, a devastating injury suffered by the breadwinner, or the death of a parent, an uncle might step in, usually by singling out one child and providing him or her with continuous support.[43] Joshua Butler was so singled out when his father died. Butler was eighteen years old and employed as a carpenter by Samuel Porter when his uncle Moses Munroe opened a bank account for him to help ease the financial burden placed on Butler's mother and her four children by the father's death. Ties of blood and obligation like these were a direct outgrowth of the black experience under slavery.[44]

That experience also included the involvement of fictive or quasi-kin, such as in-laws and cousins, which helped to develop slave communities by binding otherwise unrelated adults. As a result, slave communities were infused with conceptions of obligation that flowed initially from kin obligations rooted in blood and marriage and extended to obligations toward a fellow slave or a fellow slave's child. These familial and kin obligations that were enlarged to social obligations were maintained after emancipation.[45]

The strength of extended family ties among the former slaves of Charleston can also be deduced by observing naming patterns among them. Even during slavery, many children were named after their parents, grandparents, aunts, and uncles.[46] The naming of children for their fathers is particularly noteworthy because it puts to rest the false notion that slave fathers played a negligible role in the slave family. It also contradicts the theory that "patriarchal" status came only after black men acquired property or assimilated American attitudes and patterns of behavior following emancipation and the breakdown of their social isolation.[47] Among Charleston's slaves, 53 of 71 males born between 1820 and 1860 were named after their fathers.[48] Among a group of 4,667 blacks selected randomly from eight wards in Charleston in 1870, 62 were named after their fathers.[49] When women had children out of wedlock, they generally named their sons after a brother, the child's maternal grandfather, or his natural father.[50] Daughters were sometimes named after mothers but less often than sons after fathers. Among the survey of 4,667 blacks, 34 daughters were named after their mothers.[51] Another pattern can be seen in the repetition from generation to generation of such biblical names as Isaiah, Moses, Josiah, and Ezekiel. After emancipation, names associated with slavery, such as Primus, Bacchus, Scipio, Orpheus, and Caesar, all but vanished, rejected along with the slave identity. By 1870, of the 4,667 blacks surveyed, only 12 had one of these slave-associated names.[52] But also, as slave names disappeared after emancipation, Anglo-Saxon-sounding names such as Mary, Elizabeth, John, William, Charles, and George—names, that is, that were associated with freedom—appeared more and more.[53] Above all, as one recent scholar of the American South notes, "Naming patterns affirmed familial loyalties and affixed a stamp of approval on the lines of mutuality and kinship."[54]

The concept of social obligations among slaves that had grown out of the concept of familial obligations was transformed after emancipation into larger community obligations.[55] Some four million blacks in the South were set free by emancipation. But because of the devastation of war, the entire South was thrown into economic chaos, and disease and destitution characterized the lot of Charleston's freedmen. The Freedmen's Bureau and Northern benevolent societies worked hard to alleviate the suffering, but when these efforts were not enough, former slaves did what they could to lessen for their brethren the emotional strains of the transition from slavery to freedom, sometimes even going without the necessities of life to do so.

Black churches often took the lead in organizing charitable societies to help the destitute and sick and formed burial societies to pay burial expenses for the indigent.[56] In one instance, an individual, James Wigfall, a seventy-year-old self-employed carpenter who had lost his entire family, opened a bank account for which the deposit voucher reads, "Money is deposited for the purpose of burying the dead who have no money or friends."[57] Charleston's freedmen contributed labor and money to the establishment of an orphanage for black children in that city. The project began shortly after the evacuation of the city by Confederate forces when an extremely persistent black woman first wrote to James Redpath and then met with him to ask for his help in creating an "orphanage" where she and others could leave their children while they went to work the land in the interior. Redpath responded by acquiring two deserted buildings from the army. Since the buildings were filthy and lacked furnishings, he asked the members of a black church for twelve volunteers to clean them. The volunteers came and did the cleaning, and others contributed a few cooking utensils. A former house servant to a South Carolina governor volunteered to work at the orphanage, and a "society of colored ladies" sewed clothing for the children. The establishment of this orphanage was truly a community effort.[58] This kind of effort was crucial to the survival of former slaves throughout the South because only 0.5 percent of the four million freedmen were materially assisted by the Freedmen's Bureau during its existence.[59]

But all that freedmen did to supplement the efforts of the Freedmen's Bureau and the Northern benevolent societies to alleviate the suffering among blacks in Charleston was still not enough. The city's depressed economy and overabundance of labor that was due largely to the heavy influx of black migrants from the countryside forced most freedmen to accept a standard of living much lower than that of whites.[60] A few individual freedmen were able to save enough money to buy lots and build homes for themselves, and some groups pooled their funds to accomplish this objective. But countless former slaves were forced by circumstances to take any sort of housing they could find. This often meant renting a cheap shack that was unhygienic and overcrowded.[61] White Charlestonians were well aware of the living conditions of Charleston's freedmen and wrote down their reactions. One white noted, for example, that it was not unusual to see "as many as five different families [living] in one small building."[62] Another revealed that "a crowd of colored persons living in a house in Tradd Street . . . have made the location a perfect nuisance to the neighborhood."[63] These were not the worst cases. There were many whose plight was even worse; they could not afford to rent housing and were forced to sleep under old buildings and on the pavement of back alleys.[64] Out of these desperate circumstances, predominantly black shanty towns emerged on the outskirts of Charleston, breeding crime, disease, and early death. In these neighborhoods, the death rate among blacks far exceeded that of whites living in other parts of the city.[65] Alcohol aggravated the ill effects of the shanty towns. Blacks had more money than they had ever had as slaves as well as the freedom to buy what they wanted, and as a result, the sale of liquor was unrestrained.[66] Some of the drunkenness must surely have been an attempt to assuage the pain of poverty, disease, unemployment, and failed expectations. Nevertheless, though drunkenness was a problem among freedmen, it was more prevalent among whites in Charleston.[67]

Allowing racism instead of facts to influence them, countless white Charlestonians labeled all freedmen thieves and scoundrels.[68] Certainly some freedmen did commit crimes. But, in the first few years of Reconstruction at least, most crimes by blacks were petty transgressions on the property of others and were not violent.[69] The *Charleston Courier* frequently reported petty thefts committed by blacks. On September 3, 1866, for example, the *Courier* reported that two freedmen were charged with forcibly robbing a young woman of $17. When a portion of the money was found in their possession, they were arrested. On September 20, the paper reported the arrest of Henry Diane, who, two days earlier, had stolen clothing, a gold watch and chain, some tobacco, and $660 cash from the residence of J. Meyer. And on December 22, the paper reported that a freedman was arrested for rifling the pocketbook of another freedman. The thief was arrested, found to be in possession of the money, and held for trial. Some freedmen who were accused of theft had stolen food to support their starving families; often these were wage earners who might have been driven to such measures in part by white employers who defrauded them of wages or crop shares.[70] Others stole money or valuables to exchange for food.[71] A few freedmen associated freedom with leisure, however, and, alienated from social norms, they became swindlers and drifters.[72] Often thievery was their sole support.

It is difficult to measure the extent of black crime in Charleston because the racism so deeply ingrained in the minds of white judges and juries makes the results of the trials of Charleston's former slaves suspect. The volumes of letters written by black officials of the Freedmen's Bureau and black religious and civic leaders, as well as black defendants and their families, protesting acts of discrimination and brutality at the hands of law enforcement officials help, however, to balance the picture.[73]

Besides the difficulties provoked by these injustices, many freedmen found the economic and social problems of emancipation nearly overwhelming at times. Indeed, there are a few recorded cases of attempted suicide. Mary Williams, for example, tried twice to kill herself, once by jumping off the dock adjacent to Elliott Street in an effort to drown herself and a second time by taking laudanum, a powerful narcotic usually taken to relieve distress. Friends intervened and made sure she obtained medical help. James Wright, a black police officer beset with domestic difficulties, also tried to kill himself by taking laudanum, and he too received medical attention in time to save his life.[74]

Suicide was not a major issue within the larger black community, however. All of the difficulties freedmen were forced to face paled in comparison to the inhumane treatment they had been subjected to as slaves—the beatings, the separated families, the sexual exploitation, and the destruction of the male role as head of the family. Most former slaves were thus prepared mentally and spiritually to deal with the difficulties of freedom. Moreover, powerful affective kin ties were strong countervailing forces to suicide.

Although the typical Charleston freedman had little leisure time, most freedmen engaged in an active community life, centered mostly on schools and churches. Parents often visited schools informally to oversee the educational progress of their children or to attend, along with relatives and friends, the public examinations of students. These were festive events where socializing was as important as honoring student scholars.[75]

The church, however, in and around Charleston, was the central social institution for blacks. Sabbath services and prayer meetings provided opportunities to socialize, and so too did sitting-ups and funerals, where old friends and family members who had not seen one another for months or years could reestablish old relationships.[76] Religious societies such as Mary and Martha, the Rising Sons and Daughters of Bethlehem Star, and the Sons and Daughters of Zion Number Two sponsored sacred and secular events, including picnics and concerts. Old Fellows, Good Templars, Good Samaritans, Ancient York Masons, the Knights of Damon, the Catholic Knights of America, and a host of other fraternal organizations sponsored balls, parties, and banquets. All-black fire companies sponsored excursions around Charleston Harbor and to other cities. In addition, Charleston's Marble Skating Rink provided the setting for regular roller skating contests and promenade concerts.[77]

Athletics, particularly for spectators, were as much of a unifying force among all social and economic classes in the black community as was the church. Blacks gathered at the Washington Race Course to enjoy horse racing or joined regatta clubs, such as the Monrovia, Attacks, and Charleston Union, to watch or participate in boat races on the Ashley and Cooper rivers.[78] Baseball, however, was the all-important sport in the black community. Its significance is attested to by the number of baseball teams that black Charlestonians organized. Among the most important teams were Fulton, United, Eckford, Catchers, Pacific, Arlington, Active, and Resolute. By the mid-1870s, the black clubs had organized statewide tournaments, and in 1876 the Fulton team of Charleston won the state championship.[79] It is not difficult to imagine the special joy this victory must have given to the entire black community, particularly in the midst of worsening economic conditions and the defeat of Radical Reconstruction. In sports, the black community had something special that could not be taken away by whites. Blacks may have been frustrated and defeated in the economic and political spheres, but they were successful in the athletic arena.

Politics, supported by the church, was, however, the most powerful force unifying the black community of Charleston. The church helped to organize special commemorations for such occasions as the Fourth of July, the passage of the Emancipation Proclamation, and the ratification of the Fifteenth Amendment. Freedmen from the city and surrounding rural areas turned out at day-long celebrations in crowds that at times reached well into the hundreds and even thousands. Members of black organizations usually launched the events with parades that ended at Citadel Square, where stands and booths were set up to sell peaches, pancakes, ice cream, ginger cake, soda water, groundnuts, and beer. Here the freedmen had picnics, set off fireworks, and danced and sang to the music of fiddles, banjos, and pianos.

White Charlestonians generally left the celebrating of the Fourth of July entirely to blacks and often expressed annoyance at how they went about it. On these occasions all the formal talk was usually political. Both black and white Republican politicians addressed the freedmen with speeches praising Abraham Lincoln and the Union, praising the freedmen for their social, economic, and political progress since emancipation, and advising them about how to continue their successes, and of course always reminding them of the necessity of keeping the Radical Republicans in office. Being addressed on these occasions by black men of distinction, such as the high-ranking army officer Martin Delany and the educator Francis Cardozo, must have engendered a powerful sense of racial pride among the freedmen, while being addressed by whites of similar fame must have enhanced their self-esteem. White men coming to speak to blacks was something that had seldom happened during the antebellum period. Freedmen might have to go home at the end of the day and face a life of poverty, but at least for the time of these celebrations, they could stand among men of higher social stature and be recognized and heard. Although hundreds and thousands of freedmen attended the celebrations, there are no recorded instances of fist fights or other crowd violence.[80] Perhaps this is another indication that the black community of Charleston was not as disunited as many white contemporaries thought.

Unfortunately, however, there was no such discipline and self-restraint among the black Charlestonians who frequented the city's many saloons, lottery establishments, and houses of prostitution, especially the places on Elliott Street and the surrounding alleys, an area that was described as "the filthiest and certainly the wickedest region of the city." Here, some freedmen, fortunately a minority of the whole, frustrated with life at the bottom of society, vented their anguish, often in violence. These districts were the scenes of skirmishes, robberies, and sometimes murder.[81]

Despite all the forces that welded the black community of Charleston together racially, socially, culturally, and politically, there were forces dividing it. Blacks from the antebellum free black elite were scornful of the recently freed blacks, who in turn were distrustful of them. House servants thought themselves better than field hands, and blacks who were not very prosperous envied the well-to-do. There were also tensions between established city dwellers and rural migrants.[82]

When the special status that free blacks had enjoyed before the war was shattered by emancipation, some moved quickly to distinguish themselves from the masses of freedmen, labeling themselves the "bona fide free" and freedmen as those "sot free."[83] As late as 1880, Joseph Hayne Rainey reflected this attitude when he referred to himself as the "first colored *bonafide* member of Congress."[84] Jane Van Allen, a teacher employed by the American Missionary Association in Charleston, noted that

> many of the brown people here, think they are a great deal better than those who were slaves; and wherever you meet them, they are sure to tell you that they were free; but they think the Northern people must think the colored people are just as good as they are.[85]

A British visitor to postwar Charleston was told that there were still some French mulattoes in that city who formed an exclusive class by themselves, and that the "genteel" colored people kept very much to themselves.[86]

Differences in complexion fostered even more divisions than prewar status. Mulattoes valued their light complexions highly because these complexions revealed their white ancestry, the source of some of their advantages. This high regard for light complexions caused some to view those of a darker hue with disdain.[87] Incidents revealing these prejudices occurred daily. When, for example, two well-dressed young mulatto women and their black servant entered a railway car together, one of the young women ordered the servant to stay on the car's outer platform. When the conductor saw the servant and told her to take a seat inside, she replied, "Oh Lor' bless you massa, no—missus wouldn't 'low it." But when the conductor made it clear that riding on the outside of the car was now illegal, she reluctantly took a seat by her mistress, who seemed greatly disturbed that "Blacks were allowed to ride alongside ladies."[88] In another incident, a visitor to Charleston noted that "a couple of ebony damsels and a mulatto boy are belaboring one another in terms more vigorous than select as to each other's claims to respectability on the ground of color on the walk outside my window."[89]

While mulattoes glorified their white ancestry, those who were darker sometimes glorified their African heritage.[90] Immediately after gaining freedom, one former slave declared, "I got mannish. Wid not a drop of blood in me but de pure African, I sets out to find a mate of the pure breed."[91] Assuming much the same attitude as darker blacks would during the Black Power movement of the 1960s and 1970s, many darker blacks in postwar Charleston were scornful of the mulattoes, viewing them as anomalies,[92] a people without a racial heritage. In an incident recorded at the time, two young mulatto men arguing over who had the lighter complexion were overheard by a "jet Black youth who rather contemptuously asserted 'you ain't white people an' you never kin be niggers. You'se just nuff in at all. As foh me, I'se pure blooded Black nigger . . . lemme tell you. It makes me tired to hear two mulatto niggers talking like dat'."[93] A *New York Times* correspondent reported that it was not unusual to hear "an ebony rice field hand say of some cream colored city dandy: 'Dat white washed nigger am just like a mule. He ain't got no country and no ancestor'."[94]

As the historical record shows, these color distinctions within the black community of Charleston often had a direct effect on social class and status. Color conflicts led some members of Charleston's black community to view others with contempt and suspicion, and because of this contempt and suspicion, mulattoes sometimes remained aloof from the black masses and embraced exclusive organizations based on their light skin color. These color distinctions were very real after emancipation, but at the time whites probably overstated their extent and attached too much importance to them as well. Highly conscious of race themselves, whites could not avoid imputing importance to the deference darker-skinned blacks sometimes showed to those who were lighter skinned. Furthermore, in an effort to recruit mulattoes away from the Republican party and into their fold, conservative politicians continuously exaggerated the importance of color distinctions within the black community. But Northern white observers seem to have been the most interested in the color consciousness within the black community. As a consequence, they were the ones who did the most to publicize its existence.[95]

According to the statistical evidence, only a tiny minority of free blacks held elitist and pretentious notions. On the eve of the Civil War, 14 percent of the city's free blacks, most of whom were mulatto, belonged to an aristocracy of color, status, and wealth, amounting to only 3 percent of Charleston's total black population.[96] Because many lost property with the defeat of the Confederacy, this group's number had probably diminished further by the end of the war.[97] When all blacks were made free, the elite lost their once-privileged position, and it became more necessary than ever to distinguish themselves from former slaves and the free black masses. To this end, they formed separate churches and either continued exclusive organizations that predated the war, such as the Brown Society, or established new ones. Many continued to identify with the Southern white aristocracy, with whom they shared white ancestry and economic status. Feeling no identity with most blacks, they rarely joined the movement of racial self-help, though they were subject to much of the same racial oppression that entrapped poorer blacks. Seldom did they take up the political banner of their less fortunate brethren.[98] Members of the mulatto elite continued to place great value on their skin color and white heritage for well over half a century after Reconstruction.[99]

Most mulattoes, however, were just as proud of their African ancestry as they were of their white ancestry, and not all of them had been allowed to benefit from their color through manumission. Certainly, if mulattoes were to deny their black heritage, they would be denying a large portion of themselves. Most rejected the idea of separating themselves from whites and blacks by forming a third "mulatto community" upon emancipation, seeing themselves as a part of the larger black community with the same interests as the black masses.[100] Some even took active roles in organizing assistance for destitute freedmen. Francis Cardozo, Robert Smalls, Robert DeLarge, and many other mulattoes emerged to lead blacks in their struggle for political and civil rights. Some also became major figures in the freedmen's campaign for education, most notably Cardozo, the efficient school administrator at Saxton School and Avery Institute, where other mulattoes were teachers. Cardozo later became the state treasurer of South Carolina and then secretary of state. Smalls and DeLarge both proposed bills in Congress aimed at securing rights for blacks.[101]

On balance, the influences that united the black community were far more important than those that divided it. Blacks were bound together by a host of organizations they formed in the early years of freedom to achieve economic objectives, including burial, mutual homestead, and planting insurance societies; organizations of tradesmen; savings and loan associations; and the joint enterprises. They were also bound together by social clubs, by religious and educational institutions and the myriad social activities emanating from them, and above all by the one organization that nearly every black belonged to, the Republican party.[102]

The combination of all of these associations helped to minimize the tensions between blacks and mulattoes, freemen and freedmen, field hands and servants, and established city dwellers and rural migrants. That most free blacks were tied to former slaves by blood and marriage, and shared the former slaves' alienation from whites as well,[103] provides strong evidence that there existed a unified black community in Charleston during Reconstruction. Together, former slaves and free blacks made up a formidable front, and at the time of emancipation Charleston's black community was socially, racially, culturally, and politically united. In a real sense they were all brothers and sisters.

WE MUST HAVE OUR OWN HOUSE OF WORSHIP

The Exit of Charleston's Freedmen from White Churches

6

Reconstruction spawned many significant changes among Southern blacks, one of which was the severing of their religious ties to white churches. The massive withdrawal of Charlestonian blacks from white churches and the ultimate establishment of their own religious institutions took place in the first few years following the triumph of federal troops over the Confederacy. Sometimes this movement occurred over the protests of white church members, but more often than not, it was sanctioned and hastened by their actions and attitudes. When federal troops were withdrawn from South Carolina in 1877, marking the official end of political Reconstruction, there were virtually no black members in the white Southern Baptist, Methodist, Presbyterian, or Episcopalian churches in Charleston. For most Charleston freedmen, abandoning white churches to establish their own was as much a part of exercising their new freedom as was leaving the old plantations and the urban homes of former owners. As a group, freedmen had few resources for organizing their own churches. They were unable and unwilling, however, to solicit the help of Southern whites, and so Charleston freedmen often worshipped in makeshift surroundings until they could collect enough money to either secure or erect church buildings. Once these religious institutions were established, freedmen went to great lengths to maintain them. During the Reconstruction period, large and influential churches were created that quickly became the central institutions of the black community of Charleston, and many black ministers emerged as community leaders. An understanding of the pivotal role played by the black church in the transition from slavery to freedom is essential if one is to have a clear picture of the Reconstruction period.

The religious status of slaves during the antebellum period was a constant reminder to them of their slave status. In fact, beginning in the early colonial period, white Christians debated the question of whether slaves should be allowed to convert to Christianity. It was not long, however, before whites, responding to their economic interests, professed the belief that Christianity conferred only spiritual, not legal, freedom on the slave. Some white clergymen even maintained that slavery was divinely ordained by God, as revealed in the Bible.[1]

Throughout the antebellum period, however, Southern whites held ambivalent attitudes toward slave religion, based on the conflicting ideas of equality before God on one hand and obedience and the promise of reward in the next life on the other. Some whites feared that Christian doctrine might encourage slaves to be less docile and more assertive. Thus, they concluded, religious instruction of slaves could foster insurrection. The attempted insurrection in Charleston in 1822 led by Denmark Vesey, who was a member of the African Methodist Episcopal (A.M.E.) Church and was supported by other black church members, seemed to bear out the worst nightmares of slaveowners that religious education would make slaves less accepting of servitude. Many other Southerners, however, saw religious indoctrination as a useful method of social control.[2] As one scholar of the Reconstruction period suggests, "The biblical injunction of obedience to one's master seemed clear and the promise of reward in the life after death could be useful in keeping an oppressed class docile."[3] By the late antebellum period, this was the attitude of most Southern white clergymen. Southern Baptists and Methodists responded by authorizing missionaries to convert blacks, and Episcopalians and Presbyterians established churches specifically for blacks but supervised by whites.[4] Most slaves in Charleston, however, did not attend these churches. They were usually required to attend the churches of their masters, where they were assigned to separate sections in the rear of the church or in the gallery, and sometimes they attended separate, black services. Blacks often received special attention from white ministers, who carefully quoted to them the scriptural references supporting the contention that slaves should be obedient to their masters and content with their servitude.[5] Blacks had no voice in church affairs and were essentially spectators rather than full members of the congregation.[6]

Many blacks deeply resented the treatment they received from white churches, especially the segregated seating arrangements that were constant reminders of their inferior position in society. The earliest indication of blacks' dissatisfaction with their roles within white churches was the steady withdrawal of black Charlestonians from the Methodist Episcopal Church South to the all-black A.M.E. Church in that city in 1817.[7] This action presaged the sweeping response of newly freed slaves to white-controlled religious institutions.

Blacks were well aware of the contradictory nature of the Christian doctrine whites espoused in the effort to make them docile, and they were well aware also of how white clergymen manipulated that doctrine. This version of the gospel gave no comfort to the slaves. In most instances, they were uninspired and unmoved by the bland style of the sermons preached by white clergymen. Often, only when the worship services at the white churches ended did the slaves' worship begin in earnest, for neither their hearts nor their souls were in the white churches. The slaves' true church was an invisible institution usually located deep in the woods where blacks could release feelings that had to be suppressed in the white churches. Most slaves found so much spiritual and emotional release at these meetings that they were willing to risk the possibility of severe punishment for being caught at these unsanctioned gatherings.[8]

Blacks wanted more from the antebellum white churches in Charleston than Southerners were willing to give.[9] During the late antebellum period, they grew less and less tolerant of their subordinate status within these churches and found it more and more distasteful to occupy the designated black pews and upper galleries of white churches and to be denied a role in church affairs.[10] As a result, an entire corps of slaves longed to take flight from white religious institutions. Only in black churches would they be able to worship with dignity.

Emancipation gave the former slaves the opportunity to establish these churches, and they blossomed in Charleston and throughout the South during Reconstruction. The rapid exit of black Charlestonians from white churches presented a striking picture. In June 1865, an observer in Charleston wrote: "In fact the Colours are separated now as to churches. The Blacks now have Calhoun and Zion, Old Bethel, also I believe another Methodist church, Morris Street Baptist and perhaps some other old churches to themselves."[11] Another observer wrote: "Not only do the two races stand apart in all domestic relations, but they cannot even go to the house of God in company." Every now and then, "a Black might come to one of the white churches and creep into a corner, but gone are the old days of mixed congregations. The Blacks now occupy their own churches."[12]

Because the Baptists were primarily an unstructured sect that had traditionally maintained much greater local autonomy than the Methodists, the process of separation occurred with relative ease among this group. Baptists who wanted to secede and establish their own church had only to secure letters of dismissal documenting their good standing, enter a covenant to form a spiritual church, select a minister, and get him ordained by other ministers.[13] In Charleston, blacks fled from the white Baptist church and established their own independent Baptist organizations as soon as the Civil War was over. In the months of May and June 1865, the premier black Baptist church, Morris Street Baptist, was organized in Charleston from the black memberships of First Baptist, Wentworth Street, and Citadel Square churches. Rev. Jacob Legare was the pastor of Morris Street Church, assisted by the Rev. Edward Lawrence and Rev. Charles Smalls. The church began with only seventy-three members, but by the mid-1880s, the congregation numbered nearly three thousand.[14]

Black Baptists deserted their former masters' houses of worship in such large numbers that the Morris Street Church could not contain them all, and other churches had to be organized. In October 1865, the capable Charles Smalls was summoned and given the task of organizing the many blacks who were making only pro forma appearances in white Baptist churches. Out of his efforts grew the Calvary Baptist Church. Calvary's growth was so phenomenal that in 1867 and 1876, some members left and established two other major black Baptist churches in Charleston.[15]

The swiftness and the magnitude of the movement to form black churches in Charleston underscores the intense determination of blacks to obtain religious freedom. The churches of former slaveowners epitomized the old regime. Having been denied equal rights and privileges in the house of God during the antebellum period, blacks had no reason to believe that the situation would improve with emancipation. The only solution was to make a quick retreat from white religious bodies to avoid the inevitable humiliation and degradation. With the attainment of freedom, blacks resolved to exercise autonomy over their church affairs as in other areas of life. This could take place only in all-black churches.

Unlike the black Baptist churches, which were organized first on the local level, the black Methodist churches were built from the top down.[16] Because the African Methodist Episcopal Church had already sown the seeds of black Methodism in Charleston before being disbanded in the aftermath of the Denmark Vesey insurrection attempt in 1822,[17] the A.M.E. Church was quite successful in recruiting black Charlestonians into its fold in the early years of the Reconstruction period. Almost immediately after emancipation, the A.M.E. Church began to organize freedmen in Charleston and throughout the state of South Carolina. On May 13, 1865, Bishop Daniel Payne, accompanied by three preachers, landed in Charleston Harbor and put into action plans to organize the South Carolina Conference of the Methodist Episcopal Church. Returning to Charleston in this capacity was a personal triumph for Payne, a native black Charlestonian who, thirty years before, had been forced to leave the city for violating the law against educating blacks. The conference officially convened on May 15, 1865, and several resolutions were immediately adopted that called for the formation of a separate black church. Indeed, most blacks in attendance felt that it was of the utmost necessity to organize one.[18] Payne firmly believed that "the day had not come when all men could worship at the same altar because of the prejudices of the white churchmen of both the North and the South. Black men who had admitted to a distinction in the House of God," he added, "had lost half their manhood."[19] Many black Methodists in Charleston, old and young, shared Payne's sentiments, opening their hearts to the A.M.E. Church and flocking daily to the conference. Richard Cain, a prominent black A.M.E. minister in Charleston, described the scene in the *Christian Recorder*. "Many old mothers," he wrote, "bending towards the ground, came to the conference every morning and listened with rapturous delight to their deliberations. . . . When the conference was over, they would come forward and embrace us, and pour blessings upon us, and even kiss our hands."[20] The ordination of deacons at the conference was, to Cain, "one of the most impressive ceremonies I ever witnessed."[21]

When the conference ended, the Methodists of Bethel, Trinity, and Cumberland churches gathered in two mass meetings to decide whether to withdraw from the Methodist Episcopal Church South. After carefully considering their past and present relations with the Southern white Methodist church, and clearly agreeing with Payne that blacks worshipping at the same altar as whites were subject to degradation and humiliation, they unanimously adopted a preamble and resolutions withdrawing themselves from the M.E. Church South and reorganizing themselves as a religious body under the A.M.E. Church. It was agreed at these two meetings that the services of the congregation would be held in Zion Church every Sunday afternoon at 4:00 P.M. and 7:30 P.M., and that Cain would be the presiding elder.[22]

The growth of the A.M.E. Church in Charleston and throughout South Carolina was phenomenal. As early as May 6, 1865, Cain reported in the *Christian Recorder*, "There are at least three thousand colored members who are Methodists in this city, and the great mass of them are with us." More than twenty-five Bible class leaders with their classes, he also noted, "have transferred their relationship to the A.M.E. Church from the M.E. Church South."[23] Throughout 1865 and 1866, black Methodists in Charleston flocked to the A.M.E. Church in such great numbers that there was a strain on the existing ministry, and additional ministers had to be called to Charleston to accommodate the new members. Equally outstanding growth in African Methodism occurred among rural freedmen on John's, James, and other islands outside Charleston.[24]

The remarkable success of black Methodism in Charleston and throughout South Carolina is made clear by membership figures given at the second annual conference held in 1866 in Savannah, Georgia. Belonging to the A.M.E. Church in South Carolina were 22,388 members and 13 ministers, as well as $28,900 in property. Later conferences of the A.M.E. Church documented its continued rapid progress in the state. By 1876, church property was worth $143,875, the number of ministers had reached 1,000, and church membership was approaching 44,000. This one sect of black Methodism numbered 1,000 more in 1876 than the entire denomination of black Methodism had in 1860.[25]

Not all black Methodists in Charleston were drawn to the A.M.E. Church. Some were attracted to the Methodist Episcopal Church North. Shortly after Confederate forces evacuated Charleston, a group of black Methodists announced that they were severing all relations with the M.E. Church South and were becoming members of the M.E. Church North. When white members of Old Bethel Church built a new structure for themselves and abandoned the old one, blacks took over the old church and renamed it New Bethel Church. Black Methodists also established Wesley and Centenary churches.[26] Although these churches were affiliated with Northern white Methodists, they were still essentially all black and provided a place where their members could exercise religious autonomy and thus escape the humiliation and degradation they had experienced in white churches.

Black Presbyterians and black Episcopalians, also rejecting the dogma of black inferiority, left white churches to establish their own religious institutions after emancipation. Because of the unemotional worship style of these denominations, however, only a small number of blacks were ever attracted to either.[27] By the end of the Reconstruction period, in Charleston and throughout South Carolina, few blacks continued to maintain membership in the white Southern Presbyterian Church.[28] Most black Presbyterians worshipped apart from white Presbyterians, and eventually even these few left this church and became members of the Northern Presbyterian Church.[29] Two Presbyterian churches were formed by blacks in Charleston. One was the famous Zion Presbyterian Church, pastored by Rev. Jonathan C. Gibbs; the other was Mission Presbyterian Church, with a smaller congregation of some four hundred blacks, pastored by the politically active Rev. Ennals J. Adams.[30]

Few blacks were ever attracted to the Episcopal church, and after emancipation black Episcopalians were unceremoniously rebuffed by the white Episcopal churches in Charleston.[31] Before the Civil War, white Episcopalians had established separate churches for blacks, but only a small percentage of Charleston blacks ever attended. One of these, Calvary Church, established in 1849, continued to attract very few freedmen throughout Reconstruction. Most of Charleston's black Episcopalians, led by a group of prominent freeborn blacks, established St. Mark's Episcopal Church in May 1865. They held services in the chapel of the Orphan House, and Rev. J. B. Seabrook, a white man, was summoned to serve as their minister.[32]

The attitudes and actions of Southern white church members toward black church members helped to speed the exit of blacks from white churches. Southern Baptists and Southern Methodists were generally opposed to receiving freedmen within their churches on equal terms. They saw little reason why established church relations should be changed by war or emancipation.[33] At a meeting of the Baptist State Convention in 1866, white delegates from Charleston agreed that no changes should be made to accommodate blacks under the changed legal conditions of society. Apparently unaware of how blacks had experienced their unequal privileges in the church, or unwilling to acknowledge the inequality, white delegates said they were "prepared cordially to welcome [blacks] to all the ecclesiastical privileges with us which they have heretofore been accustomed to enjoy." Furthermore, they recommended the appointment of a joint committee on "the colored membership of our united churches so that church care and Gospel discipline may be extended to them as formerly."[34] White Southern Methodists made similar recommendations.

With the advent of emancipation, most freedmen in Charleston proved reluctant to accept a subordinate position in their religious practice, however, and their steadily growing assertiveness made white church members uncomfortable. It was evident, even in the early years of the Reconstruction period, that blacks and whites would not coexist peacefully within the same religious bodies. Rather than accommodate the demands of black parishioners, white church leaders deemed it best for church members to separate according to race. As early as 1866, white Baptists of South Carolina were hopeful that all blacks in their churches would "of their own accord seek separation and a distinct organization."[35] In an 1867 directive, the Charleston Baptist Association suggested that "the best course for the Church to pursue, would be to advise the colored members in a friendly way to withdraw and form a separate interest, if they cannot harmoniously cooperate with this church."[36] Similarly, the official organ of the white Methodist church announced that setting up independent black organizations was necessary because "the Black people will not remain in any church organization that does not admit them to the legislative and pastoral relation, [and because] the social relations of the two races preclude the idea of such equality."[37] In an effort to aid black separation, the white Methodists of Charleston, in fall 1865, extended the use of Trinity Church in Hazel Street to freedmen until they could erect their own church.[38]

During the Reconstruction period, the position taken by Baptists and Methodists on the role of blacks in their respective churches was mirrored by the Presbyterians and Episcopalians. The Presbyterian General Assembly of 1865 adopted a resolution averring that there was no need to abandon its antebellum policies and that if the black communicants should "think it best to separate from us, and organize themselves into distinct organizations, . . . this church will do all in its power to encourage, foster and assist them."[39] To this end, the Presbyterian church worked diligently, although it need not have done so, for freedmen deserted the church on their own. The Episcopalians also refused to grant blacks equality within their church doors, and as a consequence, the 3,000 black Episcopalians who attended white churches in South Carolina at the close of the war had dwindled to 262 by 1876.[40]

In retrospect, it appears that even if Southern whites had made serious efforts to accommodate black members, most blacks would have deserted white churches anyway. To the newly freed slave and freeman alike, the Southern white church epitomized the old slave regime. Margaret Sasportas, a free black Charlestonian, expressed this sentiment best. She wanted to remain in the same white church in which she had worshipped before the war, but she simply could not stay "under a Rebel Minister."[41] The only plausible solution for most black worshippers was to establish all-black churches. It made no difference to most blacks how whites viewed the situation; it was inevitable that black worshippers would withdraw. The attitudes and actions of Southern whites simply hastened the process.

As a result of the black worshippers' desire for independence and the refusal of whites to accord them equal status, the process of religious separation accelerated in the late 1860s, and by the end of the Reconstruction period, only a few blacks remained in the white churches. In 1860, there were 40,000 black members in the M.E. Church South in South Carolina, but by 1867 the number had dropped to only 8,275, and by 1873 it had plummeted to a mere 653. Similarly, the white Baptist church was down to 1,614 black members in 1874.[42]

The freedmen's withdrawal from white churches to establish their own churches created the problem of where to meet. There were few funds available to purchase or construct church buildings. Some white churches helped blacks to erect new buildings or donated old buildings they had vacated. In most instances, freedmen had to worship in makeshift surroundings until they could save enough money to secure adequate church facilities. The African Methodists of Charleston made arrangements with the Zion Presbyterian Church trustees to hold religious services in Zion Church until they could acquire a church of their own. This arrangement proved satisfactory until Gibbs took charge of Zion in summer 1865 and promptly announced that the African Methodists would no longer have access to the church building. As a consequence, the African Methodists were forced to find another place in which to hold religious services. They secured Bonum's Hall for conducting their services, but when the hall proved too small for holding Bible class meetings, seats were placed in a yard nearby to accommodate everyone. By using both locations the A.M.E. Church, at least temporarily, was able to conduct its services with a measure of success.[43]

For the long term, the African Methodists began raising money to purchase land and erect their own churches. The multiple church-building-fund campaigns organized by black Methodists in Charleston were highly successful even though many freedmen were nearly penniless. The goal of the first A.M.E. campaign was to raise ten thousand dollars to erect a new facility, Emanuel Church. R. H. Cain was to be the pastor. As early as fall 1865, fifteen hundred dollars of this amount had been obtained. Even schoolchildren lent their support by contributing coins. Blacks who could not contribute money often provided their labor instead. In fact, every person who worked on the building was black, including the architect, Robert Vesey, the son of Denmark Vesey. When the huge Emanuel Church, located on Calhoun Street between Meeting and Elizabeth Streets, was completed, it was able to serve about twenty-five hundred people.[44] But almost immediately, with the rapidly increasing membership of the A.M.E. Church, it was believed that Emanuel would not be large enough to accommodate all the members, and so another campaign was started to raise eight thousand dollars for another church and lot. By summer 1866, the Methodists had already raised two thousand dollars.[45] Given the disastrous economic conditions in Charleston and throughout the postwar South, these were remarkable achievements and a testimony to the willingness of Charleston freedmen to make whatever sacrifices were needed to construct and secure their own religious institutions.

Another group of black Charlestonians founded Centenary Methodist Church shortly after emancipation. Most of the founders belonged to Trinity Methodist Church before the war, but when that building was demolished by federal guns in the bombardment of Charleston, they held religious services wherever they could, including the building housing Baker Institute. They continued to worship at Baker Institute until Northern missionaries helped them buy the church building they named Centenary.[46]

The story of how they finally acquired the building illuminates the

Emmanuel A.M.E. Church. Avery Research Center for African-American History and Culture, College of Charleston.

Pastors of Centenary Methodist Episcopal Church, 1866–1912.
Avery Research Center for African-American History and
Culture, College of Charleston.

A black church in South
Carolina in 1860. South Carolina
Historical Society, Charleston.

racial climate of Southern society at this time and dramatizes the commitment of all former slaves to religious freedom and their determination to make whatever sacrifices were needed to secure their own religious institutions. When white church officials of Wentworth Street Baptist Church in Charleston decided to sell their church, Northern missionaries secretly arranged to buy it with funds provided in part by the black church members. Southern white church members would not knowingly sell their church to blacks, and therefore the blacks had to stay in the background while the missionaries negotiated on their behalf. But somehow the news leaked out. When the white Baptists learned that Northern missionaries were attempting to buy the church on behalf of freedmen, they raised the price so high it was nearly impossible to close the deal. On top of the increase, the Baptists also stipulated that the price had to be paid in gold by a specific date and time. Demanding payment in gold was a shrewd way to obviate the deal because it raised the price by thousands of dollars. But the freedmen only dug even deeper into their meager resources, and the missionaries found more money in the North as well.[47] That left one major problem, getting the gold from New York to Charleston on time. The ship from New York bringing the gold to Charleston was delayed, and, to make matters worse, when the ship finally arrived, it ran aground in the harbor. By this time, the deadline date for the sale had arrived, and the money had to be in the bank by noon. Men were hired to row a small boat out to the ship, unload the gold, and carry it to the bank. While the men doggedly rowed, members of the church prayed long and hard for the money to get to the appointed place on time. Many had given up savings they had hoarded for their funerals without the certainty that they would, in return, obtain their own church. Happily, the boatmen made it to the wharf, where they loaded the gold into a buggy drawn by some of the fastest horses in Charleston, and raced through the streets of the city to reach the bank in time.

Centenary Church was finally acquired by the black Methodists in April 1866, at a cost of twenty thousand dollars in gold, of which five thousand was contributed by the freedmen themselves.[48] But the worshippers had to wait still longer and donate labor before they could use the building. Because Baptists practice total immersion, there was a pool in front of the church altar at the Wentworth Street Baptist Church and the pulpit was built very high. Methodists, however, baptize by sprinkling at a fountainhead in the front of the church, and so when the black Methodists purchased Centenary Church from the Baptists, they had to convert the pool into a fountainhead. The freedmen performed this work themselves. Mamie G. Fields, a longtime resident of Charleston, recounted that, in addition, her Uncle Abram Middleton built the altar and altar rail in the church. As late as the early 1980s these structures were still standing.[49]

Freedmen offered a fertile new field for recruitment to both the independent black denominations and the Northern Protestant sects, which had been prominent in the abolitionist movement. Competition between these two groups was widespread and sometimes intense. Surprisingly, the Congregational church in Charleston was particularly persistent in its efforts to recruit former slaves into its fold. Before the war, there had been few black Congregationalists in Charleston, in part because the reasoned, self-controlled nature of Congregationalism did not have the appeal for most blacks that the more emotional character of the Baptist and Methodist denominations had, and in part because there were few white Southern Congregationalists. Slaves usually attended the churches of their masters, and so only a few slaves were introduced to Congregationalism in the antebellum South.[50] Most of the small number of black Congregationalists in Charleston attended Circular Church during the antebellum years. When the church was destroyed during the Great Fire of 1861, most blacks took the opportunity to leave the congregation, even though a new church structure was built. Many of the departing congregants were young blacks who joined other denominations. Other congregants, black and white, began to celebrate separate services in an old chapel owned by the Circular Church.[51]

In the early years after emancipation, the American Missionary Association (AMA) experienced so much success in spreading education to Charleston's freedmen that it was convinced it could make similar headway in converting freedmen to Congregationalism. This optimism, however, was ill-founded, for though the AMA worked tirelessly and gave continuous support to the Plymouth Congregational Church—the church established in 1867 by some of the congregants of the former Circular Church, with the Reverend Mr. Merritt—the Congregationalists never attracted more than a small number of black converts. There were several reasons: Plymouth was plagued by financial problems, the congregation was weakened by factionalism, most blacks found the church too bland,[52] and, above all, the Congregationalists were a white denomination with mostly white ministers. As late as 1876, Plymouth Church in Charleston could claim a membership of only just under two hundred blacks.[53] Congregationalism simply did not have the cultural appeal of the all-black Baptist and Methodist churches, where Charleston freedmen could feel a sense of Christian fellowship and leadership that was not possible in white churches. Clearly race played a major role in undermining the campaigns of white church members to enroll freedmen, as did the desire of the recently freed slaves to enjoy the autonomy that only the establishment of their own churches would yield.

The intense competition between different religious denominations to recruit freedmen into their ranks reached its zenith with a fierce confrontation between the A.M.E. Church and M.E. Church North in Charleston. Initially, relations between the two were cordial. Rev. T. W. Lewis of the M.E. Church North sent a letter welcoming Bishop Daniel Payne and others of the A.M.E. Church to the city of Charleston and later invited Bishop Payne to hold his ordination service in Trinity Church, one of the black churches under Lewis's jurisdiction. During the service, however, Lewis became greatly concerned about the enthusiastic reception that members of Trinity Church were giving to the African Methodists.[54]

Fearing the impending loss of these members to the A.M.E. Church, Lewis called all of his congregation to the church basement and attempted to prejudice them against the A.M.E. Church. First he told them to have nothing to do with the other church and accused it of being based on the distinction of color, meaning that it was founded on the principle of all-black membership to the exclusion of both whites and mulattoes. In contrast, the M.E. Church North, he said, was color blind: both blacks and whites were welcomed into the church on the basis of equality. Believing that the freedmen were still unconvinced, Lewis announced that "if they left him, they would lose their church property; that the property belonged to the M.E. Church North, and that he would hold it for that body."[55] Later that night, when the members of Old Bethel Methodist Church gave an enthusiastic reception to A.M.E. minister James Handy's sermon, Lewis again became alarmed, and he forbade the

Trinity Church members from holding any future meetings in the church without first consulting him.[56] Using any device to offset the A.M.E. Church's popularity among former slaves, agents of the M.E. Church North, according to Cain, "were offering money to freedmen as an inducement for them to leave the A.M.E. Church and join the M.E. Church, North."[57]

Unwilling to suffer these tactics and accusations without a struggle, and fearing the loss of prospective members, the A.M.E. Church in Charleston, under the direction of Cain, fought back. Cain urged the South Carolina Annual Conference of the A.M.E. Church to deny that the organization was based on color distinctions. The conference issued a denial, declaring, "We hail all men as our brothers, whatever be their complexions, and we have ever maintained, that ours is a church without distinctions of color, accepting gladly all men who believe in Christ, and work for the elevation of our race."[58] Bishop Payne responded by telling the people of Charleston that the A.M.E. Church did not exist for the purpose of separating black people from white people and that his church was for all people.[59]

Despite the M.E. Church North's malicious attacks, the African Methodists were able to organize the black Methodists of Charleston and of the state and to attract twice as many members in Charleston and its environs as did the M.E. Church North. Cain was so elated with the situation in summer 1865 that he predicted that soon the black recruits to the A.M.E. Church in Charleston would push the church membership to ten thousand.[60] Race appears to have been a central part of the decision of many blacks to join the African Methodist Church. In the words of one A.M.E. publicist, "[I]t is natural . . . for . . . the black . . . people to come to us, because blood is always more potent than money." In the contest for recruits against the A.M.E. Church, the M.E. Church North had more money but lacked the more important feature of blackness. The A.M.E. Church repeatedly hammered home the point that it had "the blood" and consequently was "the church for all the black Methodists of this country."[61]

The experience of religious fellowship among others of the same race, without white supervision, had a soothing effect on former slaves in Charleston, allowing opportunities to release pent-up frustrations. Worship in all-black churches ensured freedom and dignity as well as race pride through the models of black leadership in the congregation. But the A.M.E. Church had another draw. In the years between 1862 and 1868, it had provided missionary, educational, and material assistance, contributing nearly $167,000 to assist freedmen.[62]

Despite the unifying aspects of all-black churches, in Charleston, where a free black community had thrived before the war, church affiliation often reflected divisions of class, status, and color within the black community. Many elite freemen in the city of Charleston were members of the all-black St. Mark's Episcopal Church, whose minister was the Southern aristocrat J. B. Seabrook. The *Christian Recorder* described St. Mark's as being "composed of the flower of the city."[63] Among the families listed as members were the Dereefs, O'Hears, Marshalls, Mushingtons, Greggs, Kinlochs, Walls, Maxwells, Elfes, Leslies, Decostas, Montgomerys, Inglisses, Bennetts, McKinlays, Houstons, and Bosemons.[64] Seven of the original eight vestrymen and wardens had been free before the war, and among this same group in 1880, six of the nine were included in the upper class. Indeed, St. Mark's congregation was composed overwhelmingly of mulattoes, many of whom were as color conscious as they were class conscious.[65] They usually chose to socialize with upper-class whites or other freemen of like heritage. Coldness and aloofness characterized their attitudes toward the black masses.[66] Other elite free blacks were members of Plymouth Congregational Church and of Mission Presbyterian Church. Mission came under the jurisdiction of Rev. E. J. Adams and attracted many prominent men of the city, including Eden, Ford, Howard, Morrison, Poinsett, and Thorne.[67]

Although the lines of social distinction within the black community of Charleston influenced denominational affiliation, they were not rigidly drawn. In general, the Baptist and Methodist congregations were composed of former slaves and poor free blacks from Charleston proper, the surrounding countryside, and the nearby Sea Islands, many of whom were common laborers who had nothing to depend upon for a living but their hard-earned daily wages. They were usually members of Emanuel A.M.E. Church, under the direction of Rev. R. H. Cain, or of Morris Brown A.M.E. Church or Morris Street Baptist Church. None of the stewards or the trustees of these churches was a prominent black. As late as 1880, only two of twenty-six black A.M.E. Church officials at Emanuel and Morris Brown could be classified as members of the upper class. An exception to this rule was Centenary Methodist Church. A large percentage of its congregation had been residents of Charleston proper who had been free before the war, including such families as the Westons, Wilsons, Johnsons, Millses, Browns, Sasportases, Hamptons, McKinlays, Ransiers, Holloways, Ryans, and Wigfalls. Nine of its twenty-one stewards and trustees were listed in 1881 as members of the upper class.[68]

Cultural differences between black Charlestonians were also reflected in their religious services. Most of the black upper class, who were disproportionately freemen, interacted closely with whites of a similar class and mirrored white social behavior. As a consequence, worship services at the Episcopal, Presbyterian, Congregational, and Methodist churches attended by the black elite were characteristically liturgical and formal, and the sermons were usually deliberative. Most working-class black churchgoers were generally more comfortable in either Baptist or Methodist churches, where the characteristic form of worship was more informal and the ministers' sermons were more emotional, inviting a high level of ecstatic lay participation.[69]

The more formal, deliberative services appealed to Thomas W. Cardozo, the black AMA superintendent in Charleston, who asked that the AMA send a Northern minister to Charleston to supply the spiritual needs of himself and other AMA teachers. The teachers did not object to working in the local Sunday schools, he said, but they found the typical noisy, emotional church service not conducive to their worship.[70] In contrast, Ed Barber, a freedman in the same city, found the worship services at St. Mark's Episcopal Church distressing and uncomfortable. All of the black "society folks," according to him, went there.

> No Black nigger welcome dere, they told me. Thinkin' as how I was bright 'nough to get in, I up and goes dere one Sunday. Oh, how they did carry on, bow and scrape and ape de white folks. . . . I was uncomfortable all de time though, 'cause they was too hi-faloutin' in de ways, in de singin, and all sorts of carryin' ons.[71]

Despite these divisions, however, the black church became the central institution around which the black community of Charleston was organized. Even churches like Mission Presbyterian, Plymouth Congregational, and Centenary Methodist, with their disproportionate numbers of black upper-class members, all had smaller but substantial numbers of freedmen in their congregations as well. The different denominations often jointly sponsored religious functions and lent support to one another in other ways. Between twelve hundred and fifteen hundred blacks, for example, were in attendance on March 25, 1867, at the opening ceremony for Mission Presbyterian Church on George Street, where speakers included Rev. Francis L. Cardozo and numerous other black clergymen of other denominations.[72] This event was important in that it displayed a mass-based support for black religious autonomy, as did the early relations between the African Methodists and the black Presbyterians. Black Presbyterians of Zion Church helped members of the A.M.E. Church in Charleston by lending them the use of the Zion Church building until they could secure a permanent place of their own.[73] The most dramatic demonstration of unity among black denominations came, however, at the joint camp meetings organized by Emanuel A.M.E. Church, Morris Street Baptist, and Hayne's Chapel Baptist Church seven miles outside the city on the Old Folks' Home Farm. As many as ten thousand black people of all denominations visited the camp during the ten days it was held.[74]

After the Civil War, the black churches instituted a moral and social code for the entire black community to adhere to. The churches encouraged monogamous family life and condemned "irregular social relationships." The records of the Morris Street Baptist Church, for example, include the names of parishioners who were accused of adultery, some of whom were exonerated and others of whom were expelled from the church. Typically, once a person was accused of committing adultery, a deacon was selected to investigate the charge and report his findings to the church. Deacons Washington and Carter of Morris Street Church were the investigators in the cases of two men, F. B. Banks and Daniel Ancrum, and a woman, Bella Fraser, who were accused of adultery, found guilty by the church, and expelled. Others who were accused of committing adultery, including Henry Brown, Alliet Harris, and Catz Simmons, were exonerated.[75]

Members who were expelled from the church had to demonstrate that they had repented to the satisfaction of a committee of deacons in order to be received again into full membership. Records show that Annett Ford, Diana Fraser, Nancy Williams, Ella Moore, and Harriet Aiken, who had been expelled from Morris Street Baptist Church, were able to convince the deacons that they had repented. Accordingly, they were again received into full membership. It was not unusual also for those desiring marriage to go before the board of deacons requesting permission to marry. The name Amille Collins appears in the records as one who asked for and received permission to marry.[76]

The church also adopted a rigid stance against gambling, drinking, stealing, swearing, and card playing. Church deacons were often called upon to investigate charges against church members believed to have violated this code. The records give no outcome in the case of a parishioner named Campbell, who was accused of having stolen the goods found in his possession and was investigated by Deacon McZaeirb.[77]

As the central institution in the black community, the church provided a structured social forum and psychological outlet, a refuge in a hostile white world. The entire Sabbath was often spent in attending services and programs at the church. Other functions took place in the evenings during the rest of the week. Wednesday evening prayer services were particularly common. In addition, the church building frequently served as the community's concert hall and theater for singing programs and religious and secular plays.[78] Black churches organized picnics, barbecues, parades, baseball games, and boat excursions around Charleston Harbor. At these events, blacks could relieve the frustrations of everyday life, giving and receiving solace for the grim economic conditions and intense white racism and violence that all came in the aftermath of the war.[79]

The church was also central to the freedmen's campaign for education.[80] Much of the money blacks gave to support schools was given in collections at the churches. When ministers called upon freedmen to contribute, they gave what they could, even though many were nearly destitute. Church ministers often served as teachers, and church build-ings housed the freedmen's schools. Black ministers R. H. Cain and Jonathan C. Gibbs organized schools specifically to educate blacks.[81]

Even in times of economic hardship, blacks did not want to accept government handouts. They believed they had to oversee their own survival, and so members of churches pooled their meager resources and organized numerous benevolent and mutual aid societies,[82] further unit-ing Charleston's black community. Members of Cain's Emanuel A.M.E. Church established and maintained a home for the aged on a plantation not far from Charleston. During the early years of emancipation, when destitute blacks came to Charleston with the hope of emigrating to Africa, the congregation of Morris Street Baptist Church organized a relief society to assist them.[83] The congregation also agreed to pay for the burial services of Sally Mintz and other members like her who left no funds.[84] Black churches in Charleston extended their relief activities to other cities as well. When yellow fever epidemics broke out in Memphis and New Orleans, Charleston's black churches took up collections for the afflicted in those cities. Since most freedmen were members of the lower classes and had few economic resources, the social welfare func-tions of the church were particularly important to their daily survival.[85] Understanding this, even the impoverished would contribute what they could when called upon by their ministers.

Black churches in Charleston, particularly Zion Presbyterian and Emanuel A.M.E., were popular sites for organized political activity among freedmen and their Northern supporters. Blacks gathered at Zion to adopt resolutions thanking the Union forces for their liberation, and the church hosted the ceremonial raising of the Union flag over Fort Sum-ter.[86] Throughout the early years of freedom, blacks continued to hold mass political meetings at Zion and Emanuel, both of which could seat between fifteen hundred and two thousand people. Most meetings were held to discuss the state and welfare of the country in general and the condition of newly freed slaves in particular. At these meetings, commit-tees were often organized to devise strategies to deal with the changed conditions wrought by the war.[87] In the aftermath of a violent melee between freedmen and the white Zouave troops stationed in Charleston, for example, a large number of blacks met at Zion Church to consider what actions should be taken to cool these racial tensions. A committee was appointed to draft resolutions expressing the discontent of blacks and to request protection from the Union commander at Charleston. Apparently the freedmen were persuasive, for General Woodford in-formed them that he and the government would "afford ample protec-tion to all citizens, without regard to color."[88] These political gatherings were attended by hundreds, sometimes thousands of freedpeople, re-gardless of religious affiliation. When blacks were confronted by major problems, religious affiliation mattered little. It was more important that they marshal all available forces to combat Southern white racism.

In the first few months of emancipation, Zion Church also served as a political forum on the state level. It was the site of the Colored People's Convention in November 1865. The city was chosen because so many black Charlestonians were politically aware, and the church was chosen because it had such a large seating capacity. The goal of the convention was to protest the work of the white constitutional convention and legislature of South Carolina, and it marked the beginning of concerted political action by blacks in Reconstruction South Carolina.[89] In opening its doors to the political activities of blacks at the state level, the black church was able to bind together an even larger black community.

Clergymen were among the most effective and able black politicians during the Reconstruction period. After the war, ministers of Zion Presbyterian and Old Bethel Methodist Churches organized and carried out a huge emancipation parade that impressed even the most vocal white critics of the black community.[90] Ministers also engaged in Republican party politics in Charleston and throughout South Carolina. At a mass meeting of Charleston's freedmen held in March 1867 to organize a Union Republican party in South Carolina, black ministers Ennals Adams of Mission Presbyterian Church, and B. F. Randolph, Francis Cardozo, and R. H. Cain of Emanuel A.M.E. Church delivered addresses and seconded the platform's adoption.[91]

These and other ministers went on to hold either appointed or elective offices. In 1868, Adams was elected to the city council and later was appointed a trial justice. Samuel B. Garrett served for many years as a municipal alderman in Charleston, and J. E. Hayne served as a county school commissioner for Charleston County. Henry Cardozo and Bruce Williams were elected state senators. One of the most influential ministers, Cain (known as Daddy Cain) was, variously, a city alderman, a delegate to the state constitutional convention of 1868, a member of the state senate from 1868 to 1870, and a congressman representing South Carolina from 1873 to 1879.[92]

Of these ministers, Adams and Cain were particularly vocal in addressing the concerns of the black masses. When whites in Hamburg, South Carolina, rioted against blacks in 1876 and murdered some freedmen, Adams and Cain organized a mass meeting of freedmen in Charleston to denounce these actions. They did not directly advocate violence, but they pressed the need for self-defense against attacks by whites, and Charleston's freedmen heeded them by going to the defense of Hamburg blacks.[93]

Repeatedly, Cain championed the cause of his people. He was at the vanguard of the movement to grant land to former slaves, formulating a practical program to accomplish this objective and presenting it to the constitutional convention of 1868. Failing in this endeavor, but undaunted, Cain sought ways on his own to provide land to freedmen. In 1871, he contracted to purchase a thousand acres a short distance from Charleston, and he subdivided this area into a property that later became known as Lincolnville. His land dealings drew legal attention, and although he was not indicted at the time, when he was elected to Congress in November 1872, it was under a cloud of suspicion.[94] Cain's election despite his legal difficulties suggests that his predominantly former-slave constituency wholeheartedly supported his efforts to provide them with land as a means to economic independence and showed their gratitude and their faith in him in the form of votes. Cain was one of several black politicians upon whom the freedmen depended to advance their interests. Between 1868 and 1878, Cain was able to sell sixty lots, including one to the trustees of the A.M.E. Church in Charleston. There were about one hundred dwellings in Lincolnville by 1885, with most of them owned by blacks.[95]

Shortly after the white South Carolina State Constitutional Convention of 1865 enacted the Black Code in order to reintroduce blacks to servitude, Cain protested to General Charles Devens, a Freedmen's Bureau official. He argued that passage of the Code had caused most freedmen to seriously question their fate under Southern whites once civil rule was restored. Cain informed General Devens that "they believe that these laws were passed for the purpose of keeping them as nearly in a state of slavery as the changed state of affairs would admit." Freedmen particularly feared the Code as a powerful instrument of employers, who, for example, could refuse to pay freedmen their wages if they left plantations without cause.[96] Cain wrote persuasively against the Code, articulating these fears. He was an immensely popular preacher and politician, and the generally illiterate freedmen in Charleston counted on him and other black leaders to make their views known to white government officials.

When freedmen began refusing to contract for work with planters in protest over the Black Code, it was rumored that there would be a black insurrection by New Year's Day 1866 if conditions did not improve. Cain, who was in constant contact with freedmen in the Charleston area, knew that no such plans existed. Recognizing the danger of these rumors, Cain sought to dispel them. In a letter to Devens, he maintained that there was no cause for insurrection among freedmen, and that it would be fruitless for them to commit wrongs against a government that they "rely upon to protect them from vindictive Southern whites." He pointed out that the rumors probably originated with guilt-ridden whites who, having oppressed blacks for so long, therefore expected the former slaves to rise up and seek vengeance. In concluding his letter, Cain further ridiculed notions of an insurrection, noting, accurately, that freedmen were more concerned with laying firm foundations for the future well-being of their families by acquiring land and building homes.[97]

Like other black ministers, Cain acted as an intermediary between blacks and the white authorities and often advocated for individuals. Not long after the arrest and incarceration of Jefferson Williams, a young freedman alleged to have assaulted a nine-year-old white boy by slapping him, kicking him, and striking him with a brick, Williams's parents appealed to Cain for help. Cain protested to Robert K. Scott of the Freedmen's Bureau that Williams had been unjustly arrested and jailed without due process of law and that he had not yet received a trial. Such arrests, Cain said, could not be permitted to continue; they took place all too often and usually without redress. Cain's protests were heard and Williams was released.[98]

In this and other ways, the black church became the central institution within the black community of Charleston. During the prewar years, slaves had been largely confined to white churches, where they were virtually excluded from participation in church affairs. There is much evidence that slaves greatly resented this situation, but they had no alternative but to continue to attend the churches of their masters. Emancipation gave them the opportunity to make choices about their lives, and one of their first choices was to leave the white churches and establish all-black churches, for most Charleston freedmen believed that they had to have their own house of worship. Only in their own churches could they enjoy the dignity and freedom that were now rightfully theirs. These churches and their leaders became the nucleus of black community life, providing sacred services to blacks but functioning also as a social, economic, and political institution within the black community. The impact of the church has lasted. Today the black church still plays an integral role in black community life.

FREEDOM IS A CONSTANT STRUGGLE

Resistance and Self-Protection by Charleston's Freedmen

Violence between blacks and whites was a common feature of the Reconstruction period in Charleston and throughout the South. There were fistfights, skirmishes, and individual cases of murder; and there were small-scale battles and even riots. Black Charlestonians were often the victims of white violence, but often too they fought back and repelled white violence. Some of the clashes appeared to be undirected or unfocused, but behind most was the former slaves' drive to preserve the freedom that should have come with emancipation but that was many times threatened by the attempts of whites to reconstruct the old social order. Life for most former slaves during the Reconstruction years was a constant struggle for freedom.

For several reasons Charlestonian freedmen were able to repel white violence whereas blacks in other places were not. Charleston's black community had a reputation for aggressiveness dating from the antebellum period, when slaves had been known to physically confront whites and sometimes to murder them. The attempted insurrection led by

Denmark Vesey in 1822 was the most dramatic manifestation of slave aggressiveness and the severity of the white response a testament to the fear that reputation engendered. Many blacks would be even more aggressive once they had broken the shackles of slavery. Also during the antebellum period, Charleston was home to a nucleus of free blacks experienced in exerting leadership. After the war, that nucleus grew when many of the South's most capable and outspoken black leaders were drawn to Charleston because it was an urban center. In response to the conditions created under Reconstruction, these leaders organized the large and assertive black populace of Charleston in continual efforts to maintain the autonomy of the black community. It should be acknowledged, however, that black community leaders neither anticipated nor encouraged the many racial clashes that would develop, but they always put their organizational and leadership skills to work in support of the aims of the black community, particularly when major race riots occurred. Population was the final factor that gave blacks an edge and helped ensure victory by blacks in the numerous racial clashes in Charleston during the Reconstruction years. By 1875, at 73 percent of the total population of Charleston and the outlying areas, blacks had a clear numerical advantage over whites.[1]

In the years following the Civil War, the violence between blacks and whites brought on by emancipation was intense. Many white Charlestonians found it difficult to accept blacks as free men and women and attempted to continue to treat them as slaves. Blacks, on the other hand, were determined to resist this treatment by asserting and defending their new freedom. The Battery, a scenic shoreline park on Charleston Harbor, was one testing ground for blacks' new status. During the antebellum period, all blacks, free and slave, had been prohibited from visiting the Battery, but with the arrival of emancipation, black Charlestonians exerted their right to go there as often as they wished, much to the dismay of most whites. The customary exclusion of blacks from the Battery symbolized to them the tyranny of the old racial order. After emancipation, black youths began to congregate there, and when white youths tried to force them out, the blacks remained, fighting back by hurling brickbats.[2]

Blacks now went wherever they wanted to, and if whites tried to stop them, most blacks were quick to retaliate. In 1871, for example, a white streetcar conductor, apparently upset by the sight of a group of black firemen out enjoying an evening on the town after a picnic at Payne's farm near John Street, ordered the driver to run them over. The driver obeyed, and one of the firemen was badly injured. In retaliation, other firemen attacked the car, severely beating the conductor and driver and breaking some of the car windows.[3] In another incident, James Clarke, a white seaman, was severely beaten by a group of blacks after he suggested

Charleston in 1872. South Carolina Historical Society, Charleston.

that they had no right to be on the wharf watching black firemen embark for Georgetown.[4] These and many similar incidents indicate that whites were not willing to accept the changed behaviors of emancipated blacks, so they attempted to reinstate the traditional rules of racial decorum. But black Charlestonians would not comply. They were resolved to go where they wished, and they were willing to defend their right to do so with force if necessary.

In antebellum Charleston, white policemen were routinely abusive of blacks. Their attitude changed little during Reconstruction, and they continued to discriminate against and sometimes to physically abuse blacks. In response, freedmen often took revenge. Local newspapers regularly reported these incidents. In January 1873, for example, the *Charleston News and Courier* reported that when a policeman identified as Private Miller tried to break up a fight between a man and a woman on Philip Street near the Orphan House, the man and a group of other freedmen seized and stabbed him.[5] In May 1874, a group of black firemen beat two white policemen who tried to arrest them for being too boisterous in King Street, and in August 1876 a policeman named Fludd arrested a black man, "but a crowd of blacks made a rush for him, knocked him down three times and rescued the prisoner."[6] Black women also fought back against white policemen: in August 1876 when a white policeman named O'Conner tried to force a group of black women off the sidewalk, they attacked and beat him.[7] Often when white policemen tried to arrest individual blacks, groups of freedmen would descend upon them and rescue the prisoners.

Black Charlestonians also got into scuffles in the streets of the city with white Union soldiers, whom freedmen grew to despise once the initial euphoria of liberation had passed. Many Union soldiers were racists and usually sided with Southern whites to oppress the freedmen. According to a correspondent for the *New York Tribune,* "Whenever Union soldiers could and dared to, they maltreated and abused freedmen."[8] Black Charlestonians fought back with a vengeance against these abuses, which to them were an extension of the white authority they had been forced to accept under slavery. Vengeance was especially swift and harsh when incidents involved black women, whom slave men had been powerless to protect against whites.

One Sunday night in 1867, two United States soldiers went to the house of a black woman named Charlotte Range on Market Street, seeking her sexual favors. When she would not allow them to enter the house, the soldiers began pelting it with stones and breaking the windows. Five freedmen who were nearby came to her rescue, chasing the soldiers with stones, sticks, and an ax and driving them around the corner into Archdale Street. There a fight broke out during which one of the soldiers and one freedman were severely beaten.[9] In another incident a group of freedmen cornered a white soldier at the corner of East Bay and Elliott Streets, threatening to beat him. They might have succeeded had he not been rescued by a policeman.[10]

Some of the tension between black men and the United States soldiers was due to envy and jealousy over the soldiers' open flirtation with black women. After several successive nights of socializing between white soldiers and black women in the square on Ann Street in summer 1869, for example, a group of black men decided they could stand aside no more. On a Thursday night, the group assembled and threw bricks at the soldiers, who retaliated in kind. When one of the bricks struck a freedman, hurting him badly, he began to yell at the top of his voice, over and over, "Murder!" "Fire!" "Help!" "Murder!" His cries drew some two hundred or more freedmen, and one of them shot at the soldiers. The sound of the shot intensified the excitement, and had not cooler heads prevailed among the freedmen, a bloody riot most certainly would have ensued.[11] These incidents demonstrate that the former slaves not only would stand firm against white violence but sometimes would initiate violence against whites. Many of these confrontations between freedmen and whites were mere fistfights or skirmishes, but there would be others in which lives were lost.

Having been powerless to prevent the mental and physical abuse of black women by white men under the slave regime, as free men Charleston's blacks were determined to protect their wives and daughters from further abuse, even at the cost of killing white men in order to do so. In one such case, in 1877, the black community thought that a white man by the name of Vaughan had assaulted a black woman. When a group of freedmen saw him walking down Market Street early one morning, they accosted and questioned him about the supposed incident. Denying that he knew anything about it, Vaughan turned to walk away. But the freedmen had revenge on their minds, and when one called out, "Go for him anyhow," they chased him down King Street, where two shots were fired at him. One shot missed and the other struck him just under the right shoulder blade. He was not seriously wounded, though some believed that the freedmen had intended to kill him.[12]

Many whites were not so lucky as Vaughan and lost their lives at the hands of freedmen. William Allen, a close friend of the diarist Emma Holmes, was "chopped to pieces in his barn by ex-slaves in Charleston," and Prioleau, a prominent white Charleston physician, was also murdered by freedmen.[13] Although most former slaveowners adamantly denied that their former slaves might harbor sufficient ill will toward them to contemplate their murder, usually when a former slaveowner was murdered, the white community would immediately view one or more of his former slaves with suspicion.[14]

Such was the case when B. S. Rhetts of Charleston was murdered in 1866. The particulars of his murder are unclear, but two of his former slaves were arrested for it. On the day of the murder, Rhetts had left his home shortly after dinner to visit his farm near the race course. When he opened the gate, he was fired on twice. Bullets struck him in the left arm and in the side. With no one around to help him, Rhetts struggled to his horse, rode a short distance, and fell to the ground. He later died in the presence of his son and a doctor.[15]

With no solid clues to the identity of the murderers, the police assumed that one of Rhetts's former slaves, John Bennett, knowing Rhetts's daily routine, had hidden near the farm with another freedman, Horace Johnson, to ambush him. The two men were arrested and charged with the murder. Later events suggest that they were framed by the police. Bennett was instructed to say that Johnson, who had been involved in an earlier altercation with Rhetts, fired the fatal shots; but Bennett refused to do so. Among the correspondence files of the Freedmen's Bureau is a letter Bennett wrote to General O. O. Howard, commissioner of the Bureau, complaining that he had been imprisoned for four months without trial for a murder he denied committing.[16] The outcome of the case is not known. However, given the mistreatment of slaves in the antebellum period and the attempted mistreatment of blacks under

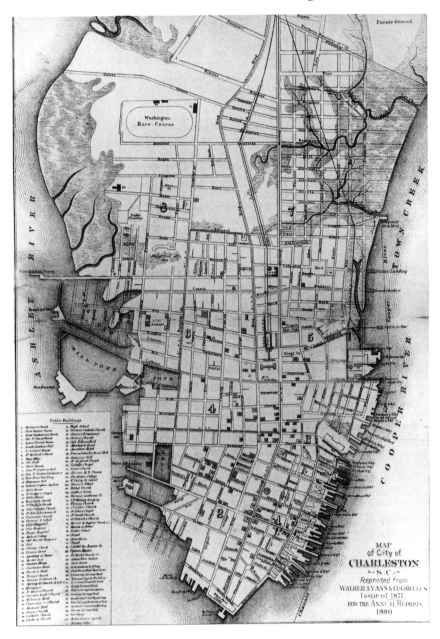

Charleston in 1877. South Carolina Historical Society, Charleston.

Reconstruction, it is very likely that these murders were attempts at retribution.

According to the many incidents between blacks and whites reported in the local newspapers, freedmen sometimes had little compunction against killing whites who humiliated or physically confronted them. The *Charleston News and Courier* described in detail a confrontation that began at nine o'clock one Saturday night in November 1877 when John Cook, the white watchman at Graham's Stable on Chalmers Street near Meeting, came upon a freedman named Tom Pope sitting in the front of the stable with a pistol in his hand. When Cook asked Pope how he got in, Pope replied that this was none of Cook's business and swung open the front door. Cook ordered him to close it, but Pope refused, saying, "I haven't got much use for you anyhow." And the reason for that, Cook implied, was that he prevented Pope from stealing feed from the horses for his own consumption. Angered by this insult, Pope struck Cook on the back of the head. A struggle ensued and Pope was thrown to the floor. But he got up, apparently drew a pistol from his hip pocket and ran out the front door, cursing. Thinking that the episode was over, Cook attempted to close the door after him, but Pope stepped back into the stable and fired a fatal shot. Pope was later overheard on the city streets boasting to other young freedmen that he had shot Mr. Graham's watchman. One day after the murder, Pope had not yet been arrested.[17] Incidents like this were few in number, but they are the extreme examples of black Charlestonians repelling behavior from whites that smacked of the repressive and humiliating conditions suffered under slavery, and blacks' refusing to be talked to or treated as beasts or subordinates.

Black soldiers in the Charleston area were even more determined than the general black population to resist any form of mental or physical cruelty at the hands of whites. These black troops were a mixture of Northern free blacks and Southern blacks who had escaped slavery. The black soldiers from the North had experienced racism and racial discrimination there but, because there they had lived under fewer restraints than had the blacks in the South, they were less tolerant of oppression by whites. All black troops saw themselves as symbols of emancipation and as men deserving of respect for their experiences in battle, and, as such, they would show themselves unwilling to countenance repression by whites. Throughout the Reconstruction period in Charleston, black soldiers were active participants in many racial clashes, often as the aggressors.

Like the rest of the black population, black soldiers despised the white policemen. Skirmishes between the two were commonplace. According to the *Charleston Daily News,* on one occasion in 1866 a black soldier roamed the streets with a pistol in hand and in the company of about ten other black soldiers as if he wanted to pick a fight with someone white. He then pushed a police officer, who ordered him to go home. He refused to go, saying "he would not mind any d——d rebel police." At that point some twenty or so additional policemen arrived, and the soldiers, realizing they were outnumbered, headed up the street. Undaunted, however, a corporal in the group was heard to call out, "Come on, let us go to the Freedmen's Bureau and get ten more of our boys; I'd like to see them take us to the Guard House." When the soldiers returned, a fight ensued between them and the policemen, and ten or twelve pistol shots were fired, leaving one policeman wounded in the shoulder.[18] The particulars of this incident are presented in the report with the biases one might expect of the region and time. The police are portrayed as paragons of restraint and the black soldiers as uncontrolled rowdies. An accurate account would probably indicate some fault on both sides, though the melee may well have been initiated by the soldiers. The tensions behind the incident were most likely rooted in the general behavior of white authorities toward black soldiers and in the desires of black soldiers to show that they would not take insults or repression at the hands of white civil authorities.

Black soldiers shared the black community's disdain for the white Union troops. Consequently, they often united with Charleston's blacks in attacks on white soldiers. These racial clashes were larger and bloodier than any skirmishes between freedmen and soldiers and often grew into race riots. The first major race riot to occur in Charleston during the Reconstruction period took place in July 1865. Details of the clash are unclear, but it apparently began brewing at a time when racial tensions were high. White soldiers had been regularly abusing freedmen in and around Charleston. The Zouaves of the 127th New York Regiment had most often been involved,[19] and so as a precaution they had been replaced by the 165th New York Regiment, Duryee's Zouaves. It rapidly became apparent, however, that this regiment could get along with the black troops and the black community no better than had their predecessors. On the night of July 8, tensions came to a head. The 165th New York Regiment happened to be assigned police duty in one of the busiest areas of Charleston and the one most often frequented by blacks, the Market Place.[20] For freedmen longing for an opportunity to do battle with these white soldiers, the chance presented itself when a Zouave appeared to have exceeded his authority by physically abusing blacks. One of the freedmen took offense, struck the Zouave, and pulled a knife on him. This action drew in members of both the Twenty-first United States Colored Troops and the Fifty-fourth Massachusetts Volunteers (a black regiment), as well as other blacks. Fearing for his life, the Zouave sent for assistance. In the violent melee that ensued, James Bing, a black proprietor of an egg stand, was killed, and a Zouave and two freedmen were wounded.[21]

For three days blacks made sporadic attacks on white civilians and soldiers, initiating a series of street brawls. There is no record of how many people were killed or wounded in these scattered fights.[22] By July 13, however, with the intervention of General W. T. Bennett, the United States military commander in Charleston, a measure of order had been restored to the city. Bennett issued orders forbidding citizens to assemble in the streets, and he ordered both blacks and whites to turn in their firearms and observe an 8:00 P.M. curfew.[23] The 165th New York Regiment was sent to Morris Island ten days after the riot and was replaced by the Forty-seventh Pennsylvania Regiment. The Twenty-first United States Colored Troops were also ordered out of the city for their role in the riot.[24] Despite these measures, Charleston would not remain quiet.

The next months were punctuated by skirmishes between blacks and whites that culminated in another riot the following summer. Again, black soldiers played a major role. The riot originated on Sunday, June 24, when a group of black and white youths assembled on the Battery and began showering each other with stones. This was not an uncommon event. Skirmishes erupted continually on the Battery over its use by black youths who refused to accede to the whites-only tradition of the area. This particular encounter grew in intensity as adults, both black and white, joined in, using sticks and other weapons. The police arrived in time to quell the fracas for the moment by arresting some of the ringleaders. Afterward, the crowd dispersed, and it appeared that the fighting was over. But, being intent upon asserting their rights, some of the freedmen who had escaped the police regrouped and summoned additional support from the black neighborhood. Eight or ten black soldiers emerged to direct this angry group. They formed a procession of two or three hundred and "riotously marched through East Bay, Tradd, Legare and other streets randomly attacking any whites in sight. Eventually, a large detachment of police, and United States Regular Troops confronted them, and were able to restore some order to the city by forcing them to disperse."[25] Unimpressed and perhaps even further angered by this show of white authority, blacks continued isolated barrages on whites, showering police with bricks and injuring a police sergeant, whose hat and club were seized as trophies.[26]

The police sergeant escaped with his life, but another white man, Richard M. Brantford, was not so fortunate, according to a local newspaper account. During the evening the fighting took place at the Battery, Brantford was spotted by a large group of freedmen led by John Jenkins and Scipio Fraser, two discharged black Union soldiers. Fraser suggested they "kill the son of a b——h" and then threw a rock at Brantford, hitting his head. Brantford hurried away as fast as he could, but he was not as swift as Jenkins and Fraser, who knocked him down and struck him in the head with a brick.[27]

Shortly thereafter, a crowd of about twenty freedmen arrived on the scene and, after battering Brantford with bricks, left him to die. According to the newspaper, later that evening Fraser was overheard bragging about the riot to other blacks. He held up a knife and said, "I, and no one else, killed the rebel son of a b——h, and he is not the first nor will he be the last I will kill." Furthermore, he added, he had killed "many a one in the army."[28] For the next three weeks or so, the streets of Charleston were not safe, with freedmen launching continual attacks on whites. The situation was bad enough that some whites left the city.[29]

These riots must be viewed in a political context, as the outgrowth of a struggle by whites to regain control over black people and by black people to maintain their right to autonomy. All of the individual selfish and cruelly senseless acts performed in these Reconstruction riots were opportunities to release frustrations, and these acts represent the political determination of blacks not to suffer under white authority. The singling out of white individuals, purely because of their race, to suffer the wrath of the rioters was akin to the treatment blacks had suffered purely because of their race.

While many of Charleston's freedmen fought in the streets to hold onto the rights won with emancipation, others asserted themselves throughout the Reconstruction years in efforts to acquire civil and political rights, preparing for battles yet to be fought by staging sit-ins, signing petitions asserting their rights, and seeking court injunctions to promote their interests.[30] As early as January 1866, several hundred freedmen in Charleston and throughout South Carolina signed a petition asking that they be "allowed the rights of citizenship" and entrusted General Rufus Saxton, former head of the Freedman's Bureau for the State of South Carolina, to deliver it to Washington. Saxton had spent nearly four years among the freedmen and believed strongly that if the federal government did not soon grant citizenship rights to freedmen, they would take matters "into their own hands."[31] In Washington, a member of Congress asked Saxton whether he thought blacks would ever acquiesce or submit quietly "to a subordinate role." Saxton replied emphatically that they would not and that, in fact, patience was growing thin and many blacks were already arming themselves. Saxton told the congressman that while he was posted in Charleston, he had been able to restrain some freedmen by persuading them to keep faith in the federal government. But this he could no longer do. Saxton had been greatly loved, trusted, and respected by the freedmen in Charleston, and his removal as head of the Freedman's Bureau for the state had only made a tense situation even worse, convincing many freedmen that the federal government was turning its back on them. The leader of the Colored Union League and other blacks had told Saxton that they feared that soon the freedmen would attempt to take their cause into their own hands.[32]

These fears were soon realized. In spring 1867, Charleston's black community united in sometimes forceful efforts to desegregate the city's streetcars. Buoyed by the rising expectations produced by the passage of the first Reconstruction Act granting blacks the right to participate in the reorganization of the former Confederate states, Charleston's blacks were now even more convinced that they were entitled to the same rights and privileges as whites.[33] As part of this campaign to secure their rights, black Charlestonians tried to obtain court injunctions against the operation of the exclusive City Railway Line. When this strategy failed, freedmen adopted another. They would, if necessary, force their way onto the streetcars and stage "sit-ins" to protest their case. If they were then forcibly removed, they would sue the company for assault and battery.[34]

Distrustful of whites, freedmen were determined to seize their rights whenever the opportunity presented itself. They were uncertain of what the future would bring: perhaps abandonment by Radical Republicans, perhaps a return to dominance by Southern whites. The initial effort to stage sit-ins on the streetcars occurred on Tuesday afternoon, March 26, 1867, in the aftermath of a meeting of freedmen numbering between fifteen hundred and two thousand. They met outdoors on the Citadel Square to ratify the Republican party platform that had been drawn up a few days earlier and to proceed with the party's formation. Both black and white speakers urged freedmen at this meeting to vote and demand equal rights.[35] It is unclear why those who engaged in the sit-ins picked this particular date for their initial action. Perhaps many were buoyed by the hope and confidence gained from the political meeting.

Whatever the reasons, at the conclusion of the mass meeting, an unnamed black barber entered a streetcar at Calhoun and Meeting Streets. When the conductor, Faber, asked him to leave, he refused. But after the conductor informed him of the company's rules that blacks could ride only on the platforms outside the cars and insisted that he get out, the barber reconsidered his earlier response and, following the advice of friends who feared that he might be forcibly removed, he got out. This was not the end of the issue; freedmen were determined to settle the matter in their favor. The campaign to desegregate the city's streetcars was mass based and well planned.[36] Although this initial move was spontaneous, the black community had been discussing the problem of the streetcars and planning for a mass intervention to resolve it.

Later that same day, when conductor Faber's car returned to Meeting Street between George and Society Streets, a huge crowd of blacks, intent upon seizing the car, rushed into it, to the great dismay of the white passengers, and refused to leave. Faber tried to get the driver to run the car off the track. When that failed, he instructed the driver to unhitch his horse, which he readily did, leaving the car on the track and returning the horse to the company's stable. This left the group of blacks frustrated and disappointed. They tried to push the car forward, but Faber, though badly outnumbered, put down the brake and stuck to his post. When the blacks began to pull Faber away from the brake, he was rescued by the timely arrival of police.[37]

While Faber's car was under attack, other blacks went after other streetcars in much the same way. Many of the women passengers, fearing insult and injury, were compelled to leave the cars. When the protesters realized that the conductors would not give in to their demands that blacks be allowed to ride on an equal basis with whites, they tried to interrupt the travel of cars by placing stones in the track. But they were soon arrested by local police and United States army troops.[38] Undeterred, freedmen again pressed the issue only six days later at the same location.[39] Two blacks, Daniel McInnis and Sidney Eckhard, forced their way inside one of the cars, disregarding all entreaties by the conductor either to get off or to ride on the platform. The conductor made no attempt to forcibly eject them but instead waited until the car was near the police station, where he summoned help, and McInnis and Eckhard were overpowered by police and arrested.[40]

As news of the arrests spread to the black community, a group of one hundred or more angry blacks congregated around the police station house and hurled stones at the policemen on duty. Troops were called to help the police disperse the crowd, but before they arrived, two of the policemen were severely beaten. When the soldiers did arrive, they took custody of three blacks who had been arrested. Angry and intent upon rescuing these men, a large group of black men and women followed the squad and threatened to injure them. In response, soldiers were dispatched to keep the freedmen in check by using their muskets if necessary.[41]

This event did not resolve the streetcar issue. Instead, it made the battle even more intense. With pressure on the Charleston City Railway Company mounting, its executives began scurrying for solutions. They proposed at first to establish separate and equal cars, or to install partitions within the cars to separate blacks and whites. But Charleston's freedmen would have nothing to do with plans they regarded as demeaning and in violation of their newly acquired civil rights. They demanded and expected nothing less than fully integrated facilities.[42] Not letting up on the railway company, blacks pressed their case in the courts.[43] The sit-ins and court actions ultimately forced the company to abandon its discriminatory policies against blacks, and one month after the "riot," the Charleston City Railway Company announced that it had decided to eliminate all racial distinctions on its cars.[44] In addition, a month after that, Major General Daniel Edgar Sickles, the military commander of South Carolina, issued an order restricting racial discrimination on street railways, railroads, and steamboats.[45]

Almost immediately, blacks took advantage of this newly guaranteed right, and they could be seen riding daily on streetcars. The *New York Daily Tribune* reported that "the whites took the new situation with good humored resignation."[46] The determination of black Charlestonians to integrate the streetcars underscores the great value that freedmen attached to the civil rights they believed they were entitled to as free men and women. Being forbidden to ride inside the streetcars was a racial and personal affront to them and a violation of their new rights. Furthermore, the campaign to desegregate the streetcars illuminates the considerable organizational capacity of black communities during the postwar period that could be brought to bear on any issue of importance to blacks. The campaign to desegregate Charleston's streetcars was well planned, mass based, and, above all, successful.

With the passage of the first Reconstruction Act on March 2, 1867, moreover, the black community of Charleston was excited by the prospect of political involvement.[47] Realizing early that their interests would best be served by the Republican party, black community leaders and some Northern whites swiftly led successful campaigns to recruit freedmen into the Republican party. At the same time, freedmen were encouraged to register and to vote.[48] Because some blacks had already been organized into Union Leagues, which were auxiliaries of the Republican party, the task of recruitment was made somewhat easier.

Soon the ranks of the Republican party were swelled by blacks, and freedmen went to the polls in large numbers in South Carolina. Most black voters, believing that the Republican party and blackness went hand in hand, were fiercely Republican, despite all obstacles, and determined to vote Republican.[49] They insisted, too, that every other black do so. Even black women, though denied the vote themselves, were active in ensuring that men would vote the Republican ticket. If a black man was a Democrat, he was seen as having betrayed the race by joining the party of the slaveowner. Black Republicans found such an alliance both distasteful and puzzling. Black Republicans detested white Democrats, and these sentiments were returned in kind. As a result, political violence between the two groups was intense and often bloody during the Reconstruction years.

While this violence led to the deaths of many black Republican politicians throughout South Carolina, black Charlestonians were resolved to prevent any such murders in their city and its environs. As a reminder to whites who might entertain such notions, a group of blacks issued a special warning. They swore "to burn the city to ashes and have no mercy on the Democrats if any prominent man in the community was murdered."[50] Apparently white Charlestonians took these threats seriously, for there were no political assassinations in Charleston. Even so, violent encounters between black Republicans and white Democrats were commonplace.[51] Henry W. Ravenel noted in his journal that in summer 1868, blacks became so "riotous" that at "the late Democratic meeting in Charleston . . . the whites found it prudent to go armed; and a threatened violent interruption of the meeting was only averted by the appeal and interference of the more prudent colored radicals."[52]

There were many violent encounters between black Republicans and both black and white Democrats. One such encounter, in Charleston in July 1869, became known as the baseball riot. The origins of the riot are unclear, but it seems to have been precipitated by the arrest of a freedman, Rafe Izzard, in an altercation between policemen, soldiers, and freedmen that broke out at the end of a baseball game. The visiting team had come to Charleston from Savannah, Georgia, with their black band, all presumably Democrats.[53]

When the black community learned that Izzard had been locked up in the guardhouse in the Citadel, a crowd of nearly three thousand blacks soon stood ready to do battle near Citadel Square. Although evidently upset over the arrest, they did not attempt to forcibly rescue him. Perhaps many blacks were simply using the arrest as an opportunity to vent their frustrations against the black and white Democrats from Georgia, whom they despised. It is possible that rumors were circulating through the black community that these Democrats had actually precipitated the events that led to the arrest. Violence did occur, however, when some black Charlestonians intercepted the black musicians from Savannah as they proceeded to a gate on Calhoun Street, throwing stones and injuring several band members. The city mayor, Gilbert Pillsbury, acknowledging that he was powerless to stop the freedmen, solicited the help of the commander of the Citadel, Colonel Andrews. Andrews sent a detachment of armed soldiers to escort the black band and Savannah baseball team to their boat.[54] To the shock of Charleston's blacks, the black band, on their departure, played "Dixie" for the whites.[55] A group of blacks on the outskirts of the crowd reacted to this perceived insult by throwing rocks and wounding several people, including some of the baseball players.[56]

This riot was both a political and a racial matter. By attacking the baseball team and the band from Savannah, Charleston's freedmen were attacking the lingering symbols of slavery and those who would like to see slavery return. Members of Savannah's baseball team were Democrats, and yet they had a team band made up of blacks. That meant the band members had apparently befriended people whose sentiments were identified as anti-black. Furthermore, the musicians were themselves Democrats, an indication that they lacked racial consciousness. And when the musicians had the audacity to play "Dixie," the anthem of the slaveholders, they compounded the insult of their association with the whites. To Charleston's freedmen, the band had betrayed their race and therefore deserved to be stoned. White Democrats from Savannah were attacked because they represented the old slave regime. As far as most blacks were concerned, the slave system, in all its formal and informal ramifications, was obsolete.

Throughout the Reconstruction period, black Charlestonians continued to rebel against any reminders of the regime of slavery. The black vote was a central issue. Charleston's freedpeople fought to protect the voting rights of all of South Carolina's blacks, while Democrats in the state fought equally hard to restore white supremacy by keeping blacks out of electoral politics, resorting even to murder to persuade blacks of the potential dangers of voting. When six black South Carolina militiamen were murdered by whites at Hamburg in Aiken County on July 8, 1876, blacks in Charleston organized a mass meeting to denounce the murders. In a warning to whites, freedmen asserted, "We tell you that it will not do to go too far in this thing—remember there are 80,000 black men in this State who can bear Winchester rifles, and know how to use them." Furthermore, they said, women and children could be called upon to repel white violence. There were 200,000 women in the state of South Carolina who could light a torch and use the knife, and 100,000 boys and girls ready to fight to retain their freedom.[57]

This was not simply rhetoric. The actions taken by Charlestonian freedmen against white authority, as an extension of that suffered under slavery, are well documented. During the outdoor meeting from which the warning to whites was issued, one freedman refused to move to allow a streetcar to pass through the crowd of blacks massed at this event. The frustrated conductor sought the aid of the police, who arrested the man, whereupon a group of freedmen rushed to his rescue, crying, "This is no Hamburg!" In five minutes the prisoner was taken from the police by force and hidden in the crowd.[58] The actions of the conductor and the policeman were most probably interpreted as another example of whites', in an echo of the slave regime, presuming to control their right to assembly.

Political violence involving Charleston's blacks reached its zenith in fall 1876 as black Charlestonians fought doggedly to protect the modest degree of political power they had gained with emancipation. At that time, Democrats appeared to be seizing power in South Carolina, largely through fraud and intimidation. Most blacks had by then become even more fiercely Republican than in earlier years, and many feared that a Democratic victory would inevitably return them to slavery. Confrontations between black Republicans and Democrats of both races were becoming particularly bloody in the waning years of the Reconstruction period. Out of these racial conflicts black Charlestonians would emerge as the aggressors and the victors.

By late August 1876, political meetings in Charleston were a regular occurrence. At a Democratic ward meeting held on September 1, several blacks delivered speeches explaining why they could no longer support the Republican party and had chosen instead to side with the Democrats. To black Republicans, the enrollment of their brothers in the Democratic party was anathema. A crowd of black Republicans waited outside the Democratic meeting house, and at the conclusion of the meeting, they attacked one of the speakers, Isaac Rivers, a twenty-nine-year-old porter, as he left the hall. The confrontation continued after another, well-attended Democratic ward meeting on September 6 in Archer's Hall on the corner of King and George Streets. Blacks who had attended Republican ward meetings that same evening wandered over to Archer's Hall to listen to the speeches. One of the speakers, J. R. Jenkins, a black Democrat, fueled the already inflamed passions by launching a verbal assault on black Republicans. Angry black Republicans went outside to wait for Jenkins in the street. Having vowed earlier to kill all black Democrats, the group now appeared ready to carry out its threat.[59]

As was customary during these days of political turmoil, a large group of whites surrounded Jenkins and other black Democrats, attempting to escort them safely home at the conclusion of the meeting. As they moved up the street, they were pursued by several black Republicans, who jeered at them until they reached St. Matthew's Church opposite the Citadel. At this point, the blacks advanced aggressively on the Democrats.

In an effort to disperse the black crowd, one of the whites fired his pistol into the air, but it had the opposite effect of attracting several hundred blacks to the scene. Both groups began throwing rocks and shooting pistols, touching off a riot. Although badly outnumbered by the black Republicans, the whites managed with the help of the police to place the black Democrats under the protection of federal troops at the Citadel Green. At this point, emboldened by steadily increasing numbers, the blacks leveled a furious missile assault. Whites responded by firing into the black crowds. The white Democrats and the police had kept the black mob at bay in the initial stage of the riot, but in the ensuing phase, blacks moved unopposed through King Street and other parts of Charleston.[60]

From midnight until the next morning, blacks gathered on street corners in large numbers, and, according to a reporter for the *New York Times*, "broke windows, robbed stores, and attacked and beat indiscriminately every white male who showed his face."[61] Although one black man, Ben Gibbes, and one white man, J. M. Buckner, died, whites suffered far greater injury in the riot than did blacks. Several whites were critically wounded, but only a few blacks received serious wounds.[62] As the black mob moved through the streets of Charleston wreaking vengeance upon whites, white Charlestonians reported hearing blacks cry, "Kill Them! Kill Them All! Dis town is Ours!"[63] After the initial stage of the riot, blacks seemed to provoke no white response to their actions. Even the hated white rifle clubs, holdovers from the antebellum militia groups, would not oppose them. As blacks roamed the streets on the night of September 6, they jeeringly asked where the rifle clubs were, but they were nowhere to be found.[64]

For the next few days, Charleston was in a turmoil as blacks continued to attack whites randomly, making it unsafe for whites to venture out on the streets, particularly at night.[65] In most white households, "people were stooping and crawling as they passed windows; a shadow on a curtain was a target for a rock or a bullet."[66] Black women also figured prominently in the riot, as they too were armed with axes or hatchets, sometimes held in aprons or concealed at their sides in the folds of their dresses.[67] White fright ran so deep that Wade Hampton, the leading white Democratic proponent of white supremacy in South Carolina and future governor of the state, "cried when he heard of the cowardice of the whites."[68]

The September 1876 riot was not to be the last between black Republicans and the Democrats in the Charleston area. An even more bloody riot occurred in October 1876 in Cainhoy, a village located a few miles from Charleston that was often the site of social gatherings and political meetings for blacks and whites. The Cainhoy riots were occasioned by a "joint discussion" political meeting, organized by whites to appeal to black voters. Under normal circumstances, the Democratic party would have attracted few blacks to a rally. But this time the Democrats had arrived at a strategy to better their access to black voters. The Charleston County Democratic party chairman, Charles H. Simonton, had asked his Republican counterpart, Charleston County sheriff Christopher Columbus Bowen, to allow the Democrats to share the speaking time at an upcoming political meeting. Bowen agreed, but only with the stipulation, which Simonton accepted, that both sides travel to the meeting unarmed and attend it unarmed. This agreement was unusual. In the waning years of the Reconstruction period, Democrats often attended joint political gatherings that were organized by Republicans. Usually there was no violence, but most participants came armed, and the atmosphere was often tense.[69]

The joint political meeting in Cainhoy, at which each party's candidate was to have equal speaking time, was scheduled for October 16. The participants left Charleston on the steamer *Pocasin* at nine o'clock in the morning. The Democratic contingent included several white men who carried no rifles, in keeping with the agreement between Simonton and Bowen, but who nonetheless had armed themselves with pistols. The Republican candidates, consisting of Bowen, William J. McKinlay (a black), and G. Galliard, were accompanied by a small contingent of friends. No trouble occurred during the river trip, and the steamer reached Cainhoy on schedule at noon.[70] A small contingent of freedmen met the boat and proceeded to the meeting site. When they arrived, they found about three or four hundred other blacks already assembled. Most were Republicans who, because they did not trust whites, had brought shotguns and muskets, which they had stashed in a dilapidated shed in the woods to the left of the speaker's stand. Most whites had come armed with their pistols.

The meeting was opened with the understanding that each party would be allowed two hours for speeches. The first speaker was W. St. Julien Jervey, a well-known Charleston Democrat, who finished his hour-long speech without interruption or disturbance.[71] But when William McKinlay, a member of one of Charleston's prominent and wealthy antebellum free black families and a Republican candidate for solicitor, stepped to the podium to deliver his speech, the atmosphere changed drastically. McKinlay had uttered only a few words when he was startled by a number of blacks crying: "Look out dar; look out dar!" McKinlay responded immediately. Pointing to a group of white men who were arming themselves, he shouted to the blacks in the crowd, "Those men have got the guns. They are going to shoot me and the rest of you," and he leaped from the stand.[72]

Realizing that the whites had stolen the guns from the shed, blacks took up the few arms they had and ran for cover. At this point, one of the guns carried by a white man accidentally discharged. This accidental shot was followed with a volley of further shots, this time apparently to gun down the scurrying blacks. One of the shots killed an elderly freedman, John Lachicotte.[73] Somehow the freedmen managed to retrieve their guns, and the tide of the battle began to change in their favor. Although the whites had initiated the shooting, they now found themselves out of ammunition, outnumbered, and, as rarely happened in Reconstruction, outgunned. Angry over the attack and over Lachicotte's death, freedmen now set out to kill all the whites responsible. They peppered the fleeing whites with several rounds of shots. The bloodied whites struggled to reach their boat and return to Charleston.

Efforts by white leaders, both Republican and Democratic, to get blacks to stop firing their weapons were futile. Freedmen ignored the pleas of the Republican Bowen and the Democratic Walker to cease their fire, wounding Walker in the leg as he fled back toward a party of whites who had sought refuge in a nearby vestry. The prominent black candidate McKinlay had to pretend he was arresting two desperate whites in order to get them to safety. The hasty retreat of the whites to their boat was chaotic. Many, too severely injured to make it on their own, were left behind with the dead. In this riot, five white men were killed and between fifteen and fifty whites were injured. Only one black man, Lachicotte, died, and only three blacks were injured, all of them Democrats.[74] Measured by almost any standard, the Cainhoy riot was a black victory. The *New York Times* conceded this fact, asserting that "for the first time in the history of the race conflicts of the South, the Negroes were victorious."[75] But this was not the first victory by blacks nor would it be the last. The upcoming November election of 1876 would lead to another round of intense political confrontations between black Republicans and Democrats of both races.

Because federal troops were present throughout South Carolina and because the Democrats wished to avoid the appearance of coercion, the November election passed with relative calm in the state, having inspired only sporadic acts of violence. The question of whether Wade Hampton or Daniel Chamberlain won the gubernatorial election in South Carolina, or whether it was Rutherford B. Hayes or Samuel Tilden who actually won the presidential election in 1876 are open to historical debate.[76] What is clear, however, is that Charleston's freedmen interpreted Hampton's election as an end not only to their political rights but to their civil rights as well. Angry and frustrated over the election results, blacks in Charleston engaged in one more violent clash with whites over this perceived threat to their political rights.

As election results trickled in, Charlestonians crowded around newspaper offices hoping to hear the latest figures. On November 8, E. W. Mackey, a local white Republican leader and former congressman, awaited election returns outside the office of the *Charleston News and Courier*. Joking with a group of Democrats about the election, he said, with a measure of certainty, that Chamberlain, the Republican candidate, had been elected, but the group insisted that Hampton had won. The Democrats soon grew tired of hearing Mackey say that Chamberlain had won, and one became so incensed that he fired his pistol at Mackey. He missed; but hearing the shots, a number of blacks and whites rushed to the scene. From this point on, confusion reigned. Blacks gathering on street corners heard rumors that Mackey had been killed by the Democrats. They moved toward the newspaper office and joined other blacks already there. When they encountered a group of white Democrats, the riot began. As in earlier racial clashes in Charleston, blacks in the streets outnumbered whites, and blacks beat and shot whites as they passed through the area of the riot. Again, black women played a key role in the riot, passing loaded rifles to men on the sidewalk. Both black men and black women were said to be following whites on the streets, shouting "Kill um! Kill um! Kill um!"[77] Black policemen entered the melee on the side of the other blacks, shooting several whites. Black police were believed to be the ones who killed Endicott H. Walter, the son of a prominent Charleston businessman, who was also injured. The younger Walter was the only fatality, though several other men were wounded.

Because of the black community's reputation for being aggressive, several companies of federal troops under the command of Colonel Henry J. Hunt of the Fifth Artillery were already stationed in the city to prevent further disturbances. When the riot began, Hunt swiftly dispatched troops to restore order to the city. The troops cleared the streets by that evening, ending Charleston's final Reconstruction-era riot.[78]

The historical record seems to indicate that Charleston's blacks were not the innocent victims of white violence during the Reconstruction period. Charleston County blacks were unique in their determination and ability to release their anger through violence. Furthermore, they enjoyed a large numerical advantage over whites and a reputation for militancy and violence dating from colonial times. The skirmishes, fistfights, and riots of the Reconstruction era were merely a continuation of efforts by the region's blacks to stand up for themselves.[79] Standing up for themselves was an ambitious undertaking in the postwar South; and to the credit of Charleston's blacks, they were largely successful. Charleston's freedmen consistently put whites on notice that they were willing to defend their newly gained rights and their freedom for as long as necessary.

It must be noted that not all Charlestonian freedmen who engaged in violence against whites did so to defend their rights. Some may have participated in these riots simply because they felt violence was a justified response to white violence against them. Some rioters apparently took advantage of the riots to vent racial hatred and to settle old scores. Some, of both races, were simply thugs with no political motivation. Still, it appears that much of the racial violence in these riots was politically motivated. The attainment and preservation of human, civil, and political rights was of great importance to freedmen, and these rights would not be surrendered without a struggle. For freedmen in Charleston, freedom was a battle. The incidents of racial violence in Charleston during the Reconstruction period suggest that freedmen had adjusted to the new social order better than had whites. Whites who treated blacks as if nothing had changed represented to blacks a direct threat to their newfound rights. The freedmen who responded in these violent ways did so at the peril of their own lives, a clear indication of the value they placed on the rights they were attempting to assert and defend.

EPILOGUE

The Light of Freedom, Justice, and Equality Brightens, Dims, and Then Darkens

Reconstruction failed in Charleston because of Republican divisiveness and Democratic opposition. Charleston Republicans were so divided that on only two occasions were they able to present a well-organized, smoothly operating, and united political party: in 1867 when Congressional Reconstruction began and in 1873 during the Cunningham campaign. It was imperative that Republicans establish a solid foundation on which to build a political organization capable of functioning effectively during Reconstruction and into the post-Reconstruction period, but they were not able to do so.[1]

Republicans were beset by disagreements and factionalism that threatened always to tear them asunder. Racial mistrust and suspicions further divided the party. White Republicans, for example, expended much time, effort, and energy persuading their black colleagues during the early years of Reconstruction that they ought not occupy the most significant positions in the party. As neophytes in the political system, the vast majority of black Republicans conceded most of the key political offices in 1868 to whites. But by 1870 several black Republicans, including Robert DeLarge and Richard Cain of Charleston, had become more assertive, and, fearing that their white colleagues intended to monopolize the political system, they demanded more significant positions for black Republicans. White Republicans such as D. T. Corbin and Charles P. Leslie were appalled by their black colleagues' assertiveness. They found it incomprehensible that blacks who had so recently been emancipated were demanding so much.[2] In all likelihood, most whites thought blacks, whom they regarded as their inferiors, ought to be satisfied with playing any role at all within the Republican party.

Intraracial political differences among blacks and mulattoes posed further problems.[3] Many of the prominent black leaders and officeholders were mulattoes. These included Francis Cardozo, Robert C. DeLarge, William McKinlay, Benjamin A. Boseman, and Edward P. Wall. Some of them were related to aristocratic white families in Charleston and owned a sizable amount of property. Although a substantial majority of black men involved in politics had a dark complexion, mulattoes tended to hold the most significant positions within the Republican party out of proportion to their actual numbers.[4] This created resentment from their darker colleagues, who never fully trusted mulattoes. Divisive differences between blacks and mulattoes rose to the surface in 1871 when Martin Delany, a black, charged mulatto men with dominating office holding at the expense of black men.[5]

Native Republicans, both black and white, greatly resented the intrusion of Republicans from Massachusetts and other Northern states. In the late 1860s and the early 1870s, local Republicans found it particularly galling that New Englanders dominated the customhouse and federal patronage in Charleston. By the mid-1870s, Cain, Delany, Cardozo, and other black Republicans, including Joseph H. Rainey and George Mears, had become convinced that cooperation with white Republicans from out of state was no longer tenable. The only feasible alternative for blacks in South Carolina, they reasoned, lay in cooperation with native whites. Some, including Delany and Mears, joined the Democratic party; others, including Cain, Cardozo, and Rainey, openly explored the notion of working with white and black Democrats, while criticizing the corruption they thought characterized Republican Reconstruction.[6]

Notwithstanding the divisive factors of race and geography, the most consistently divisive factor in the Republican party during the Reconstruction years was ambition to hold political office. The eagerness among Republicans to hold public office sometimes amounted to desperation. The Bowen and Mackey factions, led by Christopher Columbus Bowen and E. W. Mackey, developed because they represented the opposing political machines through which individuals could run for office and not because of differing views on issues or ideology. Fluidity characterized both groups, and it was not unusual for individuals to move from one faction to the other and in and out of politics. Since both groups were adamant about gaining a solid foothold in Charleston, it is not surprising that the two factions were the source of never-ending disruptions and disputes. Typically, most Reconstruction elections in Charleston were accompanied by two Republican nominating conventions, two tickets, and a dispute after the election over who won. Conflict over the distribution of patronage caused further contentiousness. Frequently the differences between factions were expressed through violence, making it virtually impossible for the victorious wing of the party to operate in an organized and efficient fashion.[7]

This infighting caused the Republicans in Charleston to lose the municipal election in 1871 to the Democrats. Republicans' cutthroat tactics, beginning at the nomination stage of the election, proved so devastating to the party that it was torn asunder. Because of Republican factionalism in 1874 and 1875, the Mackey wing of the party was compelled to fashion a fusion ticket with moderate Democrats. This alliance was successful until 1876, when Democratic gubernatorial candidate Wade Hampton convinced Democrats to abandon the Mackey Republicans and unite behind his candidacy. With so many years of Republican disunity, it was too late for the warring factions of Bowen and Mackey to unite and form an effective opposition party once the Democrats had taken control of the state and local organs of government in 1877. Once Hampton became governor in South Carolina, the Republican party in Charleston simply collapsed.[8]

Democratic opposition to the Republican party throughout much of Reconstruction was so persistent and hostile that it is highly unlikely that Republicans could have prevailed, even if they had been able to develop a stable and effective political machine. White Democrats in South Carolina, and, indeed, throughout the South, fervently believed that black men and women, whether slave or free, were their inferiors. Anything that smacked of racial, social, political, or economic equality had to be abated quickly and effectively. In the minds of most white Democrats, the Republican party stood for everything that was anathema to Southern society.[9] The Republican party's demise in Charleston also was further hastened by the exodus of black Republicans who became disillusioned with the party and either joined the Democratic party or denounced the Republicans.

The divisiveness that proved so devastating to the Republicans in Charleston was mirrored in their behavior in state government. White and black Republicans were continuously at odds, often failing to vote in concert on critical issues that came to a roll-call vote. In fact, a majority of the white Republicans opposed a majority of the blacks on at least one out of three of these issues. Moreover, the black and white Republican majorities voted against each other on six out of every ten critical votes during the administration of Franklin J. Moses, Jr., from 1872 to 1874.[10]

More destructive to the Republican party than interracial conflicts, however, was the disunity between black party members, particularly between blacks and mulattoes. Black Republicans came from disparate backgrounds and often exhibited severe intragroup strains along color and, ultimately, class lines. Those freeborn mulattoes who were relatively affluent sometimes held political views and interests that ran counter to those held by blacks from among the poorer, slave-born masses. The differences between black and mulatto members were significant enough to contribute to the failure of some of the party's legislative initiatives and to the curtailment of some of the more radical or experimental policies that were put forth.[11]

The results of the presidential election of 1876 between Republican Rutherford B. Hayes and Democrat Samuel J. Tilden, and South Carolina's gubernatorial race between Republican Daniel H. Chamberlain and Democrat Wade Hampton held dire consequences for blacks in Charleston and all of South Carolina. The Republican candidates for the South Carolina House defeated the Democratic ticket in Charleston and Charleston County by over six thousand votes. But across the state the results were different. Hampton and Chamberlain appeared to have received approximately the same number of votes. Of course, each maintained that he had won. In fact, both were so ardent about occupying the governor's mansion that for five extraordinary months South Carolina had two governors and two legislatures. A remedy to this situation would be forthcoming. Once Rutherford B. Hayes was declared the victor in the presidential election of 1876, even though initially he did not receive a majority of either popular or electoral votes, he struck a deal with Southern Democrats to head off any opposition from them to the electoral commission's decision. Hayes promised, among other things, to remove the few remaining federal troops guarding the Republican claimants in the statehouses of Louisiana and South Carolina. Accordingly, he withdrew the remaining 683 federal troops from South Carolina in April 1877, and Chamberlain resigned. Thus, political Reconstruction had come to an effective end.[12] White Southerners were essentially told by the federal government that they could deal with Southern blacks as they desired.

After Hampton became governor, to no great surprise the Democratic-controlled statehouse declared the seats of the Charleston Republican delegation vacant and ordered new elections. The Democrats elected three blacks and fourteen whites to serve in the new seventeen-member delegation. The three blacks were fortunate enough to serve three consecutive terms. And Martin Delany, because of his tireless efforts in promoting Democratic candidates in the gubernatorial race of 1876, was appointed to the position of magistrate by Governor Hampton.[13]

The end of political Reconstruction marked the end of many black political careers and the destruction of the political rights of many black citizens of Charleston. White Democrats, who now controlled state and local government, proudly charged the Republicans with having run a black-dominated, corrupt, inefficient, and barbaric government. Such a government was intolerable, they maintained, and was to be prevented from recurring at all costs. So, in an effort to destroy the potential political power of the black majority, the local white Democratic "redeemers," or former Confederates, prohibited blacks who had previously supported the Republicans from voting in municipal elections after 1877. Their efforts were successful. Neither black nor white Republicans were elected to Charleston's city council or the state legislature for decades thereafter, and many well-known black politicians left politics altogether for various reasons. Cardozo was forced out of politics after 1876 amid charges of fraud leveled at him by the Democratic administration. He moved to Washington, D.C., where he worked for the postal department and eventually became the principal of a black high school in the capital city. Although Robert Smalls ultimately returned home to Beaufort and was elected to Congress, he was convicted of corruption along with Cardozo. Delany was able to maintain his position of trial justice until 1879, when the South Carolina legislature elected Hampton to the United States Senate and purged black officeholders throughout the state. "Daddy" Cain also became a victim of this purge, vacating his seat in the United States House of Representatives at the end of his term in 1879. Shortly thereafter, he was elected bishop of the African Methodist Episcopal Church and assigned to Louisiana and Texas, where he became president of Paul Quinn College in Waco. From a financial standpoint, life after politics proved more rewarding for Cardozo, Delany, and Cain than for Alonzo J. Ransier and Robert B. Elliott. Ransier, a former South Carolina congressman and lieutenant governor, died in poverty in 1882. He struggled in vain to make a living during his last years, working both as a night watchman at the Charleston customhouse and as a city street sweeper. Elliott, the state's most brilliant political organizer, also encountered much difficulty in earning a living. He became so disenchanted with his predicament in Charleston that he eventually moved to New Orleans in search of employment as a lawyer. His search proved futile, however, for he died there in 1884, still struggling to revive his flagging career.[14]

In the post-Reconstruction period, Charleston's city council was either nearly or completely all-white. Between 1877 and 1883 only three blacks served as aldermen. They were C. H. Holloway, John R. Dourant,

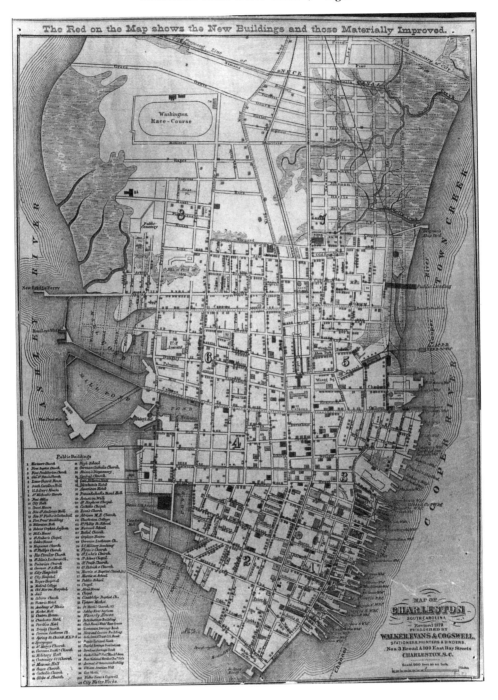

Charleston in 1879. South Carolina Historical Society, Charleston.

and Clarence Nell, all Democrats. The Democrats were now the only members of the city council, and after 1883 no black man was elected to the council until 1967. Only one black, the Democrat George Mears, was able to serve in the South Carolina legislature after 1882. With the experience and seniority of seven consecutive terms, he should have possessed a significant amount of power, but Mears was an almost totally silent member.

Different measures were employed by the state legislature to eliminate black participation in government, including fraud, intimidation, gerry-mandering, and complicated voting procedures.[15] In 1882, the South Carolina legislature enacted the eight box law, designating eight catego-ries of office holding to confuse black voters. As a result, the black vote dropped from 91,870 in 1876 to 13,740 in 1888.[16] In 1890, the ardent white supremacist Ben Tillman was elected governor, and he went on to mastermind the Constitutional Convention of 1895, which rendered the Fifteenth Amendment meaningless in the state.[17] Consequently, by the end of the nineteenth century, blacks in Charleston and throughout South Carolina had been effectively disfranchised, and in essence, were political nonentities.

The economic fate of black Charlestonians during the waning years of the Reconstruction era and in the post-Reconstruction period paralleled their fate in the political realm. Although in the early 1870s it seemed as if Charleston's economy might gradually recover, a worldwide depres-sion had a devastating impact on Charleston's weak economy that would last until 1896. Capital in the city's banks, which had totaled almost twelve million dollars in 1860, declined to less than four million dollars by election day in 1872. Moreover, in 1873 some thirty-eight firms collapsed, and payments were suspended by three of the city's four state banks. The "crash" of 1873 proved to be a financial nightmare for both black and white Charlestonians. The following year brought additional financial hardships, as sixty businesses in Charleston collapsed, and the Broad Street office of the National Freedmen's Savings Bank folded and ulti-mately closed its doors after its parent bank in Washington, D.C., failed. The fifty-three hundred blacks and two hundred whites who had depos-ited their money in the bank were informed of the bank's collapse and were understandably shocked to learn that they would not get back the modest savings they had invested there.[18]

The depression of the 1870s wreaked havoc on the lives of black and white workers in Charleston and throughout the South, with black work-ers being the hardest hit. Because of the city's declining economic for-tunes and the overabundance of labor in the city, many black workers had difficulty finding steady work. The city's depressed economy espe-cially hurt the building tradesmen. The wages paid to some workers actually declined below their prewar levels. Competition between black and white workers in Charleston in the 1870s was intense. In most occupations, blacks lost out to whites. Accordingly, by 1880 there was a drastic reduction in the number of blacks employed as bakers, masons, sawyers, tailors, millers, printers, saddlers, engineers, carpenters, sail makers, machinists, cigar makers, blacksmiths, shipwrights, wheelwrights, and cotton menders. Native white Charlestonians, however, made positive gains in all except one of the occupations in this list.[19]

Not surprisingly, in a city which was ravaged by the depression of the 1870s and where black workers lost jobs because of discrimination, blacks experienced huge reductions in real wages. Day laborers were periodically without jobs and lived in dilapidated "nigger sections." Most black Charlestonians found the odds against their being able to provide adequately for themselves and their families nearly insurmountable.[20] Some had invested their meager savings in the Freedmen's Savings Bank with the hope of using it to purchase property,[21] but this hope died when the bank collapsed in 1874. Of course, black unskilled laborers experienced the most difficulty accumulating property. The 1880 census notes, for example, that only 6.5 percent of black day laborers had accumulated any real property and 75 percent of this group held property valued below five hundred dollars. Although black skilled workers enjoyed better chances of acquiring property than other black workers, only 8 percent were able to obtain any real property.[22] Since purchasing a small farm or even a town lot was beyond the means of most former slaves, it was much easier to acquire personal items such as plows, tools, carts, mules, horses, cattle, wagons, machinery, furniture, carriages, watches, jewelry, and clothing.[23] Despite the fact that most black Charlestonians were unable to acquire real property, the small but growing number of those who were businessmen and professionals illustrated that the doors of economic opportunity that had opened could never be completely closed.[24]

Nevertheless, the organized efforts of black workers in Charleston labor unions in the waning years of the 1870s produced no significant gains for black workers. This reflected a national trend. The influence of management was growing while the influence of labor was steadily declining. Both black and white workers held little clout in a country ravaged by depression, where work was often extremely difficult to find and labor was overabundant. After the panic of 1873, union membership fell nationwide by 90 percent and by 1880 fewer than one in a hundred workers belonged to a union.[25] Once Radical Republicans were driven from political power in South Carolina in the election of 1876, the threat of significant work disruptions like the 1873 Charleston strike was effectively eliminated, while political support from conservative legislators now reinforced the control that industry had over labor. These legislators authorized industry to install a convict-lease system, which physically and mentally exploited prisoners while white planters and industrialists reaped huge profits.[26] The only benefit black workers in Charleston seemed to have gained during Reconstruction was the right of those not in prison to choose where, when, and for whom they would work. Legally, at least, they no longer had designated owners for whom they were obliged to work.

Charleston was in a relative decline by the early 1880s, despite signs of economic prosperity. Construction boomed, export trade increased sharply, the employment rate rose dramatically, and the profits of Charleston's industrial, wholesale, and retail establishments spiraled. Nevertheless, when compared with other New South urban centers, Charleston lagged behind. Near the end of the decade, the South Carolina Railway Company faced the likelihood of bankruptcy. The anemia of the local economy was due in part to the city's aging business leadership. Charleston was in such economic peril that, as late as 1880, it had not been able to completely repair the district destroyed by the fire of 1861. Moreover, Charleston was one of the two major Southern ports that continued to decline significantly up to the turn of the century.[27] The city's steady economic decline did not bode well for Charlestonians, particularly for blacks who, by the dawn of the twentieth century, were consigned to a special caste in America's class society. Economically, a large number were bound by new and insidious shackles—such as poverty, debt peonage, and convict lease—to sell their labor in a buyer's market.[28] They were also hurt by the diminishing influence of the labor unions they were allowed to join. In addition, the vast majority of black Charlestonians remained propertyless.

Blacks faced more than economic difficulties. Beginning in the late 1870s, the pace of discrimination and the enforced institutional separation of the races quickened in Charleston. By 1880, for example, the insane were strictly segregated at Roper Hospital. Segregation permeated Charleston society so thoroughly that it extended even to death. Thus, blacks were buried in the city's black cemetery and whites in the white one. The Charleston police force, despite being reorganized several times during the Reconstruction era by various mayors, was unusual for having maintained a membership that was 50 percent black and for having a black man, George Shrewsbury, as the chief of detectives. By the late 1870s, however, firemen in Charleston were segregated. The more than five hundred black firemen maintained their equipment separate from white firemen, after years during which black and white firefighters had battled fires together. In the early 1880s both black policemen and black firemen fell victim to Charleston's steady economic decline, as the dismissal of a large number of black policemen resulted from Mayor William Ashmead Courtenay's budget cuts, and most black firemen were released following major retrenchments and the city council's merger of

Charleston's volunteer companies into a paid city fire department.[29] Blacks could serve on juries during Reconstruction, but by the closing decades of the nineteenth century, even though the United States Supreme Court continued to support their right to serve, they were virtually excluded.[30] Furthermore, the judicial system used the expansion of federal powers during the Reconstruction era to protect corporations, not blacks. Enforcement of the Fourteenth and Fifteenth Amendments continued to wane, and in 1883 the United States Supreme Court declared the Civil Rights Act of 1875 unconstitutional.[31]

Despite the very bleak record of failures in the era of emancipation and Republican rule, there were some enduring accomplishments. Even though all these measures were flagrantly violated after 1877, it is difficult to imagine how the Civil Rights Acts of 1866 and 1875, the Fourteenth and Fifteenth Amendments, and the Enforcement Acts of 1870 and 1871 could have passed without Reconstruction. They became a vehicle for future federal intervention in Southern affairs.[32] Moreover, they also set a precedent for legislation promoting fair practices in housing, the 1964 Civil Rights Act, the 1965 Voting Rights Act, President Lyndon Johnson's War on Poverty, and enactment of affirmative action programs. Black and white Republicans in Charleston and throughout South Carolina helped enact a constitution that was modern, generally progressive, and comparatively democratic[33] and that, though tampered with by the "redeemers," was not substantially overhauled. Fortunately, blacks were never barred from citizenship, herded into labor reserves, or prohibited by law from moving from one part of the country to another, as were blacks in South Africa in the twentieth century.[34] Blacks in the Reconstruction era also enjoyed the freedom of assembly, a privilege they had never had under slavery. As a result, black benevolent and fraternal associations were spawned in large numbers in the South, and many survived well beyond the Reconstruction years. Furthermore, these assocations became the basis for much of the black self-help activity that continues today.

The autonomous black family survived the end of Reconstruction.[35] Indeed, the black family was significantly strengthened by then. Blacks could live as family units without fear of being separated from one another against their will. Religious institutions became the focal point of black communities. Black churches enforced black morality and became involved in education and social welfare, and their buildings were used as social centers. The black church survived the end of Reconstruction[36] and continues to play an integral role in black life. Moreover, many of the black civil rights activists of the post–World War II era emerged from active roles in the black church. One of the most striking successes of the Republican regime in Charleston and throughout South Carolina was the establishment of an educational system. While the system did not operate smoothly, its creation firmly established the principle of free public education in a state that had not had such a system before the war. It also provided the infrastructure on which later systems could be based.[37] The Avery Normal Institute, opened in Charleston during Reconstruction, survived until 1954, and several of its graduates have played and continue to play major roles in American society. The seeds of educational progress planted during the Reconstruction era could not be entirely destroyed.[38] In the years 1870 to 1900 the illiteracy rates for black Charlestonians dropped dramatically, and they would continue to drop well into the twentieth century. Nationally, Reconstruction brought the growth of many black colleges that have endured to this day and produced not only many of the black civil rights activists of the post–World War II period but also a substantial portion of the black professional class.

Blacks in Charleston and throughout the South took one step forward and two steps backward during the Reconstruction era. Emancipation arrived amid much excitement from the standpoint of blacks, and initially it appeared that real opportunities existed for blacks to make huge strides in becoming first-class American citizens. Indeed, it seemed as if the light of freedom, justice, and equality for blacks was bright. But in the waning years of Reconstruction, the light grew dimmer, and in the closing decades of the nineteenth century it was all but extinguished. The gallant struggle of black Charlestonians to acquire first-class American citizenship represented their first civil rights movement. That they did not ultimately prevail, after such a promising start, is the real tragedy of the Reconstruction period in Charleston. Sadly, the American nation as a whole allowed an opportunity to lay the foundation for a truly egalitarian society to elude it.

APPENDIX

TABLE 1. Free Blacks in Charleston, South Carolina,
by Sex and Age, 1850, 1860

Year/Sex	Under 15	Age 15–49*	50 & Older	Total
1850	1,421	1,644	376	3,441
Male	659	585	111	1,355
Female	762	1,059	265	2,086
1860	1,310	1,505	417	3,232
Male	582	526	128	1,236
Female	728	979	289	1,996

Sources: Calculated from U.S. Bureau of the Census, *Compendium of the Seventh Census of 1850* (Washington, D.C., 1854), p. 397; U.S. Bureau of the Census, *Eighth Census of the U.S., Population of 1860* (Washington, D.C., 1864).

Note: The 1860 Federal Census lists free blacks at 3,237, but my own count, used here, produced 3,232 free blacks. This discrepancy could be attributed to the fact that the 1860 published census counted five Native Americans as blacks, but I did not.

*Most common marriage ages.

TABLE 2. Antebellum Population of Charleston, South Carolina,
by Race and Legal Status, and as a Percentage
of Total Population, 1820–1860

Year	Whites Raw Total	(%)	Blacks Raw Total	(%)	Free Blacks	Slaves	Raw Total
1820	10,653	(43)	14,127	(57)	1,475	12,652	24,780
1830	12,828	(42)	17,661	(58)	2,107	15,554	30,489
1840	13,031	(45)	16,231	(55)	1,558	14,673	29,262
1850	20,012	(47)	22,973	(53)	3,441	19,532	42,985
1860	23,376	(58)	17,146	(42)	3,237	13,909	40,522

Sources: U.S. Bureau of the Census, *Seventh Census*; U.S. Bureau of the Census, *Population of the U.S. in 1860 Compiled from the Eighth Census* (Washington, D.C., 1864).

Note: The 1860 figures in table 1 are based on my count; here they are based on the published census data.

TABLE 3. Slaves in Charleston, South Carolina, District,
by Sex and Age, 1850, 1860

Year/Sex	Under 15	Age 15–49*	50 & Older	Total
1850	15,278	23,020	6,078	44,376
Male	7,299	10,725	2,685	20,709
Female	7,979	12,295	3,393	23,667
1860	13,854	18,945	4,491	37,290
Male	6,660	9,169	2,128	17,957
Female	7,194	9,776	2,363	19,333

Sources: Calculated from U.S. Bureau of the Census, *Seventh Census,* pp. 337–38; U.S. Bureau of the Census, *Eighth Census,* pp. 450–51.

*Most common marriage ages.

TABLE 4. Slaves in Charleston, South Carolina, by Sex and Age, 1850, 1860

Year/Sex	Under 15	Age 15–49*	50 & Older	Total
1850	5,560	11,017	2,955	19,532
Male	2,517	4,976	1,138	8,631
Female	3,043	6,041	1,817	10,901
1860	4,537	7,544	1,830	13,911
Male	2,170	3,668	743	6,581
Female	2,367	3,876	1,087	7,330

Sources: Calculated from U.S. Bureau of the Census, *Compendium of the Seventh Census,* p. 397; U.S. Bureau of the Census, *Seventh Census,* pp. 337–38.

Note: Figures are based on published census data for 1860, which list the total number of slaves in 1860 at 13,911. My count is 13,909. This discrepancy could be attributed to the fact that in one instance two Native Americans were counted as blacks, and in another they were not.

*Most common marriage ages.

TABLE 5. Population Distribution of Charleston, South Carolina, by Ward, Race, and Legal Status, 1850

	Whites	Slaves	Free Blacks	Total Blacks	Total Population
Ward 1	2,807	2,446	165	2,611	5,418
Ward 2	2,750	3,209	319	3,528	6,278
Ward 3	4,386	3,241	518	3,759	8,145
Ward 4	5,499	5,796	997	6,793	12,292
All Wards	15,442	14,692	1,999	16,691	32,133
Neck	4,570	4,840	1,442	6,282	10,852
City Total	20,012	19,532	3,441	22,973	42,985

Source: Frederick A. Ford, *Census of the City of Charleston, South Carolina, for the Year 1861, Illustrated by Statistical Tables, Prepared under the Authority of the City Council* (Charleston, S.C.: Evans and Cogswell, 1861), p. 8.

TABLE 6. Population Distribution of Charleston, South Carolina, by Ward, Race, and Legal Status, 1860

	Whites	Free Blacks	Slaves	Total
Ward 1	2,397	79	1,120	3,596
Ward 2	2,048	100	2,727	4,875
Ward 3	3,816	276	1,648	5,740
Ward 4	4,687	726	3,253	8,666
Ward 5	2,591	635	1,445	4,671
Ward 6	3,371	822	2,000	6,193
Ward 7	1,852	188	534	2,574
Ward 8	2,448	548	879	3,875
City Total	23,210	3,374	13,606	40,190

Sources: Ford, *Census of the City of Charleston,* p. 8; U.S. Bureau of the Census, *Population of the U.S. in 1860 Compiled from the Eighth Census,* p. 452.

TABLE 7. Percentage Change in Black and White Population of Charleston, South Carolina, 1860–1870

	White			Black		
	1860	1870	% Change	1860	1870	% Change
Ward 1	2,391	2,314	−3.22	1,199	1,817	51.54
Ward 2	2,048	2,167	5.81	2,824	2,583	−8.53
Ward 3	3,816	3,424	−10.27	1,726	2,690	55.85
Ward 4	4,687	4,885	4.22	3,979	5,774	45.11
Ward 5	2,564	2,287	−10.80	2,078	3,774	81.62
Ward 6	3,367	3,470	3.06	2,781	5,315	91.12
Ward 7	1,845	2,000	8.40	690	1,187	72.03
Ward 8	2,448	2,202	−10.05	1,383	3,033	119.31

Source: Calculated from U.S. Bureau of the Census, *The Statistics of the Population of the United States in 1870* (Washington, D.C., 1873), p. 258.

Note: In 1860, 155 whites, 486 blacks, and 52 Native Americans lived in Charleston Neck, which was merged with the city of Charleston in that year. Therefore, it was difficult to place them specifically in any of the city's eight wards. Figures also may not be exact because Native Americans were often counted among the black population. The 52 Native Americans in Charleston Neck were not counted here.

TABLE 8. Black and White Population of Charleston, South Carolina,
by Sex, 1870

| | White | | Black | | |
	Males	Females	Males	Females	Total
Ward 1	1,063	1,220	765	1,086	4,134
Ward 2	1,015	1,151	1,124	1,494	4,784
Ward 3	1,643	1,763	1,178	1,532	6,116
Ward 4	2,245	2,608	2,388	3,415	10,656
Ward 5	1,231	1,060	1,750	2,020	6,061
Ward 6	1,710	1,832	2,356	2,949	8,847
Ward 7	971	1,005	527	682	3,185
Ward 8	1,099	1,102	1,367	1,675	5,243
Total	10,977	11,741	11,455	14,853	49,026

Source: Calculated from U.S. Bureau of the Census, Population of the United States in 1870 Compiled from the Ninth Census (Washington, D.C., 1872).

Note: Most published accounts of the 1870 federal census of Charleston list the number of whites at 22,749, blacks at 26,173, and Native Americans at 34, for a total of 48,956. My count of this census revealed 22,718 whites and 26,308 blacks, for a total of 49,026. Some Native Americans may have been counted in each of the other categories in the manuscript census, but this does not account for the difference in total found.

TABLE 9. Percentage of Male Residents Aged 18 and Older in All-Black Households in Charleston, South Carolina, Who Were Employed in 1870

| | Total Black Men | Employed Black Men | |
		Raw No.	% of Total
Ward 1	34	33	97.1
Ward 2	68	65	95.6
Ward 3	80	76	95.0
Ward 4	119	116	97.5
Ward 5	117	92	78.6
Ward 6	118	111	94.1
Ward 7	116	74	63.8
Ward 8	109	102	93.6
Total	761	669	87.9

Source: Calculated from U.S. Bureau of the Census, Population of the United States in 1870.

TABLE 10. Franklin Street School Tuition Payments, 1867, 1868, 1869

Date	Tuition Collected	No. Students Paying
October 1867	$37.00	N.A.
February 1868	N.A.	288*
April 1868	35.10	140
December 1868	12.60	51
January 1869	18.14	75
February 1869	20.38	90
March 1869	33.45	148

Sources: Teachers Monthly School Reports, October 1867; December, April 1868; January, February, March 1869, Superintendent of Education, South Carolina, Teachers Monthly School Reports, Box 27, Bureau of Refugees, Freedmen, and Abandoned Lands Records, National Archives, Washington, D.C. (hereafter, FBP); *Charleston Courier,* February 12, 1868; Kate B. Savage to Major E. L. Deane, June 30, 1870, Box 26, FBP.

Note: Enrollment figures are available only for February 1868.

*Out of an enrollment of 666.

TABLE 11. School-Aged Children Enrolled in Schools in Charleston, South Carolina, by Ward and Race, 1870

	Total	Student Enrollment			
		Black	% of Total	White	% of Total
Ward 1	716	273	38.1	443	61.9
Ward 2	655	286	43.7	369	56.3
Ward 3	943	357	37.9	586	62.1
Ward 4	1,275	608	47.7	667	52.3
Ward 5	1,035	641	61.9	394	38.1
Ward 6	1,842	1,006	54.6	836	45.4
Ward 7	473	163	34.5	310	65.5
Ward 8	949	512	54.0	437	46.0
Total	7,888	3,846	48.8	4,042	51.2

Source: U.S. Bureau of the Census, *A Compendium of the Ninth Census, 1870* (Washington, D.C., 1873), p. 474.

TABLE 12. Rate of Illiteracy among Blacks, Aged Ten or Older, in Fifteen Southern Cities with Populations in Excess of 25,000, 1890–1900

City*	1890 No.	1890 % Illiterate	1900 No.	1900 % Illiterate	1890–1900 % pt. Change
Charleston, S.C.	8,400	34.7	7,462	29.7	−5.0
Little Rock, Ark.	3,096	40.1	3,314	27.4	−12.7
Chattanooga, Tenn.	4,044	40.7	3,278	30.5	−10.2
San Antonio, Tex.	1,502	41.1	1,281	21.0	−20.1
Houston, Tex.	3,459	42.7	3,634	29.8	−12.9
New Orleans, La.	21,882	43.1	22,758	36.1	−7.0
Memphis, Tenn.	10,407	44.2	14,116	25.1	−19.1
Nashville, Tenn.	10,755	45.4	8,065	32.4	−13.0
Richmond, Va.	12,127	45.7	8,588	32.2	−13.5
Norfolk, Va.	6,122	47.2	6,399	38.4	−8.8
Atlanta, Ga.	10,766	48.9	10,119	35.1	−13.8
Savannah, Ga.	9,511	51.3	7,885	34.1	−17.2
Birmingham, Ala.	4,756	51.5	5,533	40.3	−11.2
Augusta, Ga.	6,913	55.4	5,781	38.8	−16.6
Mobile, Ala.	6,027	55.7	6,187	44.1	−11.6

Source: U.S. Bureau of the Census, *Eleventh Census of the United States Population in 1890* (Washington, D.C., 1894), p. 60; U.S. Bureau of the Census, *Twelfth Census of the United States Population in 1900* (Washington, D.C., 1903), p. 43.

*In ascending order of their 1890 black illiteracy rate.

TABLE 13. Percentage of Residents Who Were Married, by Race and by Racial Composition of Household, in Charleston, South Carolina, 1870

	% Residents Married in Racially Unmixed Households Blacks	Whites	% Residents Married in Mixed-Race Households Blacks	Whites
Ward 1	64.2	65.0	47.2	48.3
Ward 2	59.6	60.1	40.3	46.5
Ward 3	58.1	46.2	62.5	57.8
Ward 4	51.4	57.6	57.4	58.7
Ward 5	47.6	55.8	41.1	51.4
Ward 6	53.1	56.2	22.2	59.1
Ward 7	57.5	62.5	31.8	48.3
Ward 8	57.2	57.2	35.2	52.6
Average	56.1	57.6	42.2	52.8

Source: U.S. Bureau of the Census, *Ninth Census.*

TABLE 14. Average Number of Children per Married Couple and Average Number of Residents in Racially Unmixed Households, in Charleston, South Carolina, 1870

	Average Number Children per Couple		Average Number Household Residents	
	Black Households	White Households	Black Households	White Households
Ward 1	2.6	3.1	10.8	5.6
Ward 2	2.8	2.6	12.1	7.8
Ward 3	2.2	3.1	8.6	6.0
Ward 4	2.1	3.3	8.2	6.0
Ward 5	2.5	3.2	7.1	5.8
Ward 6	2.4	3.0	5.0	6.0
Ward 7	2.6	2.8	5.1	5.2
Ward 8	2.6	2.8	6.1	5.4
All Wards	2.5	3.0	7.9	6.0

Source: U.S. Bureau of the Census, *Ninth Census.*

TABLE 15. Work Status of Women, by Race, in Racially Unmixed Households in Charleston, South Carolina, 1870

	Black Women		White Women	
	% Working	% at Home	% Working	% at Home
Ward 1	19.1	80.8	13.6	86.3
Ward 2	56.6	43.4	16.8	83.1
Ward 3	45.4	54.5	18.6	81.3
Ward 4	83.9	16.0	8.1	91.8
Ward 5	46.3	53.6	13.0	86.8
Ward 6	53.0	46.9	17.2	82.7
Ward 7	46.4	53.5	6.3	93.6
Ward 8	60.5	39.4	19.8	80.1
Average	51.4	48.5	14.2	85.7

Source: U.S. Bureau of the Census, *Ninth Census.*

Note: The designation "Working" applies to those who received wages for work outside the home; "at Home" applies to those who received no wages. Percentages may not add to 100 because of rounding.

TABLE 16. Work Status of Males Ten to Seventeen Years Old, by Race, in Racially Unmixed Households in Charleston, South Carolina, 1870

	Black Males		White Males	
	% Working	% at Home	% Working	% at Home
Ward 1	8.3	91.6	—	100.0
Ward 2	11.1	88.8	18.5	81.4
Ward 3	13.8	86.1	19.4	80.5
Ward 4	29.0	70.9	22.8	77.1
Ward 5	9.0	90.9	14.2	85.7
Ward 6	17.2	82.7	24.0	76.0
Ward 7	11.3	88.6	7.8	92.1
Ward 8	17.1	82.8	4.8	95.1
Average	14.6	85.3	13.9	86.0

Source: U.S. Bureau of the Census, Ninth Census.

Note: Given the traditional American family's sexual division of labor, the census designation of "at home" to mean unemployed may be more accurate for men than for women. Even so, it is impossible to know the extent to which men "at home" might be informally contributing to the economic and social production of their families.

TABLE 17. Work Status of Females Ten to Seventeen Years Old, by Race, in Racially Unmixed Households in Charleston, South Carolina, 1870

	Black Females		White Females	
	% Working	% at Home	% Working	% at Home
Ward 1	—	100.0	—	100.0
Ward 2	19.4	80.5	11.5	88.4
Ward 3	16.2	83.7	7.6	92.3
Ward 4	40.8	59.1	3.1	96.8
Ward 5	3.0	96.9	13.3	86.6
Ward 6	20.4	79.5	5.0	95.0
Ward 7	6.1	93.8	—	100.0
Ward 8	20.4	79.5	3.6	96.3
Average	15.8	84.1	5.5	94.4

Source: U.S. Bureau of the Census, Ninth Census.

NOTES

INTRODUCTION

1. On the roles played by both black and white political leaders during Reconstruction, see William R. Brock, *An American Crisis: Congress and Reconstruction, 1865–1867* (New York: Harper and Row, 1963); Richard N. Current, *Those Terrible Carpetbaggers* (New York: Oxford University Press, 1988); Edmund L. Drago, *Black Politicians and Reconstruction in Georgia: A Splendid Failure* (Baton Rouge: Louisiana State University Press, 1982); William C. Harris, *The Day of the Carpetbagger: Republican Reconstruction in Mississippi* (Baton Rouge: Louisiana State University Press, 1979); William C. Hine, "Frustration, Factionalism, and Failure: Black Political Leadership and the Republican Party in Reconstruction Charleston, 1865–1877" (Ph.D. diss., Kent State University, 1979); Thomas C. Holt, *Black over White: Negro Political Leadership in South Carolina during Reconstruction* (Urbana: University of Illinois Press, 1977); Peggy Lamson, *The Glorious Failure: Black Congressman Robert Brown Elliot and the Reconstruction in South Carolina* (New York: Norton Books, 1973); Eric L. McKitrick, *Andrew Johnson and Reconstruction, 1865–1867* (Chicago: University of Chicago Press, 1960); Howard N. Rabinowitz, ed., *Southern Black Leaders of the Reconstruction Era* (Urbana: University of Illinois Press, 1982); Okon Edet Uya, *From Slavery to Public Service: Robert Smalls, 1839–1915* (New York: Oxford University Press, 1971); and Charles Vincent, *Black Legislators in Louisiana during Reconstruction* (Baton Rouge: Louisiana State University Press, 1976). On Charleston's free black elite, see Michael P. Johnson and James L. Roark, *Black Masters: A Free Family of Color in the Old South* (New York: W. W. Norton, 1984); Michael P. Johnson and James L. Roark, eds., *No Chariot Let Down: Charleston's Free People of Color on the Eve of the Civil War* (Chapel Hill: University of North Carolina Press, 1984); Larry Koger, *Black Slaveowners: Free Black Slavemasters in South Carolina, 1790–1860* (Jefferson, N.C.: McFarland, 1985); and Bernard E. Powers, *Black Charlestonians: A Social History, 1822–1885* (Fayetteville: University of Arkansas Press, 1994). On the daily lives of the illiterate black masses during emancipation and Reconstruction, see Eric Foner, *Reconstruction: America's Unfinished Revolution, 1863–1877* (New York: Harper and Row, 1988); Leon F. Litwack, *Been in the Storm So Long: The Aftermath of Slavery* (New York: Vintage Books, 1980); and Joel Williamson, *After Slavery: The Negro in South Carolina during Reconstruction, 1861–1877* (Chapel Hill: University of North Carolina Press, 1965).

2. W. Robert Higgins, "Charleston: Terminus and Entrepôt of the Colonial Slave Trade," in Martin L. Kilson and Robert I. Rotberg, eds., *The African Diaspora:*

Interpretive Essays (Cambridge, Mass.: Harvard University Press, 1976), pp. 114–18, 131; G. S. Dickerman, "A Glimpse of Charleston History," *Southern Workman* 2 (November 1962): 15; Don H. Doyle, "Leadership and Decline in Post-War Charleston, 1865–1910," in Walter J. Fraser, Jr. and Winfred B. Moore, Jr., eds., *From the Old South to the New: Essays on the Transitional South* (Westport, Conn.: Greenwood Press, 1981), p. 93.

3. Import trade to Charleston decreased 51.7 percent from 1815 to 1825, and the value of domestic export goods declined from $11.0 million in 1816 to only $7.5 million in 1826. Charleston was losing its retail trade to several upland towns in this era as well as suffering from declining port activity. Donald A. Grinde, Jr., "Building the South Carolina Railroad," *South Carolina Historical Magazine* 77, no. 2 (April 1976): 84; John A. Eisterhold, "Charleston: Lumber and Trade in a Declining Southern Port," *South Carolina Historical Magazine* 74, no. 2 (April 1973): 71; Walter J. Fraser, Jr., *Charleston! Charleston! The History of a Southern City* (Columbia: University of South Carolina Press, 1989), pp. 232, 235; Charles S. Sydnor, *The Development of Southern Sectionalism* (Baton Rouge: Louisiana State University Press, 1948), p. 23.

4. Fraser, *Charleston! Charleston!* pp. 220, 235; Michael P. Johnson, "Planters and Patriarchy: Charleston, 1800–1860," *Journal of Southern History* 46, no. 1 (February 1980): 47–48, 51–53; Ernest M. Lander, Jr., "Charleston: Manufacturing Center of the Old South," *Journal of Southern History* 26, no. 3 (August 1960): 330; Michael P. Johnson, "Wealth and Class in Charleston in 1860," in Fraser and Moore, *From the Old South to the New*, p. 67; Marvin L. Cann, "The End of a Political Myth: The South Carolina Gubernatorial Campaign of 1938," *South Carolina Historical Magazine* 72, no. 3 (July 1971): 139; Hine, "Frustration, Factionalism, and Failure," pp. 5–6.

5. Hine, "Frustration, Factionalism, and Failure," pp. 10–11; Richard C. Wade, *Slavery in the Cities: The South, 1820–1860* (Oxford: Oxford University Press, 1964), pp. 28–54; Koger, *Black Slaveowners*, pp. 160–86; Johnson and Roark, *No Chariot Let Down*, pp. 14–15; Fraser, *Charleston! Charleston!* pp. 200–203, 242–43.

6. Peter Kolchin, *First Freedom: The Responses of Alabama's Blacks to Emancipation and Reconstruction* (Westport, Conn.: Greenwood Press, 1972), p. xviii.

7. For more works that advance this viewpoint, see W. E. B. Du Bois, *Black Reconstruction: An Essay toward a History of the Part Which Black Folk Played in the Attempt to Reconstruct Democracy in America, 1860–1880* (New York: Harcourt Brace, 1935); Claude F. Oubre, *Forty Acres and a Mule: The Freedmen's Bureau and Black Land Ownership* (Baton Rouge: Louisiana State University Press, 1978); Drago, *Black Politicians*; and William R. Brock, "The Waning of Radicalism," and C. Vann Woodward, "The Political Legacy of Reconstruction," in Kenneth M. Stampp and Leon F. Litwack, eds., *Reconstruction: An Anthology of Revisionist Writings* (Baton Rouge: Louisiana State University Press, 1969), pp. 496–515.

I. THE DARK BEFORE THE DAWN

1. Walter B. Hill, "Family, Life, and Work Culture: Black Charleston, South Carolina, 1880–1910" (Ph.D. diss., University of Maryland, College Park, 1989), p. 13. For statistics, see Appendix, table 1.

2. U.S. Bureau of the Census, *A Compendium of the Seventh Census of 1850* (Washington, D.C., 1854), p. 397; U.S. Bureau of the Census, *Eighth Census of the U.S. Population of 1860* (Washington, D.C., 1864); Larry Koger, *Black Slaveowners: Free Black Slavemasters in South Carolina, 1790–1860* (Jefferson, N.C.: McFarland, 1985), p. 31.

3. U.S. Bureau of the Census, *Eighth Census*.

4. Walter Fraser, Jr., *Charleston! Charleston! The History of a Southern City* (Columbia: University of South Carolina Press, 1989), pp. 199–200.

5. U.S. Bureau of the Census, *Eighth Census*.

6. Ibid.

7. For a discussion of the role played by free blacks in Charleston society during the antebellum period, see Horace E. Fitchett, "The Free Negro in Charleston, South Carolina" (Ph.D. diss., University of Chicago, 1950); Ira Berlin, *Slaves without Masters: The Free Negro in the Antebellum South* (New York: Pantheon Books, 1974); Marina Wikramanayake, *A World in Shadow: The Free Black in Antebellum South Carolina* (Columbia: University of South Carolina Press, 1973); Michael P. Johnson and James L. Roark, "'A Middle Ground': Free Mulattoes and the Friendly Moralist Society of Antebellum Charleston," *Southern Studies* 21, no. 3 (Fall 1982): 246–62; and Robert L. Harris, Jr., "Charleston's Free Afro-American Elite: The Brown Fellowship Society and the Humane Brotherhood," *South Carolina Historical Magazine* 82, no. 4 (October 1981): 289–310.

8. Hill, "Family, Life," p. 12.

9. Fraser, *Charleston! Charleston!* p. 186.

10. Hill, "Family, Life," pp. 12–13; Leonard Price Stavisky, "Industrialism in Ante-Bellum Charleston," *Journal of Negro History* 36, no. 3 (July 1951): 309.

11. Kenneth R. Manning, *Black Apollo of Science: The Life of Ernest Just* (New York: Oxford University Press, 1983), p. 7; Edmund L. Drago, *Initiative, Paternalism, and Race Relations: Charleston's Avery Normal Institute* (Athens: University of Georgia Press, 1990), pp. 12–13.

12. U.S. Bureau of the Census, *Seventh Census of the U.S., Population of 1850* (Washington, D.C., 1853); U.S. Bureau of the Census, *Eighth Census*.

13. U.S. Bureau of the Census, *Eighth Census*.

14. Frederick A. Ford, *Census of the City of Charleston, South Carolina, for the Year 1861, Illustrated by Statistical Tables, Prepared under the Authority of the City Council* (Charleston, S.C.: Evans and Cogswell, 1861), pp. 15–20.

15. Koger, *Black Slaveowners*, p. 23.

16. U.S. Bureau of the Census, *Seventh Census*.

17. Koger, *Black Slaveowners*, p. 23.

18. U.S. Bureau of the Census, *Eighth Census*.

19. Barbara J. Fields, *Slavery and Freedom on the Middle Ground: Maryland during the Nineteenth Century* (New Haven: Yale University Press, 1985), pp. 24–26.

20. Richard C. Wade, *Slavery in the Cities: The South, 1820–1860* (New York: Oxford University Press, 1964), pp. 117–18.

21. James Stuart, *Three Years in North America* (Edinburgh: Robert Cadell and Company, 1833) 2:143.

22. Norrece T. Jones, Jr., *Born a Child of Freedom, Yet a Slave: Mechanisms of Control and Strategies of Resistance in Antebellum South Carolina* (London and Hanover, Conn.: Wesleyan University Press, 1990), p. 39.

23. John W. Blassingame, ed., *Slave Testimony: Two Centuries of Letters, Speeches, Interviews, and Autobiographies* (Baton Rouge: Louisiana State University Press, 1977), pp. 698, 699, 618–19.

24. Rev. Philo Tower, *Slavery Unmasked: Being a Truthful Narrative of a Three Years' Residence and Journeying in Eleven Southern States* (Rochester, N.Y.: E. Darrow and Brother, 1856), pp. 113–14.

25. Stuart, *Three Years* 2:144.

26. Ibid., p. 145.

27. Charles Lyell, *Travels in North America in the Years 1841–42* (New York: Wiley and Putnam, 1845) 1:46.

28. Blassingame, *Slave Testimony*, pp. 374–377.

29. Adam Hodgson, *Letters from North America Written during a Tour in the United States and Canada* (London: Hurst, Robinson, and Co., 1824) 1:97.

30. August Meier and Elliott M. Rudwick, *From Plantation to Ghetto: An Interpretative History of American Negroes* (New York: Hill and Wang, 1966), pp. 65–66.

31. Wade, *Slavery in the Cities*, pp. 30, 32–33, 36–38, 45–46, 49–50, and 53. For in-depth discussions of slave and free black life in Southern cities, see Jonathan Beasley, "Blacks—Slave and Free—Vicksburg," *Journal of Mississippi History* 38, no. 1 (February 1976): 9–16; Donnie D. Bellamy, "Macon, Georgia, 1823–1860: A Study in Urban Slavery," *Phylon* 45, no. 4 (December 1984): 303–307; Merton E. Coulter, "Slavery and Freedom in Athens, Georgia, 1860–1866," *Georgia Historical Quarterly* 49 (1965): 264–93; Whittington B. Johnson, "Free Blacks in Antebellum Savannah: An Economic Profile," *Georgia Historical Quarterly* 64, no. 4 (Winter 1980): 418–31; Paul D. Lack, "An Urban Slave Community: Little Rock, 1831–1862," *Arkansas Historical Quarterly* 41, no. 3 (Autumn 1982): 259–71; John T. O'Brien, "Reconstruction in Richmond: White Restoration and Black Protest, April–June 1865," *Virginia Magazine of History and Biography* 89, no. 3 (July 1981): 259–81; Terry I. Seip, "Slaves and Free Negroes in Alexandria, 1850–1860," *Louisiana History* 10, no. 2 (Spring 1969): 147–65; and Richard Tansey, "Out-of-State Free Blacks in Late Antebellum New Orleans," *Louisiana History* 22, no. 4 (Fall 1981): 369–86.

32. J. L. Dawson and H. W. DeSaussure, *Census of the City of Charleston for the Year 1848* (Charleston, S.C.: J. B. Nixon, 1849), pp. 31–36. The 1848 Charleston Census does not give an accurate account of the city's total population or of its occupational structure, and therefore it is an invalid source for conclusions about the employment status of prewar urban blacks. Consequently, I have cited the 1848 Charleston census only to show which occupational groups included slaves or free blacks. For a critique of the inadequacies of the 1848 Charleston census, see Anne W. Chapman, "Inadequacies of the 1848 Charleston Census," *Southern Historical Magazine* 81, no. 1 (January 1980): 24–34.

33. William C. Hine, "Frustration, Factionalism, and Failure: Black Political Leadership and the Republican Party in Reconstruction Charleston, 1865–1877" (Ph.D. diss., Kent State University, 1979), p. 10.

34. Bernard E. Powers, *Black Charlestonians: A Social History, 1822–1885* (Fayetteville: University of Arkansas Press, 1994), p. 10; Claudia Dale Goldin, *Urban Slavery in the American South, 1820–1860* (Chicago: University of Chicago Press, 1976), p. 44.

35. Powers, *Black Charlestonians*, p. 11. Although both slaves and free blacks were sometimes able to find employment in Southern industry, they usually had to toil long hours under hazardous working conditions. Robert S. Starobin, *Industrial Slavery in the Old South* (New York: Oxford University Press, 1970), pp. 36–37.

36. Starobin, *Industrial Slavery*, p. 31; Goldin, *Urban Slavery*, p. 45.

37. Starobin, *Industrial Slavery*, p. 32.

38. Ibid., p. 19.

39. Wade, *Slavery in the Cities*, pp. 29–31.

40. Manning, *Black Apollo of Science*, p. 7.

41. Blassingame, *Slave Testimony*, p. 373.

42. Ibid., p. 699.

43. Ira Berlin, ed., *Freedom: A Documentary History of Emancipation, 1861–1867*, n.s., vol. 1, *The Destruction of Slavery* (Cambridge: Cambridge University Press, 1985), p. 811.

44. George P. Rawick, ed., *The American Slave: Composite Autobiography*, vol. 14, *South Carolina Narratives*, pt. 3 (Westport, Conn.: Greenwood Publishing Company, 1972), p. 233.

45. Loren Schweninger, "Slave Independence and Enterprise in South Carolina, 1780–1865," *South Carolina Historical Magazine* 93, no. 2 (April 1992): 118.

46. Joel Williamson finds the heavy rate of defection among servants of the domestic class in the Reconstruction period astonishing, but he does not explore the possible factors that led to it. Joel Williamson, *After Slavery: The Negro in South Carolina during Reconstruction, 1861–1877* (Chapel Hill: University of North Carolina Pres, 1965), pp. 34–39.

47. Norman R. Yetman, ed., *Life under the Peculiar Institution: Selections from the Slave Narrative Collection* (New York: Holt, Rinehart and Winston, 1970), p. 148.

48. J. Benwell, *An Englishman's Travels in America: His Observations of Life and Manners in the Free and Slave States* (London: Binns and Goodwin, 1853), p. 201.

49. Fredrika Bremer, *The Homes of the New World: Impressions of America* (New York: Harper and Brothers, 1854) 1:265–266.

50. Stuart, *Three Years* 2:135, 142–143.

51. William Loren Katz, *American Slavery As It Is: Testimony of a Thousand Witnesses* (New York: American Anti-Slavery Society, 1839), pp. 23, 53, 54.

52. Captain Basil Hall, *Travels in North America in the Years 1827 and 1828* (Edinburgh: Cadell and Company, 1829) 3:167; Bremer, *Homes of the New World* 1:395; Adolph B. Benson, ed., *America of the Fifties: Letters of Fredrika Bremer* (New York: The American-Scandinavian Foundation, 1924), p. 151.

53. George C. Rogers, Jr., *Charleston in the Age of the Pinckneys* (Norman: University of Oklahoma Press, 1969), pp. 146–47; James Redpath, *The Roving Editor; or, Talks with Slaves in Southern States* (New York: A. B. Burdick, 1859), pp. 53–54.

54. Sir William Howard Russell, *My Diary: North and South* (Boston: T.O.H.P. Burnham, 1863), p. 110.

55. Stuart, *Three Years* 2:132–33. Although some slaves did uphold the curfew, others did not. Between September 1836 and September 1837, 573 were convicted of this offense or of being at large in some illegal place. The slaves' disregard for the curfew was an even greater problem in Charleston Neck, which

before 1850 was an infrequently patrolled unincorporated area just north of Boundary Street. According to the mayor, slaves violating the curfew were sometimes fined only one dollar, and where corporal punishment was meted out at all, it was usually moderate. Powers, *Black Charlestonians,* pp. 22–23.

56. For descriptions of the workhouse in Charleston, see Stuart, *Three Years* 2:143–44; Redpath, *The Roving Editor,* pp. 53–54; Rogers, *Charleston,* pp. 148–49. It was the knowledge of what went on in the workhouse that drove Sarah and Angelina Grimké into the arms of the abolitionists. Rogers, *Charleston,* p. 149.

57. Katz, *American Slavery,* pp. 53–54.

58. Bremer, *Homes of the New World* 1:278.

59. Rev. G. Lewis, *Impressions of America and the American Churches* (New York: Negro Universities Press, 1968), pp. 112–13.

60. Bremer, *Homes of the New World* 1:278, 295.

61. For an excellent piece of scholarship on runaway slaves in Charleston and in other parts of South Carolina, see Michael P. Johnson, "Runaway Slaves and the Slave Communities in South Carolina, 1799 to 1830," *William and Mary Quarterly* 38, no. 3 (July 1981): 418–41. Many blacks may have taken these actions because they seemed logical under the circumstances. Slaves had few alternatives because they could not fully use the legal system to counter white injustices. For two provocative works on the plight of blacks in the legal system in the antebellum South, see Daniel Flanigan, "Criminal Procedure in Slave Trials in the Ante-Bellum South," *Journal of Southern History* 40, no. 4 (November 1974): 537–64; Michael S. Hindus, "Black Justice under White Law: Criminal Prosecutions of Blacks in Ante-Bellum South Carolina," *Journal of American History* 63, no. 3 (December 1976): 575–99.

62. *Charleston Courier,* September 30, 1828.

63. *Charleston Courier,* March 15, 1831; March 20, 1833.

64. *Charleston Courier,* March 20, 1833.

65. Sir Charles Lyell, *A Second Visit to the United States of North America* (London: John Murray, 1849) 1:204.

66. Benwell, *An Englishman's Travels,* pp. 206–207.

67. Rosser H. Taylor, *Ante-Bellum South Carolina: A Social and Cultural History* (Chapel Hill: University of North Carolina Press, 1942), pp. 178–79; Powers, *Black Charlestonians,* pp. 29–32. Vesey's hopes depended on Charleston's carelessness. This point is explored in William W. Freehling, *Prelude to Civil War: The Nullification Controversy in South Carolina, 1816–1836* (New York: Harper and Row, 1965), pp. 56–57. For thorough accounts of the Vesey conspiracy, see James Hamilton, Jr., *An Account of the Late Intended Insurrection among a Portion of the Blacks of This City Published by Authority of the Corporation of Charleston* (Charleston, S.C.: A. E. Miller, 1822), pp. 1–49; and Achates, *Reflections Occasioned by the Late Disturbances in Charleston* (Charleston, S.C.: A. E. Miller, 1822), pp. 5–29. A series of letters that chronicles the firsthand view of a prominent white Charlestonian on the Vesey conspiracy can be found in the Haywood Papers, the Southern Historical Collection (hereafter, SHC), University of North Carolina, Chapel Hill. For an article that attempts to argue that the Vesey conspiracy never existed but was instead only rumor translated into a belief of a widespread conspiracy, see Richard C. Wade, "The Vesey Plot: A Reconsideration," *Journal of Southern History* 30, no. 2 (May 1964): 143–61.

68. Steven A. Channing, *Crisis of Fear: Secession in South Carolina* (New York: Simon and Schuster, 1970), pp. 45–46. The South Carolina Association was formed in 1823 as a result of the Vesey conspiracy to keep the black population in check. This Charleston-based society counted among its members many of the most prominent men in the state. It possessed an elaborate organization, and it published rules and eventually a legislative charter. For a time, it boasted auxiliaries throughout the low country. Alan F. January, "The South Carolina Association: An Agency for Race Control in Antebellum Charleston," *South Carolina Historical Magazine* 78, no. 3 (July 1977): 191.

69. John A. Scott, ed., *Journal of a Residence on a Georgian Plantation in 1838– 1839,* by Francis Anne Kemble (New York: Alfred A. Knopf, 1961), p. 39.

70. James Johnston Pettigrew to ———, April 16, 1849, Pettigrew Family Papers, SHC, University of North Carolina, Chapel Hill, quoted in Channing, *Crisis of Fear,* pp. 45–46.

71. Tower, *Slavery Unmasked,* pp. 111–13.

72. Stuart, *Three Years* 2:141–42.

73. Hodgson, *Letters from North America* 1:98–99.

74. Yetman, *Life under the Peculiar Institution,* p. 149.

75. Jones, *Born a Child of Freedom,* pp. 18–19.

76. Drago, *Initiative,* p. 31.

77. Michael P. Johnson and James L. Roark, eds., *No Chariot Let Down: Charleston's Free People of Color on the Eve of the Civil War* (Chapel Hill: University of North Carolina Press), pp. 6–7.

78. Meier and Rudwick, *From Plantation to Ghetto,* pp. 67–68.

79. Ibid. For an examination of the plight of free blacks in the South Carolina court system, see Donald J. Senese, "The Free Negro and the South Carolina Courts, 1790–1860," *South Carolina Historical Magazine* 68, no. 3 (July 1967): 140–53.

80. Meier and Rudwick, *From Plantation to Ghetto,* p. 68. Phillis Cox was a black woman born free in Pennsylvania, who through a tragic series of events was sold and held as a slave in Charleston. As a youth in Charleston, Daniel Payne's father met the same fate and remained a slave there until he reached adulthood and purchased his freedom for one thousand dollars. Free blacks could be legally sold into slavery for nonpayment of the capitation tax or the taxes that whites were also subject to. Powers, *Black Charlestonians,* pp. 55–56.

81. Goldin, *Urban Slavery,* p. 34; Wikramanayake, *A World in Shadow,* p. 74.

82. Wikramanayake, *A World in Shadow,* p. 74.

83. Johnson and Roark, *No Chariot Let Down,* pp. 6–7. More than three-quarters of Charleston's free blacks were propertyless; only about one out of six heads of household owned a slave or real estate worth two thousand dollars or more. Ibid., p. 6.

84. Johnson and Roark, *No Chariot Let Down,* p. 6.

85. Wikramanayake, *A World in Shadow,* pp. 78–79.

86. Wikramanayake, *A World in Shadow,* p. 89; Hine, "Frustration, Factionalism, and Failure," p. 16; Johnson and Roark, *No Chariot Let Down,* p. 6.

87. Johnson and Roark, *No Chariot Let Down,* p. 10.

88. Ibid., pp. 12–13. Free blacks were also under attack outside Charleston. Away from the city, free blacks were widely scattered and less capable of sustain-

ing a community for self-defense. Upcountry planters typically looked upon free blacks as ill-disciplined rogues, likely to steal corn and livestock and to set a bad example for slaves by their free, idle, dissolute existence. Upcountry whites believed that free blacks subverted the racial subordination that was the essence of slavery, and their representatives argued in the state legislature that nothing would be lost and much gained if freedom were prohibited to all blacks. Ibid., pp. 13–14. Richard Tansey argues that when white patrons in New Orleans abandoned their support of free blacks in the 1850s, free blacks did not suffer a decline in their economic and social status during this period because certain economic forces took the place of white patronage in shielding free blacks from their adversaries. Tansey, "Out-of-State Free Blacks," pp. 369–86.

89. Johnson and Roark, *No Chariot Let Down*, p. 14; Powers, *Black Charlestonians*, p. 65. In January 1861, several steamers arrived in New York from Charleston carrying free blacks who apparently had decided that "safety was to be found only in getting out of the reach of the slave power." It was estimated that no fewer than two thousand had left the state of South Carolina since economic and legal restrictions were placed on free blacks during the war. In addition to the restrictions and the prospects of war, rumors arose that the property of the free blacks would be seized by the Confederacy and that free blacks would be sold into slavery. Charles H. Wesley, *Negro Labor in the United States, 1850–1925: A Study in American Economic History* (New York: Vanguard Press, 1927), pp. 97–98.

90. Johnson and Roark, *No Chariot Let Down*, pp. 14–15. The sixteen wealthiest free blacks in Charleston in 1859 had a combined total of sixty-nine slaves and $244,595 in real estate. *List of Taxpayers for Charleston* (Charleston, S.C.: Evans and Cogswell, 1861), reprinted in Hine, "Frustration, Factionalism, and Failure," p. 15.

91. Memorial of Free Blacks to J. H. Boatright, Mayor, City of Charleston, January 10, 1861. Papers of Francis Wilkinson Pinckens and Milledge Luke Bonham, 1837–1920, Library of Congress, Washington, D.C. Within a matter of days, two other nearly identical petitions had been submitted to the mayor of Charleston and then forwarded to the state legislature, where no action was taken. Hine, "Frustration, Factionalism, and Failure," p. 17.

92. Powers, *Black Charlestonians*, p. 66.

93. *Charleston Mercury,* September 5, 1861.

94. Powers, *Black Charlestonians*, p. 67.

95. Benjamin Quarles, *The Negro in the Civil War* (New York: Russell and Russell, 1968), p. 264. The free black elite in Louisiana also supported the Confederate cause. As a group, free blacks in New Orleans were even more deeply entrenched in the economic order than those in Charleston. As in Charleston, many held themselves aloof from the masses of free blacks and slaves. E. Franklin Frazier, *The Free Negro Family: A Study of Family Origins before the Civil War* (Nashville: Fisk University Press, 1932), p. 33. It also appears that some free blacks in cities such as Charleston and New Orleans might have gone into military service for the Confederacy because they saw this as the best way to ensure their security, for many white Southerners viewed them with suspicion, thinking they supported the Union cause. White intimidation might also have played a role. Powers, *Black Charlestonians*, pp. 62–66; Peter Ripley, *Slaves and Freedmen in Civil War Louisiana* (Baton Rouge: Louisiana State University Press, 1976), p. 103; and Manoj K.

Joshi and Joseph P. Reidy, "To Come Forward and Aid in Putting Down This Unholy Rebellion: The Officers of Louisiana's Free Black Native Guard during the Civil War Era," *Southern Studies* 21, no. 3 (fall 1982): 327–28. Free black troops in Charleston and New Orleans never fought for the Confederacy. Instead they were usually employed as military laborers. Powers, *Black Charlestonians*, p. 66; Joshi and Reidy, "To Come Forward," p. 328.

96. Fraser, *Charleston! Charleston!* p. 255.

97. Redpath, *The Roving Editor*, p. 52.

98. Fraser, *Charleston! Charleston!* p. 252; Stephen Colwell, *The Freedmen of South Carolina: An Address Delivered by J. Miller M'Kim in Sansom Hall, July 9, 1862* (Philadelphia: Willis P. Hazard, Bookseller, Publisher and Importer, 1862), p. 1.

99. Fraser, *Charleston! Charleston!* p. 252.

100. Ibid.

101. Ibid., pp. 252–53; Colwell, *Freedmen*, pp. 1–2.

102. Fraser, *Charleston! Charleston!* p. 252.

103. Blassingame, *Slave Testimony*, pp. 359–60.

104. John F. Marszalek, ed., *The Diary of Miss Emma Holmes* (Baton Rouge: Louisiana State University Press, 1979), p. 393; J. E. Hilary Skinner, *After the Storm; or, Jonathan and His Neighbours in 1865–1866* (London: Richard Bentley, 1866) 2:336.

105. Marszalek, *Diary of Miss Emma Holmes*, p. 393.

106. Blassingame, *Slave Testimony*, pp. 699–700.

107. Ibid., p. 618.

108. Marszalek, *Diary of Miss Emma Holmes*, p. 139; Quarles, *The Negro in the Civil War*, p. 70.

109. Okon Edet Uya, *From Slavery to Public Service: Robert Smalls, 1839–1915* (New York: Oxford University Press, 1971), pp. 11–20; James M. McPherson, *The Negro's Civil War: How American Negroes Felt and Acted during the War for the Union* (New York: Pantheon Books, 1965), pp. 154–57; Quarles, *The Negro in the Civil War*, pp. 71–74; Elizabeth Ware Pearson, ed., *Letters from Port Royal, 1862–1868* (New York: Arno Press and the New York Times, 1969), pp. 45–46; Powers, *Black Charlestonians*, p. 67.

110. Fraser, *Charleston! Charleston!* pp. 258–59.

111. Ibid., p. 259.

112. William L. Barney, *Battleground for the Union: The Era of the Civil War and Reconstruction, 1848–1977* (Englewood Cliffs, N.J.: Prentice Hall, 1990), p. 184.

113. Allen C. Guelzo, *The Crisis of the American Republic: A History of the Civil War and Reconstruction Era* (New York: St. Martin's Press, 1995), pp. 137, 298; Barney, *Battleground*, p. 186.

114. Blassingame, *Slave Testimony*, p. 618.

115. Blassingame, *Slave Testimony*, pp. 377–78.

116. Fraser, *Charleston! Charleston!* p. 259.

117. Marszalek, *Diary of Miss Emma Holmes*, p. 284.

118. Fraser, *Charleston! Charleston!* p. 259.

119. Berlin, *Freedom*, pp. 809–10.

120. Ibid., pp. 811–12.

121. Quarles, *The Negro in the Civil War*, p. 270.

122. Blassingame, *Slave Testimony*, p. 360.

123. Richard Wheeler, ed., *Voices of the Civil War* (New York: Thomas Y. Crowell Company, 1976), p. 12; C. Vann Woodward, ed., *Mary Chesnut's Civil War* (New Haven and London: Yale University Press, 1981), p. 48; Quarles, *The Negro in the Civil War,* p. 52.

124. Berlin, *Freedom,* p. 812.

125. Fraser, *Charleston! Charleston!* p. 265.

126. Ibid.

127. Howard C. Westwood, "Captive Black Union Soldiers in Charleston—What to Do?" *Civil War History* 28, no. 1 (March 1982): 28; Fraser, *Charleston! Charleston!* p. 263.

128. Fraser, *Charleston! Charleston!* pp. 263–64.

129. Marszalek, *Diary of Miss Emma Holmes,* pp. 281–82.

130. Westwood, "Captive Black Union Soldiers," pp. 39, 40, 41, 43, 44.

131. Blassingame, *Slave Testimony,* pp. 371–72.

132. United States Colored Troops, 137th Infantry Regiment, Co. "A," Record Group 94; U.S. Colored Troops, 136th Infantry Regiment, Regimental Box, Record Group 94.

2. THANK GOD WE ARE A FREE PEOPLE

1. Walter J. Fraser, Jr., *Charleston! Charleston! The History of a Southern City* (Columbia: University of South Carolina Press, 1989), pp. 268–69.

2. Ibid., p. 268; Charles Fox, *Record of the Service of the Fifty-fifth Regiment of Massachusetts Volunteer Infantry* (Cambridge, Mass.: Press of John Wilson and Son, July 1868), p. 57.

3. Benjamin Quarles, *The Negro in the Civil War* (New York: Russell and Russell, 1968), pp. 325–26; Lieutenant Colonel A. G. Bennett to Captain J. W. Dickinson, February 24, 1865, Department of the South Papers, National Archives, Washington, D.C. (hereafter, DSP).

4. For a history of these black troops and others, see Luis F. Emilio, *A Brave Black Regiment: History of the Fifty-fourth Regiment of Massachusetts Volunteer Infantry, 1863–1865* (New York: Arno Press and the New York Times, 1969); Joseph T. Wilson, *The Black Phalanx: A History of the Negro Soldiers of the United States in the Wars of 1775–1812, 1861–1865* (New York: Arno Press and the New York Times, 1968); Dudley Taylor Cornish, *The Sable Arm: Negro Troops in the Union Army, 1861–1865* (New York: Longman's Green, 1956); James M. McPherson, *The Negro's Civil War: How American Negroes Felt and Acted during the War for the Union* (New York: Pantheon Books, 1965); and Fox, *Record of the Service of the Fifty-fifth.*

5. Quarles, *The Negro in the Civil War,* p. 326.

6. E. Milby Burton, *The Siege of Charleston, 1861–1865* (Columbia: University of South Carolina Press, 1970), p. 322.

7. Viola Caston Floyd, "The Fall of Charleston," *South Carolina Historical Magazine* 66, no. 1 (January 1965): 2.

8. Quarles, *The Negro in the Civil War,* p. 327. The reactions of the newly freed slaves to the entry of the Union forces into Richmond and Petersburg were similar to that of the former slaves in Charleston. For a discussion of some of these responses, see John T. O'Brien, "Reconstruction in Richmond: White Restoration and Black Protest, April–June 1865," *Virginia Magazine of History and*

Biography 89, no. 3 (July 1981): 259–81; and Chaplain James. M. Guthrie, *Camp-fires of the Afro-American; or, The Colored Man as a Patriot* (Philadelphia: Afro-American Publishing Company, 1899), pp. 624–25.

9. Frank [Francis] A. Rollin, *Life and Public Services of Martin R. Delany, Sub-Assistant Commissioner Bureau Relief of Refugees, Freedmen, and of Abandoned Lands, and Late Major 104th U.S. Colored Troops* (Boston: Lee and Shepard, 1868), pp. 198–99. Fox, *Record of the Service of the Fifty-fifth*, p. 56.

10. *New York Tribune*, March 2, 1865; Leon F. Litwack, *Been in the Storm So Long: The Aftermath of Slavery* (New York: Vintage Books, 1980), pp. 121–22; Quarles, *The Negro in the Civil War*, pp. 327–28.

11. Fox, *Record of the Service of the Fifty-fifth*, p. 56. Most blacks were happy to see both the black and the white Union soldiers, but relations were not always good between the former slaves and white troops. For an in-depth discussion of the relations between the former slaves and the white Union forces, see George P. Rawick, ed., *The American Slave: A Composite Autobiography*, 19 vols. (Westport, Conn.: Greenwood Press, 1972).

12. Emilio, *A Brave Black Regiment*, p. 284.

13. Worthington Chauncey Ford, ed., *War Letters, 1862–1865, of John Chipman Gray and John Codman Ropes* (Cambridge, Mass.: The Riverside Press, 1927), pp. 459–60.

14. [Gabriel] Manigault Diary, 1865–1868, Gabriel Manigault Papers, Southern Historical Collection, University of North Carolina, Chapel Hill (hereafter, SHC).

15. Quarles, *The Negro in the Civil War*, p. 328.

16. Ibid.; Rollin, *Life and Public Services*, p. 189.

17. Rollin, *Life and Public Services*, p. 189.

18. Ibid., p. 192.

19. Joel Williamson, *After Slavery: The Negro in South Carolina during Reconstruction, 1861–1877* (Chapel Hill: University of North Carolina Press, 1965), p. 47.

20. *Charleston Courier*, April 3, 1865; *New York Times*, April 11, 1865; William C. Hine, "Frustration, Factionalism, and Failure: Black Political Leadership and the Republican Party in Reconstruction Charleston, 1865–1877" (Ph.D. diss., Kent State University, 1979), p. 33.

21. *New York Tribune*, April 4, 1865; *New York Times*, March 30, April 4, 1865; Litwack, *Been in the Storm So Long*, pp. 177–78; Williamson, *After Slavery*, pp. 47–48. Black communities in other cities also staged post-emancipation parades. For accounts of these, see Williamson, *After Slavery*, p. 49; *New York Times*, January 3, 1864 (regarding Norfolk); January 23, August 1, 1864 (regarding Savannah); July 12, 1865 (regarding Louisville); July 14, 1865 (regarding Raleigh); and *New York Tribune*, January 13, 1865 (regarding Key West); July 8, 1865 (regarding Mobile); July 12, 1865 (regarding Raleigh and Columbia).

22. Litwack, *Been in the Storm So Long*, p. 178.

23. *Charleston Courier*, May 2, 1865.

24. Charles F. Horner, *The Life of James Redpath and the Development of the Modern Lyceum* (New York and Newark, N.J.: Barse and Hopkins Publishers, 1926), pp. 113–15.

25. Ira Berlin, *Slaves without Masters: The Free Negro in the Antebellum South* (New York: Pantheon Books, 1974), p. 391.

26. Hine, "Frustration, Factionalism, and Failure," p. 39.

27. Berlin, *Slaves without Masters*, p. 391.

28. Williamson, *After Slavery*, p. 49.

29. Elizabeth Hyde Botume, *First Days amongst the Contrabands* (Boston: Lee and Shepard, 1893), p. 172.

30. Rollin, *Life and Public Services*, p. 193. For excellent discussions of the ceremonial raising of the Union flag over Fort Sumter, see Quarles, *The Negro in the Civil War*, pp. 336–39; and Okon Edet Uya, *From Slavery to Public Service: Robert Smalls, 1839–1915* (New York: Oxford University Press, 1971), pp. 27–29.

31. Litwack, *Been in the Storm So Long*, p. 178.

32. Rollin, *Life and Public Services*, pp. 194–95.

33. Williamson, *After Slavery*, p. 47.

34. Rollin, *Life and Public Services*, p. 195.

35. The fact that many former slaves idolized Abraham Lincoln and really felt that God had sent him to deliver them from bondage is made clear in Rawick, *The American Slave*.

36. Quarles, *The Negro in the Civil War*, p. 339.

37. Fox, *Record of the Service of the Fifty-fifth*, pp. 74–75.

38. Rollin, *Life and Public Services*, p. 205; Quarles, *The Negro in the Civil War*, p. 345; Henry L. Swint, ed., *Dear Ones at Home: Letters from Contraband Camps* (Nashville: Vanderbilt University Press, 1966), p. 189. The great love many blacks had for Abraham Lincoln eventually found expression in the beautiful Emancipation Monument erected with their offerings in Washington, D.C. Guthrie, *Campfires of the Afro-American*, p. 626. For descriptions of black reactions to the death of Abraham Lincoln in Beaufort, S.C., Michelville, S.C., Savannah, Ga., and the Sea Islands of South Carolina, see Quarles, *The Negro in the Civil War*, pp. 344–45; Swint, *Dear Ones at Home*, p. 189; and Rupert Sargent Holland, ed., *Letters and Diary of Laura M. Towne: Written from the Sea Islands of South Carolina, 1862–1884* (Cambridge, Mass.: The Riverside Press, 1912), p. 162.

39. Fox, *Record of the Service of the Fifty-fifth*, pp. 74–75.

40. Rollin, *Life and Public Services*, pp. 204–205.

41. Ibid., p. 222; Victor Ullman, *Martin R. Delany: The Beginnings of Black Nationalism* (Boston: Beacon Press, 1971), p. 311; *Charleston Courier*, March 1, 10, 1865.

42. Litwack, *Been in the Storm So Long*, p. 430; Botume, *First Days*, pp. 204–205. For an account of an Emancipation Parade on January 1, 1866, in Richmond, see Laura S. Haviland, *A Woman's Life-Work: Labors and Experiences* (Cincinnati: Walden and Stowe, 1881), pp. 401–402.

43. N. R. Middleton to his daughter, July 6, 1866, N. R. Middleton Papers, SHC.

44. Williamson, *After Slavery*, pp. 46–47. For some discussion of black assertiveness in Richmond during the early months of the war, see O'Brien, "Reconstruction in Richmond," p. 263; for the same in New Orleans, see John W. Blassingame, *Black New Orleans, 1860–1880* (Chicago: University of Chicago Press, 1973), pp. 26–27.

45. Eric Foner, "The Meaning of Freedom," *Radical History Review* 39 (Fall 1987): 94.

46. Mary Abigail Dodge, *Wool-Gathering* (Boston: Estes and Lauriat, 1877), p. 221.

47. Daniel E. Huger Smith, Alice R. Huger Smith, and Arney R. Childs, eds., *Mason Smith Family Letters, 1860–1868* (Columbia: University of South Carolina Press, 1950), pp. 179, 236.

48. William Heyward to James Gregorie, June 4, 1868, Gregorie-Elliot Papers, SHC.

49. Ellison Capers to his wife, September 10, 1865, Ellison Capers Papers, Duke University, Durham, N.C. (hereafter, DU).

50. Holland, *Letters and Diary of Laura M. Towne,* pp. 160–61.

51. Henry W. Ravenel to Augustin Louis Taveau, June 27, 1865, A. L. Taveau Papers, DU.

52. Litwack, *Been in the Storm So Long,* p. 259.

53. Williamson, *After Slavery,* p. 50.

54. A. T. Smythe to his wife, August 19, 1865, A. T. Smythe Letters, South Carolina Historical Society, Charleston (hereafter, SCHS).

55. Ellison Capers to his wife, September 10, 1865, Ellison Capers Papers, DU.

56. N. R. Middleton to his daughter, January 10, 1866, N. R. Middleton Papers, SHC.

57. Carl Schurz, *Report on the Condition of the South* (reprint, New York: Arno Press and the New York Times, 1969), p. 27.

58. Litwack, *Been in the Storm So Long,* pp. 336–51.

59. Bernard E. Powers, *Black Charlestonians: A Social History, 1822–1885* (Fayetteville: University of Arkansas Press, 1994), p. 104.

60. Litwack, *Been in the Storm So Long,* p. 347.

61. Jacob Schirmer Diary Index, January 11, 1873, SCHS.

62. Williamson, *After Slavery,* p. 37.

63. John F. Marszalek, ed., *The Diary of Miss Emma Holmes* (Baton Rouge: Louisiana State University Press, 1979), p. 455.

64. Smith, Smith, and Childs, *Mason Smith Family Letters,* p. 192.

65. Litwack, *Been in the Storm So Long,* p. 219.

66. Rev. A. Toomer Porter, *The History of a Work of Faith and Love in Charleston, South Carolina* (New York: D. Appleton and Company, 1882), pp. 58–59.

67. Anonymous letter, September 2, 1866, Wilmot S. Holmes Collection, SHC.

68. Williamson, *After Slavery,* p. 37.

69. Ibid., p. 34. For a provocative piece of scholarship that identifies some of the reasons for the heavy defections among the domestic class, see Daniel E. Sutherland, "A Special Kind of Problem: The Response of Household Slaves and Their Masters to Freedom," *Southern Studies* 20, no. 2 (Summer 1981): 151–66.

70. Powers, *Black Charlestonians,* p. 103.

71. Schirmer Diary, October 1866, SCHS.

72. Manigault Diary, 1865–1868, Gabriel Manigault Papers, SHC.

73. Powers, *Black Charlestonians,* pp. 103–104.

74. Ibid., p. 103.

75. Smith, Smith, and Childs, *Mason Smith Family Letters,* p. 173.

76. Powers, *Black Charlestonians,* p. 104.

77. Ibid.

78. Schirmer Diary, October 1866, SCHS.

79. Manigault Diary, 1865–1868, Gabriel Manigault Papers, SHC.

80. Williamson, *After Slavery*, p. 36.

81. Sidney Andrews, *The South since the War as Shown by Fourteen Weeks of Travel and Observation in Georgia and the Carolinas* (Boston: Ticknor and Fields, 1866), p. 23.

3. WE ONLY ASK FOR A CHANCE

1. John T. Trowbridge, *A Picture of the Desolated States and the Work of Restoration, 1865–1868* (Hartford, Conn.: L. Stebbins, 1868), p. 513; Sidney Andrews, *The South since the War As Shown by Fourteen Weeks of Travel and Observation in Georgia and the Carolinas* (Boston: Ticknor and Fields, 1866), p. 2; Robert Somers, *The Southern States since the War, 1870–71* (reprint, Tuscaloosa: University of Alabama Press, 1965), pp. 37–38.

2. Frederic Bancroft and William A. Dunning, eds., *The Reminiscences of Carl Schurz* (New York: McClare Co., 1908), 3:164–65; Worthington Chauncey Ford, ed., *War Letters, 1862–1865, of John Chipman Gray and John Codman Ropes* (Cambridge, Mass.: The Riverside Press, 1927), pp. 459–60; Alicia Hopton Middleton, ed., *Life in Carolina and New England during the Nineteenth Century: As Illustrated by Reminiscences and Letters of the Middleton Family of Charleston, South Carolina, and of the De Wolf Family of Bristol, Rhode Island* (Bristol, R.I.: Privately printed, 1929), pp. 158–59; Viola Caston Floyd, "The Fall of Charleston," *South Carolina Historical Magazine* 66, no. 1 (January 1965): 2; Luis F. Emilio, *A Brave Black Regiment: History of the Fifty-fourth Regiment of Massachusetts Volunteer Infantry, 1863–1865* (New York: Arno Press and the New York Times, 1969), p. 284; Arney Robinson Childs, ed., *The Private Journal of Henry William Ravenel, 1859–1887* (Columbia: University of South Carolina Press, 1947), p. 205; John H. Kennaway, *On Sherman's Track; or, The South after the War* (London: Seeley, Jackson, and Halliday, 1867), pp. 178–79; Somers, *Southern States*, pp. 37–38; Andrews, *The South since the War*, p. 2; Trowbridge, *Picture of the Desolated States*, pp. 513–14.

3. E. Milby Burton, *The Siege of Charleston, 1861–1865* (Columbia: University of South Carolina Press, 1970), p. 324.

4. D. E. Huger Smith, *A Charlestonian's Recollections, 1846–1913* (Charleston, S.C.: Carolina Art Association, 1950), pp. 115–116; Emilio, *A Brave Black Regiment*, p. 285; William Heyward to Gregorie Elliot, April 2, 1867, Gregorie-Elliot Papers; William B. Elliot to Hal Elliot, February 2, 1868, Elliot-Gonzales Papers, Southern Historical Collection, University of North Carolina, Chapel Hill (hereafter, SHC).

5. Smith, *A Charlestonian's Recollections*, pp. 115–16.

6. David D. Wallace, *South Carolina: A Short History, 1520–1948* (Columbia: University of South Carolina Press, 1961), p. 556.

7. Whitelaw Reid, *After the War: A Southern Tour, May 1, 1865, to May 1, 1866* (Cincinnati: Moore, Wilstach, and Baldwin, 1866), p. 67; Francis B. Simkins and Robert H. Woody, *South Carolina during Reconstruction* (Chapel Hill: University of North Carolina Press, 1932), pp. 18–19; Colonel, 103rd U.S.C.T., to Rev. James P., March 6, 1865; Colonel William Gurney to George D. Cragin, April 3, 1865, Part 1, Box 1, Department of the South Papers, National Archives, Washington, D.C. (hereafter, DSP); J. P. O'Neale to Mr. R. N. Gourdin, June 3, 1865, Robert

Newman Gourdin Papers, Duke University Library, Durham, North Carolina (hereafter, DU).

8. Wallace, *South Carolina,* p. 556. As late as April 1867, it was estimated that 100,000 people in South Carolina had not tasted meat in the last thirty days. *New York Times,* April 19, 1867.

9. F. Barham Zincke, *Last Winter in the United States* (London, 1868), p. 97; Simkins and Woody, *South Carolina during Reconstruction,* p. 18.

10. Robert Goodwyn Rhett, *Charleston: An Epic of Carolina* (Richmond: Garrett and Massie, 1940), pp. 308–309; Martin Abbott, *The Freedmen's Bureau in South Carolina, 1865–1872* (Chapel Hill: University of North Carolina Press, 1967), pp. 35–43; William Heyward to Gregorie Elliott, April 2, 1867, Gregorie-Elliott Papers, SHC.

11. The migration of rural blacks into urban areas was a phenomenon throughout the South. For further discussion, see Jonathan Woolard McLeod, "Black and White Workers: Atlanta during Reconstruction" (Ph.D. diss., University of California at Los Angeles, 1987), pp. 13–18; John T. O'Brien, "From Bondage to Citizenship: The Richmond Black Community, 1865–1867" (Ph.D. diss., University of Rochester, 1974), pp. 84–90; Peter J. Rachleff, *Black Labor in the South: Richmond, Virginia, 1865–1890* (Philadelphia: Temple University Press, 1984), pp. 14–15; John W. Blassingame, "Before the Ghetto: The Making of the Black Community in Savannah, Georgia, 1865–1880," *Journal of Social History* 6, no. 4 (Summer 1973): 463–65; and Yollette Trigg Jones, "The Black Community, Politics and Race Relations in the 'Iris City' Nashville, Tennessee, 1870–1954" (Ph.D. diss., Duke University, 1985), pp. 41–42.

12. Leon F. Litwack, *Been in the Storm So Long: The Aftermath of Slavery* (New York: Vintage Books, 1980), p. 312; Bernard E. Powers, *Black Charlestonians: A Social History, 1822–1885* (Fayetteville: University of Arkansas Press, 1994), pp. 100–103; Eric Foner, "The Meaning of Freedom," *Radical History Review* 39 (Fall 1987): 95–96; Edmund L. Drago, *Black Politicians and Reconstruction in Georgia* (Baton Rouge: Louisiana State University Press, 1982), pp. 106–108; Lester C. Lamon, *Blacks in Tennessee, 1791–1970* (Knoxville: University of Tennessee Press, 1981), pp. 29–30; O'Brien, "From Bondage to Citizenship," pp. 84–90, 93–94.

13. Andrews, *The South since the War,* pp. 97–99.

14. John T. Trowbridge, *The South: A Tour of Its Battle-Fields and Ruined Cities, a Journey through the Desolated States, and Talks with the People* (Hartford, Conn.: L. Stebbins, 1866), p. 537.

15. Henry M. Christman, ed., *The South As It Is, 1865–1866* (New York: Viking Press, 1965), p. 223.

16. Emilio, *A Brave Black Regiment,* p. 285.

17. John Marszalek, ed., *The Diary of Miss Emma Holmes* (Baton Rouge: Louisiana State University Press, 1979), pp. 453–54.

18. Childs, ed., *Journal of Henry W. Ravenel,* pp. 254–55.

19. Ibid., p. 244.

20. Andrews, *The South since the War,* pp. 24–25.

21. Elias Horry Deas to ———, August 12, 1865, Elias Horry Deas Papers, South Carolinian Library, University of South Carolina, Columbia (hereafter, SCL).

22. Elias Horry Deas to Anne Deas, July 12 and August 12, 1865, Deas Papers, SCL.

23. Litwack, *Been in the Storm So Long,* p. 314.

24. U.S. Bureau of the Census, *The Statistics of the Population of the United States in 1870* (Washington, D.C., 1873), p. 258.

25. Ibid.

26. Alrutheus Ambush Taylor, *The Negro in South Carolina during the Reconstruction* (New York: Russell and Russell, 1969), pp. 12–13.

27. Roger L. Ransom and Richard Sutch, *One Kind of Freedom: The Economic Consequences of Emancipation* (Cambridge: Cambridge University Press, 1977), pp. 40–55.

28. Taylor, *The Negro in South Carolina,* pp. 12–13.

29. Powers, *Black Charlestonians,* p. 102.

30. Taylor, *The Negro in South Carolina,* p. 13; Jane Van Allen to Mr. Whipple, November 28, 1866, American Missionary Association Papers, Duke University Library, Durham, N.C. (hereafter, AMAP).

31. Emilio, *A Brave Black Regiment,* p. 312; Taylor, *The Negro in South Carolina,* p. 13; Henderson B. Donald, *The Negro Freedman: Life Conditions of the American Negro in the Early Years after Emancipation* (New York: Henry Schuman, 1952), p. 158; Somers, *The Southern States,* pp. 52–53. By examining military records and those of the United States Census and the Freedmen's Bureau, one scholar found that, initially, blacks did die in great numbers, especially those living in cities at the end of the Civil War, but many scholars have exaggerated the loss of life during Reconstruction. In actuality, according to the 1870 census, black mortality began to move downward toward the lower mortality rates of whites. Michael Anthony Cooke, "The Health of Blacks during Reconstruction, 1862–1870" (Ph.D. diss., University of Maryland at College Park, 1983), p. iii.

32. Major James M. Johnston to A. L. Crawford, December 31, 1866, Assistant Commissioner Letters Received, Bureau of Refugees, Freedmen, and Abandoned Lands Records, National Archives, Washington, D.C. (hereafter, FBP).

33. P. Rector to Brvt. Lieut. Col. A. K. Smith, January 23, 1866, Roll 44, Assistant Commissioner Letters Received, FBP.

34. Litwack, *Been in the Storm So Long,* pp. 316–24. Government policies to force blacks back to the plantations under labor contracts and to prevent black urban migration appear to have been universal phenomena in the Reconstruction South. For further discussion, see John Robert Kirkland, "Federal Troops in the South Atlantic States during Reconstruction 1865–1877" (Ph.D. diss., University of North Carolina, Chapel Hill, 1967), pp. 331–34; O'Brien, "From Bondage to Citizenship," pp. 119–20; Penelope K. Majeske, "Your Obedient Servant: The United States Army in Virginia during Reconstruction, 1865–1867" (Ph.D. diss., Wayne State University, 1980), pp. 34–35, 40–42; John W. Blassingame, *Black New Orleans, 1860–1880* (Chicago: University of Chicago Press, 1973), pp. 50–53; William A. Byrne, "The Burden and Heat of the Day: Slavery and Servitude in Savannah, 1733–1865" (Ph.D. diss., Florida State University, 1979), pp. 363–64; Denoral Davis, "Against the Odds: Postbellum Growth and Development in a Southern Black Urban Community, 1865–1900" (Ph.D. diss., SUNY-Binghamton, 1987), pp. 32–35; McLeod, "Black and White Workers," pp. 19–22; Drago, *Black Politicians,* pp. 110–11; and Ernest Walter Hooper, "Memphis, Tennessee: Fed-

eral Occupation and Reconstruction, 1862–1870" (Ph.D. diss., University of North Carolina, Chapel Hill, 1957), pp. 136–37.

35. Simkins and Woody, *South Carolina during Reconstruction*, p. 30.

36. Brigadier General W. T. Bennett to Lieut. Colonel W.L.M. Burger, January 29, 1866; Brigadier General W. T. Bennett to Captain M. W. Acie, February 8, 1866, Box 160, DSP.

37. Trowbridge, *Picture of the Desolated States*, p. 537.

38. C. P. Wothampton to Rev. E. P. Smith, June 15, 1868; C. P. Wothampton to Rev. E. P. Smith, June 30, 1868; Elizabeth Boorne to Rev. E. P. Smith, August 29, 1868; Elizabeth Boorne to Rev. E. P. Smith, September 10, 1868; Elizabeth Boorne to Rev. E. P. Smith, June 12, 1869, AMAP; F. L. Cardozo to Major General R. K. Scott, February 11, 1867; G. Pillsbury to Brev. Maj. General R. K. Scott, February 22, 1867; Edward L. Deane to Brev. Maj. General R. K. Scott, March 23, 1867; Reuben Tomlinson to Brev. Maj. General R. K. Scott, April 6, 1867, Roll 44, FBP.

39. Monthly Reports of Rations, Clothing and Medicines Which Were Issued to Freed People in Charleston, South Carolina, in October and November, 1868, South Carolina, Box 60, FBP; Lists of Destitutes in the Berkley, Walamasaw, Goose Creek and Cooper River Parishes of South Carolina to Which Rations Were Issued in the Period of May–August 1866, South Carolina, Box 61, FBP. In addition, in order to lessen the burden on government assistance, if relatives could be located the aged or the infirm were sometimes sent to live with those relatives. Colonel William Stome to Brigadier General H. W. Smith, September 6, 1866; F. Pegre Porcher to ———, June 22, 1866; Records of the Assistant Commissioner for the State of South Carolina, Personnel Rosters, January to July 1868; Records Relating to Transportation, October 1886 to November 1868 and Other Records, 1865 to 1867, Roll 44, FBP. Also, in other parts of South Carolina, Georgetown in particular, blacks took government rations only when in dire need because of unemployment or chronic illness. South Carolina Chief Medical Officer Miscellaneous, 1865–1868, Inspector Letters Received 1868, Asst. Quarter-Master and Disbursing Officer Miscellaneous 1867–1869, Box 16, FBP.

40. Trowbridge, *Picture of the Desolated States*, p. 538.

41. Ibid., p. 537.

42. W. A. Ketterson to Major R. H. Willougby, March 27, 1865; Captain H. James Weston to Captain E. S. Henry, April 17, 1865, DSP; Daniel E. Huger Smith, Alice R. Huger Smith, Arney R. Childs, eds., *Mason Smith Family Letters, 1860–1868* (Columbia: University of South Carolina Press, 1950), pp. 227, 233. In most instances, contemporary sources identify women in the postwar South by the names of their husbands, usually preceded by "Mrs." or "the Widow" and rarely by their own first names.

43. Trowbridge, *Picture of the Desolated States*, p. 538.

44. O. D. Kinsman to Ralph Ely, January 23, 1866, Assistant Commissioner Letters Received, FBP.

45. William C. Hine, "Frustration, Factionalism, and Failure: Black Political Leadership and the Republican Party in Reconstruction Charleston, 1865–1877" (Ph.D. diss., Kent State University, 1979), pp. 31–32; Joel Williamson, *After Slavery: The Negro in South Carolina during Reconstruction, 1861–1877* (Chapel Hill: University of North Carolina Press, 1965), pp. 74–79; Simkins and Woody, *South*

Carolina during Reconstruction, pp. 48–52, 58–59. Other Southern legislatures passed various forms of Black Codes in 1865 and 1866. Among the most important completed works on these codes are Theodore B. Wilson, *The Black Codes of the South* (Tuscaloosa: University of Alabama Press, 1965); Vernon L. Wharton, *The Negro in Mississippi, 1865–1890* (New York: Harper and Row, 1947), pp. 80–96; Joe M. Richardson, *The Negro in the Reconstruction of Florida, 1865–1877* (Tallahassee: Florida State University Press, 1965), pp. 43, 135–36, 143, 205; C. Peter Ripley, *Slaves and Freedmen in Civil War Louisiana* (Baton Rouge: Louisiana State University Press, 1976), pp. 189–92; Howard N. Rabinowitz, *Race Relations in the Urban South, 1865–1890* (New York: Oxford University Press, 1978), pp. 34–35, 38; Arnold H. Taylor, *Travail and Triumph: Black Life and Culture in the South since the Civil War* (Westport, Conn.: Greenwood Press, 1976), pp. 6–7; and W. E. B. Du Bois, *Black Reconstruction: An Essay toward a History of the Part Which Black Folk Played in the Attempt to Reconstruct Democracy in America, 1860–1880* (New York: Harcourt, Brace, 1935), pp. 166–80.

46. Hine, "Frustration, Factionalism, and Failure," p. 31; Litwack, *Been in the Storm So Long,* pp. 366–70.

47. Litwack, *Been in the Storm So Long,* pp. 367–68.

48. Ibid.; Hine, "Frustration, Factionalism, and Failure," pp. 31–32.

49. Litwack, *Been in the Storm So Long,* p. 367.

50. Hine, "Frustration, Factionalism, and Failure," pp. 31–32; Litwack, *Been in the Storm So Long,* p. 367.

51. Hine, "Frustration, Factionalism, and Failure," p. 39.

52. *South Carolina Leader,* November 25, 1865; Williamson, *After Slavery,* p. 77; Hine, "Frustration, Factionalism, and Failure," pp. 38–39, 41. For a complete account of the proceedings of this convention, see "Proceedings of the Colored People's Convention of the State of South Carolina," Charleston (November 1865), Moorland-Spingarn Reading Room, Howard University.

53. General Charles Devens to BBG James C. Beecher, December 24, 1865; Colonel W. L. M. Burger to Charles Bennett, Jr., December 28, 1865; Rev. R. H. Cain to General Charles Devens, December 29, 1865, DSP.

54. Rev. T. Willard Lewis to General Charles Devens, December 26, 1865, DSP.

55. Rev. R. H. Cain to General Charles Devens, December 29, 1865, DSP.

56. Elizabeth Hyde Botume, *First Days amongst the Contrabands* (Boston: Lee and Shepard, 1893), p. 201; Rev. T. Willard Lewis to General Charles Devens, December 26, 1965; Rev. William Lyall to General Charles Devens, December 27, 1865; Colonel W. L. M. Burger to Charles Bennett, Jr., December 28, 1865; Rev. R. H. Cain to General Charles Devens, December 29, 1865, DSP.

57. Rev. William Lyall to General Charles Devens, December 27, 1865, DSP.

58. Rev. William Lyall to General Charles Devens, December 27, 1865, DSP.

59. Williamson, *After Slavery,* p. 74.

60. Ibid., p. 79.

61. Mary Abigail Dodge, *Wool-Gathering* (Boston: Estes and Lauriat, 1877), p. 221.

62. *Charleston Courier,* April 25, 1865.

63. Williamson, *After Slavery,* pp. 66–67.

64. *The National Freedman,* May 1, 1865, p. 133.

65. Foner, "The Meaning of Freedom," p. 101.

66. *Charleston News and Courier,* March 31, April 9, April 21, 1873; Rhett, *Charleston,* pp. 306, 308; Williamson, *After Slavery,* pp. 44–46; May Alice Harris Ridley, "The Black Community of Nashville and Davidson County, 1860–1870" (Ph.D. diss., University of Pittsburgh, 1982), p. 101; Blassingame, *Black New Orleans,* pp. 59–60; Byrne, "The Burden," pp. 349–50; O'Brien, "From Bondage to Citizenship," pp. 79, 81–84, 251–53; Rabinowitz, *Race Relations,* pp. 63, 66, 77; Edmund Drago, *Black Politicians,* pp. 107–108; Stephen V. Ash, *Middle Tennessee Society Transformed, 1860–1870: War and Peace in the Upper South* (Baton Rouge: Louisiana State University Press, 1988), p. 139; Charles H. Wesley, *Negro Labor in the United States 1850–1925: A Study in American Economic History* (New York: Vanguard Press, 1927), pp. 116–55.

67. *Christian Recorder,* September 30, 1865.

68. *Charleston News and Courier,* March 31, 1873.

69. Ibid., April 9, 1873.

70. Ibid., April 21, 1873.

71. Ibid., May 22, 1873.

72. Ibid., February 24, 1875.

73. Ibid., January 18, 1876.

74. Ibid., July 2, 1873.

75. Ibid., May 31, 1873.

76. Ibid., November 8, 1875; Donald, *The Negro Freedman,* p. 21.

77. *Christian Recorder,* August 19, 1865.

78. Ibid., August 19, 1865.

79. Ibid.

80. Ibid.

81. Caroline Gilman to Eliza, September 17, 1865, Letters of Caroline Gilman, South Carolina Historical Society, Charleston (hereafter, SCHS).

82. Powers, *Black Charlestonians,* p. 103.

83. Ibid.

84. Andrews, *The South since the War,* pp. 24–25.

85. Ibid., pp. 25–26.

86. J. W. Alvord, *Letters from the South Relating to the Condition of the Freedmen Addressed to Major General O. O. Howard* (Washington, D.C.: Howard University Press, 1870), p. 9.

87. Ibid. For excellent scholarship on the problem of labor and immigration in South Carolina during Reconstruction, see Robert H. Woody, "The Labor and Immigration Problem of South Carolina during Reconstruction," *Mississippi Valley Historical Review* 18 (1931): 195–212.

88. Powers, *Black Charlestonians,* p. 121.

89. Ibid., pp. 120–21.

90. Ibid., p. 121.

91. *Charleston Daily Republican,* August 17, 1871.

92. Edward P. Wall to Brt. Major General R. K. Scott, June 22, 1868, Assistant Commissioner Letters Received, FBP.

93. *Charleston News and Courier,* September 21, 1876.

94. W. G. Marts to Rev. Dr. Strieby, July 7, 1877, AMAP.

95. For some of the best studies of the importance of land to former slaves, see Abbott, *The Freedmen's Bureau,* pp. 52–65; Williamson, *After Slavery,* pp. 54–63;

Simkins and Woody, *South Carolina during Reconstruction*, pp. 227–31; Claude F. Oubre, *Forty Acres and a Mule: The Freedmen's Bureau and Black Land Ownership* (Baton Rouge: Louisiana State University Press, 1982); Wesley, *Negro Labor,* pp. 138–39; Donna Johanna Benson, "Before I Be a Slave: A Social Analysis of the Black Struggle for Freedom in North Carolina, 1860–1865" (Ph.D. diss., Duke University, 1984), pp. 169–70, 173–75; Jacqueline Baldwin Walker, "Blacks in North Carolina during Reconstruction" (Ph.D. diss., Duke University, 1979), pp. 63–65; Richard Bailey, "Black Legislators During the Reconstruction of Alabama, 1867–1878" (Ph.D. diss., Kansas State University, 1984), pp. 125–30: Byrne, "The Burden," pp. 364–68; O'Brien, "From Bondage to Citizenship," pp. 90–91; Foner, "The Meaning of Freedom," pp. 102–104; and Mary Jennie McGuire, "Getting Their Hands on the Land: The Revolution in St. Helena Parish, South Carolina, 1861–1900" (Ph.D. diss., University of South Carolina, 1985), pp. 1–2.

96. Abbott, *The Freedmen's Bureau,* p. 52.

97. Rev. T. Willard Lewis to General Charles Devens, December 26, 1865, DSP.

98. Reid, *After the War,* p. 147.

99. Ibid., p. 59.

100. Abbott, *The Freedmen's Bureau,* pp. 54–55; Williamson, *After Slavery,* pp. 59–63; Victor Ullman, *Martin R. Delany: The Beginnings of Black Nationalism* (Boston: Beacon Press, 1971), pp. 317–19; Litwack, *Been in the Storm So Long,* pp. 400–402; Simkins and Woody, *South Carolina during Reconstruction,* pp. 227–28.

101. Abbott, *The Freedmen's Bureau,* pp. 55–56; Oubre, *Forty Acres,* p. 189; Williamson, *After Slavery,* pp. 79–81; Simkins and Woody, *South Carolina during Reconstruction,* pp. 229–30. As indicated earlier, most former slaves were never granted land. Northern missionaries and federal officials did launch some projects at Port Royal, South Carolina, and Davis Bend, Mississippi, designed to demonstrate that blacks could make the transition from slavery to freedom. Tracts of land were distributed in these areas to blacks who were to make themselves economically independent through its use. See Willie Lee Rose, *Rehearsal for Reconstruction: The Port Royal Experiment* (New York: Vintage Books, 1964); Janet Sharp Hermann, *The Pursuit of a Dream* (New York: Oxford University Press, 1981); Janet Sharp Hermann, "Reconstruction in Microcosm: Three Men and a Gin," *Journal of Negro History* 65, no. 4 (Fall 1980): 312–35; Stephen Joseph Ross, "Freed Soil, Freed Labor, Freed Men: John Eaton and the Davis Bend Experiment," *Journal of Southern History* 44, no. 2 (May 1978): 213–32; and James T. Currie, "Benjamin Montgomery and the Davis Bend Colony," *Prologue* 10, no. 1 (Spring 1978): 5–21.

102. Oubre, *Forty Acres,* p. 188.

103. Du Bois, *Black Reconstruction,* p. 352.

104. Thomas C. Holt, *Black over White: Negro Political Leadership in South Carolina during Reconstruction* (Urbana: University of Illinois Press, 1977), pp. 162–64; Thomas C. Holt, "Negro Legislators in South Carolina during Reconstruction," in Howard N. Rabinowitz, ed., *Southern Black Leaders of the Reconstruction Era* (Urbana: University of Illinois Press, 1982), p. 239.

105. Holt, *Black over White,* pp. 163–64.

106. Ibid., p. 164.

107. Ibid., pp. 122–51. Many of Georgia's black political leaders also aspired to become a part of the capitalist class in Georgia. On such sensitive issues as land

reform and confiscation, they too refused to vote on behalf of the interests of freedmen since it would have been detrimental to their own economic interests. Drago, *Black Politicians,* pp. 86–91.

108. Charles Bennett, Jr., to Colonel W. L. M. Burger, December 28, 1865, DSP; Foner, "The Meaning of Freedom," p. 103; *Charleston Daily News,* July 23, 24, 1867.

109. Gabriel Manigault Diary, 1865–1868, Gabriel Manigault Papers, SHC.

110. Ibid. Former slaves in many parts of the South attempted to make good the "promise" of land through their own self-active behavior of occupying old estates, as well as showing their disappointment in the government's lack of action in other ways. See Abbott, *The Freedmen's Bureau,* pp. 57–60; Trowbridge, *The South,* pp. 538–45; *Charleston Courier,* February 1, 6, 1866; Litwack, *Been in the Storm So Long,* pp. 406–407; and Foner, "The Meaning of Freedom," p. 103.

111. Trowbridge, *The South,* pp. 544–45.

112. Somers, *The Southern States,* p. 54. For full accounts of the Freedmen's Savings Bank, see Walter L. Fleming, *The Freedmen's Savings Bank: A Chapter in the Economic History of the Negro Race* (Chapel Hill: University of North Carolina Press, 1927); and Carl R. Osthaus, *Freedmen, Philanthropy, and Fraud: A History of the Freedmen's Savings Bank* (Urbana: University of Illinois Press, 1976). For detailed accounts of the numerous depositors of the Freedmen's Savings Bank, see Registers of Signatures of Depositors in Branches of the Freedmen's Savings and Trust Company, 1865–1874, Record Group 101, NA.

113. Alvord, *Letters from the South,* p. 9.

114. *New York Tribune,* June 30, 1869; Hollis R. Lynch, ed., *The Black Urban Condition: A Documentary History, 1866–1971* (New York: Thomas Y. Crowell, 1973), p. 5; Donald, *The Negro Freedman,* p. 43.

115. Loren Schweninger, *Black Property Owners in the South, 1790–1915* (Urbana: University of Illinois Press, 1990), pp. 25, 26, 59, 235.

116. The steadily growing amount of money deposited in the Charleston branch of the Freedmen's Savings Bank chronicled in the *Charleston Courier* lends credence to the claim that freedmen were serious about saving money. *Charleston Courier,* June 27, July 18, October 22, November 25, 1867.

117. Somers, *The Southern States,* p. 55.

118. Carl R. Osthaus, *Freedmen, Philanthropy and Fraud,* p. 98.

119. *The Christian Recorder,* April 21, 1866; August 26, 1865; J. E. Hilary Skinner, *After the Storm* 2:342; Henderson H. Donald, *The Negro Freedman,* pp. 23, 42; *New York Tribune,* May 31, 1871; Somers, *The Southern States,* p. 54. The same eagerness to save and invest earnings shown by Charleston's freedmen was shown by freedmen throughout the South. See Patricia W. Romero and Willie Lee Rose, eds., *Susie King Taylor: Reminiscences of My Life—A Black Woman's Civil War Memoirs* (New York: Markus Wiener, 1988), pp. 15, 123–24, 127, 138; Alvord, *Letters from the South,* pp. 9–10; Blassingame, *Black New Orleans,* pp. 66–67; Oubre, *Forty Acres,* pp. 159–60, 164–65, 167–70; Bailey, "Black Legislators," pp. 128–29; Wesley, *Negro Labor,* pp. 142–45; Davis, "Against the Odds," pp. 59–63; Ridley, "Black Community," pp. 134–35; and Blassingame, "Before the Ghetto," pp. 467–68.

120. *Charleston Courier,* January 5, 7, 8, 1867; *Charleston Daily News,* January 5, 1867; *New York Times,* January 8, 1867.

121. *Charleston Daily News,* January 5, 1867.

122. *Charleston Mercury,* January 7, 1867.

123. *Charleston Courier,* January 8, 1867; *Charleston Daily News,* January 7, 8, 1867.

124. William C. Hine, "Black Organized Labor in Reconstruction Charleston," *Labor History* 25, no. 4 (Fall 1984): 505.

125. *Charleston Courier,* February 25, 1868; *Charleston Mercury,* February 25, 1868.

126. *Charleston Daily News,* February 25, 1868.

127. *Charleston Daily News,* February 27, 29, 1868; *Charleston Courier,* February 27, 29, 1868; *Charleston Mercury,* February 27, 1868.

128. *Charleston Daily Republican,* September 27, October 14, 1869; *Charleston Daily News,* October 14, 15, 16, 1869.

129. *Charleston Daily News,* October 27, 1869; *Charleston Daily Republican,* October 27, 28, November 5, 1869.

130. Hine, "Black Organized Labor," p. 512. Throughout the South during the Reconstruction era, black longshoremen and other black workers engaged in strikes. See Jenell H. Shofner, "Militant Negro Laborers in Reconstruction Florida," *Journal of Southern History* 39, no. 3 (August 1973): 397–408; Herbert Northrup, "The New Orleans Longshoremen," *Political Science Quarterly* 57, no. 4 (December 1942): 527–28; Sterling D. Spero and Abram L. Harris, *The Black Worker: The Negro and the Labor Movement* (New York: Columbia University Press, 1931), p. 183; Drago, *Black Politicians,* pp. 123–25; Litwack, *Been in the Storm So Long,* pp. 437–42; Peter Kolchin, *First Freedom: The Responses of Alabama's Blacks to Emancipation and Reconstruction* (Westport, Conn.: Greenwood Press, 1972), p. 130; Richardson, *The Negro in the Reconstruction of Florida,* pp. 69–70; Rachleff, *Black Labor,* pp. 42–44; and Eric Foner, *Reconstruction: America's Unfinished Revolution, 1863–1877* (New York: Harper and Row, 1988), p. 107.

131. *Charleston Daily News,* September 27, October 5, 1869; *Charleston Daily Republican,* October 1, 5, 1869.

132. *Charleston Daily News,* October 7, 1869; *Charleston Daily Republican,* October 6, 7, 1869.

133. Black workers and white workers after the Civil War generally viewed one another as competitors; as a result, membership of both races in a single union local was a rarity. This pattern continued well into the twentieth century. See Spero and Harris, *The Black Worker,* pp. 16–469; Charles H. Wesley, *Negro Labor in the United States,* pp. 156–91; and Wilbert L. Jenkins, "The Relationship between Blacks and the American Trade Union Movement as Presented through the Editorial Pages of the *Crisis* Magazine, 1917–1936" (paper prepared at Michigan State University, 1984).

134. *Charleston Daily Republican,* October 27, 29, 1869.

135. Ibid., November 2, 1869.

136. Hine, "Black Organized Labor," pp. 510–11.

137. Ibid., pp. 511–12.

138. Ibid., pp. 512–13.

139. *Charleston Daily Republican,* December 8, 1869; January 20, 1870.

140. Ibid., January 20, 1870.

141. Hine, "Black Organized Labor," p. 513.

142. *Charleston News and Courier,* September 3, 1873.

143. Ibid., September 12, 15, 1873.

144. Ibid., September 9, 10, 11, 1873.

145. Ibid., September 11, 12, 1873.

146. Ibid., September 15, 1873.

147. Ibid., September 11, 15, 16, 20, 1873.

148. Ibid., January 27, 31, February 2, 1874.

149. Ibid., February 6, 13, 16, 19, 1877.

150. Hine, "Black Organized Labor," p. 517.

151. *The South Carolina Leader,* October 7, 1865; *The South Carolina Leader,* December 9, 1865; *Charleston Courier,* May 13, 1865; Reid, *After the War,* pp. 83, 581–586; Botume, *First Days,* p. 205; L. Maria Child, *The Freedmen's Book* (Boston: Ticknor and Fields, 1865), pp. 262–63.

4. WE GOTTA GET US SOME BOOK LERNIN'

1. Ira Berlin, ed., *Herbert G. Gutman: Power and Culture—Essays on the American Working Class* (New York: Pantheon Books, 1987), p. 260.

2. W. E. B. Du Bois, *Black Reconstruction: An Essay toward a History of the Part Which Black Folk Played in the Attempt to Reconstruct Democracy in America, 1860–1880* (New York: Harcourt, Brace, 1935), p. 123.

3. Berlin, *Herbert G. Gutman,* p. 260. For revisionist studies that, although excellent, still tend to focus much attention on the activities of Northern whites in Southern freedmen's schooling rather than on the efforts of the blacks themselves, see Warren B. Armstrong, "Union Chaplains and the Education of the Freedmen," *Journal of Negro History* 52, no. 2 (April 1967): 104–15; John W. Blassingame, "The Union Army as an Educational Institution for Negroes, 1862–1865," *Journal of Negro Education* 34, no. 2 (Spring 1962): 152–59; Sandra E. Small, "The Yankee Schoolmarm in Freedmen's Schools: An Analysis of Attitudes," *Journal of Southern History* 45, no. 3 (August 1979): 381–402; Ronald E. Butchart, *Northern Schools, Southern Blacks, and Reconstruction: Freedmen's Education, 1862–1875* (Westport, Conn.: Greenwood Press, 1980); Peter C. Ripley, *Slaves and Freedmen in Civil War Louisiana* (Baton Rouge: Louisiana State University Press, 1976), pp. 126–37; William Preston Vaughn, *Schools for All: The Blacks and Public Education in the South, 1865–1877* (Lexington: University Press of Kentucky, 1974), pp. 1–49; and Robert C. Morris, *Reading, 'Riting, and Reconstruction: The Education of Freedmen in the South, 1861–1870* (Chicago: University of Chicago Press, 1981), pp. 1–84.

4. Berlin, *Herbert G. Gutman,* p. 261; *American Missionary Magazine,* November 1870, p. 244.

5. Mamie Garvin Fields and Karen Fields, *Lemon Swamp and Other Places: A Carolina Memoir* (New York: The Free Press, 1983), p. 2. For more information on educational activism among blacks before the Civil War, see C. W. Birnie, "The Education of the Negro in Charleston, South Carolina, Prior to the Civil War," *Journal of Negro History* 12, no. 1 (January 1927): 13–21; Janet Cornelius, "We Slipped and Learned to Read: Slave Accounts of the Literacy Process, 1830–1865," *Phylon* 44, no. 3 (1983): 171–86; John T. O'Brien, "Reconstruction in Richmond: White Restoration and Black Protest, April–June 1865," *Virginia Magazine of History and Biography* 89, no. 3 (July 1981): 264; Berlin, *Herbert G.*

Gutman, pp. 261–62; and Peter Kolchin, *First Freedom: The Responses of Alabama's Blacks to Emancipation and Reconstruction* (Westport, Conn.: Greenwood Press, 1972), p. 80.

6. Butchart, *Northern Schools, Southern Blacks*, p. 176.

7. Joel Williamson, *After Slavery: The Negro in South Carolina during Reconstruction, 1861–1877* (Chapel Hill: University of North Carolina Press, 1965), p. 219; Thomas Holt, "Negro State Legislators in South Carolina during Reconstruction" in Howard N. Rabinowitz, ed., *Southern Black Leaders of the Reconstruction Era* (Urbana: University of Illinois Press, 1982), pp. 241–42; Peggy Lamson, *The Glorious Failure: Black Congressman Robert Brown Elliott and the Reconstruction in South Carolina* (New York: Norton Books, 1973), p. 56. Black leaders throughout the South attached much significance to the acquisition of education by former slaves. For other examples, see Edmund L. Drago, *Black Politicians and Reconstruction in Georgia* (Baton Rouge: Louisiana State University Press, 1982), pp. 97–98, 105; and Charles Vincent, *Black Legislators in Louisiana during Reconstruction* (Baton Rouge: Louisiana State University Press, 1976), pp. 87–92.

8. Berlin, *Herbert G. Gutman*, p. 269. For detailed studies of the work of the Freedmen's Bureau on black education in South Carolina and throughout the South, see Martin Abbott, "The Freedmen's Bureau and Negro Schooling in South Carolina," *South Carolina Historical Magazine* 62, no. 2 (April 1956): 65–81; Martin Abbott, *The Freedmen's Bureau in South Carolina, 1865–1872* (Chapel Hill: University of North Carolina Press, 1967), pp. 82–98; Butchart, *Northern Schools, Southern Blacks*, pp. 97–114; and George R. Bentley, *A History of the Freedmen's Bureau* (New York: Octagon Books, 1970), pp. 169–84.

9. Berlin, *Herbert G. Gutman*, p. 269. For an excellent study of the educational efforts of the Freedmen's Aid Societies in South Carolina, see Luther P. Jackson, "The Educational Efforts of the Freedmen's Bureau and Freedmen's Aid Societies in South Carolina, 1862–1872," *Journal of Negro History* 8, no. 1 (January 1923): 1–40.

10. Berlin, *Herbert G. Gutman*, p. 272; Morris, *Reading, Riting*, pp. 102–104.

11. Joe M. Richardson, "Francis L. Cardozo: Black Educator during Reconstruction," *Journal of Negro Education* 48, no. 1 (Winter 1979): 74; Thomas W. Cardozo to Rev. M. E. Strieby, June 16, 1865, American Missionary Association Papers, Duke University Library, Durham (hereafter, AMAP).

12. Richardson, "Francis L. Cardozo," p. 75; Joe M. Richardson, *Christian Reconstruction: The American Missionary Association and Southern Blacks, 1861–1890* (Athens: University of Georgia Press, 1986), p. 200. Thomas W. Cardozo was fired by AMA officials amid rumors that he had seduced a female student in Flushing, New York. After being relieved of his duties, Thomas Cardozo operated a store in Charleston until it was mysteriously destroyed in December 1865. He eventually moved to Mississippi, where he became the state superintendent of education. The records are not clear as to whether Lewis Tappan Night School for freedmen was absorbed by Saxton School or ceased to exist altogether. Richardson, "Francis L. Cardozo," p. 74.

13. Berlin, *Herbert G. Gutman*, p. 272.

14. Bernard E. Powers, *Black Charlestonians: A Social History, 1822–1885* (Fayetteville: University of Arkansas Press, 1994), pp. 148–49.

15. Ibid., pp. 139, 149.

16. F. Randolph to Bvt. Major General R. Saxton, August 3, 1865, Assistant Commissioner Letters Received, Bureau of Refugees, Freedmen, and Abandoned Lands Records, National Archives, Washington, D.C. (hereafter, FBP).

17. Richard Cain quoted in Richardson, *Christian Reconstruction*, p. 246.

18. William Weston to Thomas Cardozo, June 24, 1865, AMAP.

19. Henry L. Swint, ed., *Dear Ones at Home: Letters from Contraband Camps* (Nashville: Vanderbilt University Press, 1966), p. 217.

20. Sarah J. Foster to Rev. E. P. Smith, January 3, 1868, AMAP.

21. Powers, *Black Charlestonians*, p. 145.

22. *New York Times*, July 3, 1874.

23. Mortimer A. Warren to Mr. Cravath, October 22, 1870, AMAP.

24. E. J. Warren to Rev. E. M. Cravath, October 24, 1870, AMAP.

25. *American Missionary Magazine*, November 1870, p. 245.

26. John W. Alvord, *Semi-Annual Reports on Schools for Freedmen: Numbers 1–10, January 1866–July 1870* (July 1, 1867; reprint, New York: AMS Press, 1980), p. 27.

27. *American Missionary Magazine*, November 1870, p. 245.

28. Ibid.

29. P. A. Alcott to Mr. Whipple, December 28, 1865, AMAP; *American Missionary Magazine*, February 1866, p. 30.

30. *American Missionary Magazine*, February 1866, pp. 30–31; P. A. Alcott to Mr. Whipple, December 28, 1865, AMAP.

31. Edmund L. Drago, *Initiative, Paternalism, and Race Relations: Charleston's Avery Normal Institute* (Athens: University of Georgia Press, 1990), p. 74.

32. A. T. Porter to My Dear Major, September 28, 1869; A. T. Porter to My Dear Major, October 4, 1869, Superintendent of Education, South Carolina, Unentered Letters Received, Box 26, FBP.

33. Lottie and Kate Rollin to Major General R. F. Scott, January 14, 1868, Superintendent of Education, South Carolina, Letters Received, Box 25A, FBP.

34. Norm C. Smith to Bvt. Maj. General R. K. Scott, December 7, 1867, Superintendent of Education, South Carolina, Letters Received, Box 25A, FBP.

35. Alvord, *Semi-Annual Reports* (July 1, 1867), p. 27. It was fairly common for freedmen to travel miles to obtain an education. *The Reports of the Committees of the House of Representatives, 39th Congress, 1865–1866* (Washington, D.C.: U.S. Government Printing Office, 1866), p. 239.

36. Many of the same sacrifices made by black Charlestonians to become educated were made by blacks throughout the South. See Berlin, *Herbert G. Gutman*, pp. 260–97; James M. Smallwood, *Time of Hope, Time of Despair: Black Texans during Reconstruction* (New York: Kennikat Press, 1981), pp. 84–89; Richardson, *Christian Reconstruction*, pp. 237–38; Kolchin, *First Freedom*, pp. 84–91; Donna J. Benson, "Before I Be a Slave: A Social Analysis of the Black Struggle for Freedom in North Carolina, 1860–1865" (Ph.D. diss., Duke University, 1984), pp. 228–33; William A. Byrne, "The Burden and Heat of the Day: Slavery and Servitude in Savannah, 1733–1865" (Ph.D. diss., Florida State University, 1979), pp. 343–48; Maxine D. Jones, "A Glorious Work: The American Missionary Association and Black North Carolinians, 1863–1880" (Ph.D. diss., Florida State University, 1982), pp. 64–72; James D. Anderson, *The Education of Blacks in the South, 1860–1935* (Chapel Hill: University of North Carolina Press, 1988), pp. 4–19; and Roberta Sue Alexander, "Hostility and Hope: Black Education in North

Carolina during Presidential Reconstruction, 1865–1867," *North Carolina Historical Review* 53, no. 2 (April 1976): 123–32.

37. John W. Alvord discovered many of these schools during his tours through the South. Berlin, *Herbert G. Gutman,* p. 270. Susie King Taylor, a former slave from Savannah, Georgia, operated a "pay school" for freedmen in Savannah in 1866. Patricia W. Romero and Willie Lee Rose, eds., *Susie King Taylor: Reminiscences of My Life—A Black Woman's Civil War Memoirs* (New York: Markus Wiener, 1988), p. 124.

38. Jacqueline Baldwin Walker, "Blacks in North Carolina during Reconstruction" (Ph.D. diss., Duke University, 1979), p. 97.

39. John W. Alvord, *Letters from the South Relating to the Condition of the Freedmen Addressed to Major General O. O. Howard* (Washington, D.C.: Howard University Press, 1870), p. 7.

40. Arthur Sumner to Mr. Reuben Tomlinson, June 28, 1868, Rough Draft of Annual Report of the Shaw School, Charleston, South Carolina, for the Term Ending June 26, 1868, Box 25A, FBP; Reuben Tomlinson to Brev. Maj. General R. K. Scott, July 1, 1868, Roll 29, FBP; Burchill R. Moore, "A History of the Negro Public Schools of Charleston, South Carolina, 1867–1942" (M.A. thesis, University of South Carolina, 1942), p. 11; Josephine W. Martin, "The Educational Efforts of the Major Freedmen's Aid Societies and the Freedmen's Bureau in South Carolina, 1862–1870" (Ph.D. diss., University of South Carolina, 1971), pp. 184–85; Powers, *Black Charlestonians,* p. 139.

41. Berlin, *Herbert G. Gutman,* pp. 260–61.

42. J. E. Hilary Skinner, *After the Storm; or, Jonathan and His Neighbors in 1865–1866* (London: Richard Bentley, 1866) 2:338.

43. Powers, *Black Charlestonians,* p. 139.

44. In June 1868, Cain Institute enrolled 260 freedmen and employed six black teachers and a black principal, W. D. Harris. W. D. Harris, Teachers Monthly School Report, June 1868, Superintendent of Education, South Carolina, Teachers Monthly School Reports, Box 27, FBP.

45. Anderson, *Education of Blacks,* p. 8; *Christian Recorder,* September 29, 1866; *Charleston Courier,* June 28, 1867; M. Van Horne, Teachers Monthly School Report, January 1868, Superintendent of Education, South Carolina, Teachers Monthly School Reports, Box 27, FBP.

46. Powers, *Black Charlestonians,* p. 140.

47. Berlin, *Herbert G. Gutman,* p. 272.

48. Martin, "Educational Efforts," p. 173; Jackson, "Educational Efforts of the Freedmen's Bureau," p. 35.

49. J. H. Bates to Colonel J. R. Edie, November 17, 1868, Box 25A, FBP; Jackson, "Educational Efforts of the Freedmen's Bureau," p. 27.

50. J. H. Bates, Teachers Monthly School Report, October 1868, Superintendent of Education, South Carolina, Teachers Monthly School Reports, Box 27, FBP.

51. Ibid., November, December 1868.

52. Ibid., January, February, May 1869; January 1870.

53. Arthur Sumner, Teachers Monthly School Reports, November, December 1867, Superintendent of Education, South Carolina, Teachers Monthly School Reports, Box 26, FBP.

54. Ibid., January, April, June, October, November, December 1868; January, February, June, October, December 1869, Boxes 26–27.

55. Ibid., January 1870; January 1871, Box 27.

56. M. Van Horne, Teachers Monthly School Report, January 1868, Superintendent of Education, South Carolina, Teachers Monthly School Reports, Box 27, FBP.

57. W. D. Harris, Teachers Monthly School Report, June 1868, Superintendent of Education, South Carolina, Teachers Monthly School Reports, Box 27, FBP.

58. Alvord, *Semi-Annual Reports* (January 1, 1868), p. 26; *Charleston Courier*, November 5, 1866; *Charleston Daily News,* January 20, 1869; Rev. A. Toomer Porter, *The History of a Work of Faith and Love in Charleston, South Carolina* (New York: D. Appleton and Company, 1882), p. 6; Rev. A. Toomer Porter, *Led On! Step by Step: Scenes from Clerical, Military, Educational, and Plantation Life in the South 1828–1898* (New York and London: G. P. Putnam's Sons, 1899), pp. 220–24; Francis Simkins and Robert Woody, *South Carolina during Reconstruction* (Chapel Hill: University of North Carolina Press, 1932), p. 424; Jackson, "Educational Efforts of the Freedmen's Bureau," p. 27; Williamson, *After Slavery,* pp. 214–15; Moore, "History of Negro Public Schools," pp. 14–15; Abbott, "The Freedmen's Bureau and Negro Schooling," p. 74.

59. Kate B. Savage to Major E. L. Deane, June 30, 1870, Superintendent of Education, South Carolina, Teachers Monthly School Reports, Box 26, FBP.

60. Richardson, "Francis L. Cardozo," pp. 76–80, 83; David Macrae, *The Americans at Home* (New York: E. P. Dutton, 1952), pp. 266–67; Richardson, *Christian Reconstruction,* pp. 116–18.

61. Berlin, *Herbert G. Gutman,* p. 272.

62. Francis L. Cardozo to Rev. S. Hunt. August 3, 1866, AMAP.

63. Francis L. Cardozo to Rev. S. Hunt, November 30, 1866, AMAP.

64. Berlin, *Herbert G. Gutman,* p. 272.

65. Francis L. Cardozo to William E. Whiting, March 1, 1867, AMAP.

66. Ellen W. Pierce, Teachers Monthly School Report, March 1868; Lizzie F. Pratt, Teachers Monthly School Report, March 1868; Jennie Paimelert, Teachers Monthly School Report, March 1868, AMAP.

67. Francis L. Cardozo, Teachers Monthly School Report, March 1868, Superintendent of Education, South Carolina, Teachers Monthly School Reports, Box 27, FBP.

68. Martin, "Educational Efforts," pp. 188–90; Jackson, "Educational Efforts of the Freedmen's Bureau," p. 25; Wayne E. Reilly, ed., *Sarah Jane Foster: Teacher of the Freedmen, a Diary and Letters* (Charlottesville: University Press of Virginia, 1990), p. 180.

69. Drago, *Initiative, Paternalism,* pp. 48–52.

70. S. B. Corey, Teachers Monthly School Report, October 1868; Ellen M. Pierce, Teachers Monthly School Reports, November and December 1868, Superintendent of Education, South Carolina, Teachers Monthly School Reports, Box 27, FBP.

71. Ellen M. Pierce, Teachers Monthly School Report, January 1869, Superintendent of Education, South Carolina, Teachers Monthly School Reports, Box 27, FBP.

72. Mortimer A. Warren, Teachers Monthly School Reports, February, April,

June, October 1869, Superintendent of Education, South Carolina, Teachers Monthly School Reports, Box 27, FBP.

73. Ibid., January 1870.

74. M. A. Warren to Mr. Smith, February 5, 1870, AMAP.

75. Mortimer A. Warren, Teachers Monthly School Report, March 1870, AMAP.

76. *Charleston Daily Republican,* October 5, 1870.

77. See, for example, Mortimer A. Warren, Teachers Monthly School Reports, February 1869; January 1870, Superintendent of Education, South Carolina, Teachers Monthly School Reports, Box 27, FBP; and Mortimer A. Warren, Teachers Monthly School Reports, June, October 1869; March 1870, AMAP.

78. *Charleston Courier,* June 28, 1867.

79. *Charleston Daily Republican,* April 8, 1870.

80. *South Carolina Leader,* November 25, 1865.

81. John H. Kennaway, *On Sherman's Track; or, The South after the War* (London: Seeley, Jackson, and Halliday, 1867), p. 58.

82. *The Reports of the Committees of the House of Representatives,* p. 247; Vaughn, *Schools for All,* p. 15.

83. Vaughn, *Schools for All,* p. 15; Williamson, *After Slavery,* pp. 234–35.

84. Williamson, *After Slavery,* p. 236; Vaughn, *Schools for All,* p. 15.

85. Francis L. Cardozo to Rev. George Whipple, October 21, 1865; Francis L. Cardozo to Rev. S. Hunt, December 2, 1865; Francis L. Cardozo to Rev. S. Hunt, December 9, 1865, AMAP.

86. Francis L. Cardozo to Rev. George Whipple, January 27, 1866, AMAP; Alvord, *Semi-Annual Reports* (July 1, 1867), p. 24.

87. Alvord, *Letters from the South,* pp. 6–7; *American Missionary Magazine,* May 1870, p. 98.

88. Powers, *Black Charlestonians,* p. 152

89. *Christian Recorder,* September 29, 1866; Francis L. Cardozo to Rev. S. Hunt, March 10, 1866, AMAP; Richard B. Drake, "The American Missionary Association and the Southern Negro, 1861–1888" (Ph.D. diss., Emory University, 1957), p. 230.

90. *American Missionary Magazine,* August 1866, p. 175; Alvord, *Semi-Annual Reports* (July 1, 1867), p. 28; *Charleston Daily News,* May 10, 1866; Richardson, *Christian Reconstruction,* p. 117; A. Knighton Stanley, *The Children Is Crying: Congregationalism among Black People* (Philadelphia: The Pilgrim Press, 1979), p. 75.

91. Alvord, *Semi-Annual Reports* (July 1, 1867), p. 28; *American Missionary Magazine,* September 1867, pp. 207–208.

92. Francis L. Cardozo to Rev. S. Hunt, March 10, 1866, AMAP.

93. *National Freedman,* February 15, 1866, p. 56.

94. Elizabeth G. Rice, "A Yankee Teacher in the South: An Experience in the Early Days of Reconstruction," *Century Magazine* 62, no. 1 (May 1901): 152–53.

95. Hattie C. Foote to Rev. E. M. Cravath, October 24, November 18, 1873, AMAP.

96. Mortimer A. Warren to Mr. Smith, May 21, 1869, AMAP.

97. Alvord, *Semi-Annual Reports* (July 1, 1867), pp. 28–29; *American Missionary Magazine,* September 1867, p. 208.

98. Sarah W. Stansbury to Mr. Smith, January 30, 1867, AMAP.

99. Drago, *Initiative, Paternalism,* p. 64; Sarah W. Stansbury to Mr. Smith, January 30, 1867, AMAP.

100. Jane Van Allen to Mr. Smith, February 16, 1867, AMAP; Drago, *Initiative, Paternalism,* p. 63.

101. Powers, *Black Charlestonians,* p. 153.

102. James Ford to Rev. E. M. Cravath, April 17, 1875, AMAP.

103. Ibid.

104. Henry M. Christman, ed., *The South As It Is: 1865–1866* (New York: Viking Press, 1965), p. 218.

105. Powers, *Black Charlestonians,* p. 140.

106. Jacob Schirmer Diary, June 19, 1866, South Carolina Historical Society, Charleston.

107. Phebe A. Alcott to Mr. Hunt, November 29, 1865, AMAP.

108. Francis L. Cardozo to Rev. S. Hunt, December 13, 1865, AMAP.

109. Francis L. Cardozo to Rev. George Whipple, January 27, 1866, AMAP.

110. Ibid.

111. Actually, the Freedmen's Bureau and benevolent associations had ended their major educational efforts by 1869 because of a shortage of funds. Officially, the Bureau ended its educational work in April 1870. Alvord resigned as superintendent of schools the following October, and his state superintendents sold the Bureau-owned properties and closed their offices. Vaughn, *Schools for All,* pp. 16–18.

112. W. D. Harris to Rev. George Whipple, November 7, 1868, AMAP.

113. Arthur Sumner to Reuben Tomlinson, June 28, 1868, "Rough Draft of Annual Report of the Shaw School, Charleston, South Carolina, for the Term Ending June 26, 1868," Superintendent of Education, South Carolina, Letters Received, Box 25A, FBP.

114. Mortimer A. Warren to Mr. Smith, October 18, 1869, AMAP.

115. Mortimer A. Warren to Mr. Cravath, December 8, 1871, AMAP.

116. Mortimer A. Warren to Brother Cravath, December 16, 1871, AMAP.

117. Amos W. Farnham to Rev. M. E. Strieby, January 23, 1877, AMAP.

118. Anderson, *Education of Blacks,* p. 19.

119. William W. Taylor, Teachers Monthly School Report, October 1867; M. Van Horne, Teachers Monthly School Report, October 1867, Superintendent of Education, South Carolina, Teachers Monthly School Reports, Box 26, FBP.

120. Arthur Sumner, Teachers Monthly School Reports, November, December 1867, Superintendent of Education, South Carolina, Teachers Monthly School Reports, Box 26, FBP.

121. Arthur Sumner, Teachers Monthly School Reports, January, April, June, October, November, December 1868; January, February, June, October, December 1869; January 1870; January 1871, Superintendent of Education, South Carolina, Teachers Monthly School Reports, Boxes 26 and 27, FBP.

122. Ellen M. Pierce, Teachers Monthly School Report, January 1869; Mortimer A. Warren, Teachers Monthly School Reports, February, April, June, October 1869; January, March 1870, Superintendent of Education, South Carolina, Teachers Monthly School Reports, Box 27, FBP.

123. William W. Taylor, Teachers Monthly School Reports, January, February, March 1869; Kate B. Savage, Teachers Monthly School Reports, October 1869;

January 1870; January 1871, Superintendent of Education, South Carolina, Teachers Monthly School Reports, Box 27, FBP.

124. J. H. Bates, Teachers Monthly School Reports, October, November, December 1868, Superintendent of Education, South Carolina, Teachers Monthly School Reports, Box 27, FBP.

125. Ibid., January, February, May 1869.

126. Ibid., January 1870.

127. U.S. Bureau of the Census, *The Statistics of the Population of the United States in 1870* (Washington, D.C., 1873), p. 427.

128. Lady Duffus Hardy, *Down South* (London: Chapman and Hall Limited, 1883), pp. 52–53.

129. Simkins and Woody, *South Carolina during Reconstruction,* p. 316.

130. U.S. Bureau of the Census, *Ninth Census of the U.S. Population in 1870* (Washington, D.C., 1872); U.S. Bureau of the Census, *A Compendium of the Ninth Census, 1870* (Washington, D.C., 1873), pp. 474–75.

131. U.S. Bureau of the Census, *Eleventh Census of the United States Population in 1890* (Washington, D.C., 1894), pp. 58, 60.

132. U.S. Bureau of the Census, *Twelfth Census of the United States Population in 1900* (Washington, D.C., 1903), pp. 28–29.

133. Ibid., p. 25.

134. V. P. Franklin, *Black Self-Determination: A Cultural History of African-American Resistance* (Brooklyn, N.Y.: Lawrence Hill Books, 1992), p. 175.

135. Drago, *Initiative, Paternalism,* pp. 53–56.

5. WE ARE ALL BROTHERS AND SISTERS

1. See, for example, E. Franklin Frazier, "The Negro Slave Family," *Journal of Negro History* 15, no. 2 (April 1930); E. Franklin Frazier, *The Negro Family in the United States* (Chicago: University of Chicago Press, 1939); Kenneth Stampp, *The Peculiar Institution: Slavery in the Antebellum South* (New York: Vintage Books, 1956); Stanley Elkins, *Slavery: A Problem in American Institutional and Intellectual Life* (Chicago: University of Chicago Press, 1958); Henderson H. Donald, *The Negro Freedman: Life Conditions of the American Negro in the Early Years after Emancipation* (New York: Henry Schuman, 1952); and Richard C. Wade, *Slavery in the Cities: The South, 1820–1860* (New York: Oxford University Press, 1964).

2. Carl N. Degler, *At Odds: Women and the Family in America from the Revolution to the Present* (New York: Oxford University Press, 1980), pp. 114–28; George P. Rawick, *From Sundown to Sunup: The Making of the Black Community* (Westport, Conn.: Greenwood Press, 1972), pp. 77–94.

3. Robert W. Fogel and Stanley L. Engerman, *Time on the Cross: The Economics of American Negro Slavery* (Boston: Little, Brown, 1974), pp. 128, 141, 144; C. Peter Ripley, "The Black Family in Transition: Louisiana, 1860–1865," *Journal of Southern History* 41, no. 3 (August 1975): 369–71; C. Peter Ripley, *Slaves and Freedmen in Civil War Louisiana* (Baton Rouge: Louisiana State University Press, 1976), pp. 146–59; Eugene D. Genovese, *Roll Jordan, Roll: The World the Slaves Made* (New York: Pantheon Books, 1974), pp. 450–57; John W. Blassingame, *The Slave Com-*

munity: Plantation Life in the Antebellum South (New York: Oxford University Press, 1979), pp. 151–53; Robert H. Abzug, "The Black Family during Reconstruction," in Nathan Huggins, Martin Kilson, and Daniel M. Fox, eds., *Key Issues in the Afro-American Experience* (New York: Harcourt Brace Jovanovich, 1971) 2:28–29.

4. Blassingame, *The Slave Community*, pp. 151, 179–191; Walter Hill, "A Sense of Belonging: Family Functions and Structure in Charleston, S.C., 1880–1910" (paper prepared at Howard University, 1984), pp. 1–2.

5. Herbert G. Gutman, *The Black Family in Slavery and Freedom, 1750–1925* (New York: Vintage Books, 1976), pp. 93–95.

6. Herbert G. Gutman, "Persistent Myths about the Afro-American Family," *Journal of Interdisciplinary History* 6, no. 1 (Summer 1975): 191–210; Peter Kolchin, *First Freedom: The Response of Alabama's Blacks to Emancipation and Reconstruction* (Westport, Conn.: Greenwood Press, 1972), pp. 68–69; James M. Smallwood, *Time of Hope, Time of Despair: Black Texans during Reconstruction* (London: Kennikat Press, 1981), pp. 115–16.

7. James H. Croushore and David Morris Porter, eds., *A Union Officer in the Reconstruction* (New Haven: Yale University Press, 1948), p. 36.

8. Hill, "A Sense of Belonging," pp. 4–5.

9. Ibid.

10. Ira Berlin, Steven F. Miller, and Leslie S. Rowland, "Afro-American Families in the Transition from Slavery to Freedom," *Radical History Review* 42 (Fall 1988): 89–90; Barry A. Crouch and Larry Madaras, "Reconstructing Black Families: Perspectives from the Texas Freedmen's Bureau Records," *Prologue* 18, no. 2 (Summer 1986): 112–14; Arnold H. Taylor, *Travail and Triumph: Black Life and Culture in the South since the Civil War* (Westport, Conn.: Greenwood Press, 1976), pp. 161–62; John H. Franklin and Alfred A. Moss, Jr., *From Slavery to Freedom: A History of Negro Americans*, 6th ed. (New York: Alfred A. Knopf, 1988), p. 208; Genovese, *Roll Jordan, Roll,* p. 451; August Meier and Elliott M. Rudwick, *From Plantation to Ghetto: An Interpretive History of American Negroes* (New York: Hill and Wang, 1976), pp. 77–78.

11. Croushore and Porter, *A Union Officer,* pp. 37–38.

12. Whitelaw Reid, *After the War: A Southern Tour, May 1, 1865, to May 1, 1866* (Cincinnati: Moore, Wilstach, and Baldwin, 1866), pp. 220–21.

13. J. E. Hilary Skinner, *After the Storm; or, Jonathan and His Neighbors in 1865–1866* (London: Richard Bentley, 1866) 2:336.

14. See, for example, Ira Berlin, Francine C. Cary, Stephen F. Miller, and Leslie S. Rowland, "Family and Freedom: Black Families in the American Civil War," *History Today,* January 1987, pp. 8–15.

15. Hill, "A Sense of Belonging," pp. 4–5.

16. Milton Ford to General G. Thomas, May 6, 1867, Department of the South Papers, National Archives, Washington, D.C. (hereafter, DSP).

17. John Bennett to Major O. O. Howard, November 10, 1866, DSP.

18. Donald, *The Negro Freedman*, pp. 58–59; Smallwood, *Time of Hope*, pp. 113–14; John W. Blassingame, *Black New Orleans, 1860–1880* (Chicago: University of Chicago Press, 1973), p. 86.

19. Donald, *The Negro Freedman*, p. 57.

20. Kolchin, *First Freedom*, p. 59.

21. *Charleston Daily Republican,* February 19, 1870, cited in Joel Williamson, *After Slavery: The Negro in South Carolina during Reconstruction, 1861–1877* (Chapel Hill: University of North Carolina Press, 1965), p. 307.

22. *Charleston News and Courier,* September 7, 1875.

23. Taylor, *Travail and Triumph,* p. 163.

24. Elizabeth H. Botume, *First Days amongst the Contrabands* (Boston: Lee and Shepherd, 1893), pp. 153–56.

25. Records of the Freedmen's Savings Bank, Charleston Branch, 1865–1874, Record Group 101, National Archives, Washington, D.C. (hereafter, CB).

26. *Charleston News and Courier,* December 1, 1874; April 29, 1873; May 14, 1873; *Charleston Courier,* June 2, 4, 5; July 22, 1867; *Charleston News and Courier,* April 5, 1873.

27. Williamson, *After Slavery,* p. 309.

28. *Charleston Courier,* November 11, 1867.

29. Smallwood, *Time of Hope,* p. 113.

30. *Charleston Courier,* June 4, 1867.

31. Eric Foner, *Reconstruction: America's Unfinished Revolution, 1863–1877* (New York: Harper and Row, 1988), p. 85.

32. Donald, *The Negro Freedman,* p. 21.

33. Jacqueline Jones, *Labor of Love, Labor of Sorrow: Black Women, Work, and the Family, from Slavery to the Present* (New York: Vintage Books, 1985), pp. 58–60; Foner, *Reconstruction,* p. 86.

34. Foner, *Reconstruction,* p. 86.

35. Kolchin, *First Freedom,* p. 62; Jones, *Labor of Love,* pp. 58–59; Gutman, *The Black Family,* pp. 167–68.

36. Foner, *Reconstruction,* p. 86.

37. *New York Tribune,* May 31, 1871, cited in Donald, *The Negro Freedman,* p. 21.

38. Foner, *Reconstruction,* pp. 86–87.

39. Records of the Freedmen's Savings Bank, CB.

40. Ibid.

41. Records of the Freedmen's Savings Bank, CB; Peter J. Rachleff, *Black Labor in the South: Richmond, Virginia, 1865–1890* (Philadelphia: Temple University Press, 1984), p. 20.

42. Records of the Freedmen's Savings Bank, CB.

43. Rachleff, *Black Labor,* p. 21.

44. Records of the Freedmen's Savings Bank, CB; Gutman, *The Black Family,* pp. 198–229.

45. Gutman, *The Black Family,* pp. 201, 204, 220–29.

46. Gutman, *The Black Family,* pp. 185–96; Degler, *At Odds,* p. 124; Rachleff, *Black Labor,* p. 22; Records of the Freedmen's Savings Bank, CB.

47. Gutman, *The Black Family,* p. 190.

48. Records of the Freedmen's Savings Bank, CB.

49. U.S. Bureau of the Census, *Ninth Census of the U.S., Population of 1870* (Washington, D.C., 1872).

50. Rachleff, *Black Labor,* p. 22; Records of the Freedmen's Savings Bank, CB.

51. U.S. Bureau of the Census, *Ninth Census.*

52. Ibid.

53. Gutman, *The Black Family,* p. 186; Williamson, *After Slavery,* p. 310; Rachleff, *Black Labor,* p. 22; Records of the Freedmen's Savings Bank, CB.

54. Rachleff, *Black Labor,* p. 22.

55. Gutman, *The Black Family,* pp. 220–29.

56. E. Franklin Frazier, *The Negro Church in America* (New York: Schocken Books, 1974), pp. 41–42; Geo. A. William to Major E. L. Deane, July 16, 1867, Assistant Commissioner Letters Received, Bureau of Refugees, Freedmen, and Abandoned Lands Records, National Archives, Washington, D.C.; *Charleston News and Courier,* April 29; September 6, 11, 1878.

57. Records of the Freedmen's Savings Bank, CB.

58. Gutman, *The Black Family,* pp. 227–28.

59. Ibid., p. 226.

60. Bernard Powers, *Black Charlestonians: A Social History, 1822–1885* (Fayetteville: University of Arkansas Press, 1994), pp. 118–21, 161–62; Foner, *Reconstruction,* p. 82.

61. Powers, *Black Charlestonians,* pp. 101, 162; Foner, *Reconstruction,* p. 82.

62. Powers, *Black Charlestonians,* p. 162.

63. Ibid.

64. Ibid.

65. Foner, *Reconstruction,* p. 82.

66. John W. Alvord, *Letters from the South Relating to the Condition of the Freedmen Addressed to Major General O. O. Howard* (Washington, D.C.: Howard University Press, 1870), p. 9.

67. Ibid., pp. 9–11. According to a summary of crimes committed in Charleston from October through December 1869, seventy-two whites were arrested for public drunkenness compared to only fourteen blacks. Ibid., p. 12.

68. Alvord, *Letters from the South,* pp. 10–11.

69. Williamson, *After Slavery,* pp. 322, 324.

70. Smallwood, *Time of Hope,* p. 122.

71. Williamson, *After Slavery,* pp. 322, 323.

72. Ibid., p. 46.

73. Capt. O. S. B. Wall (104 US.CT) to Major R. Saxton, August 9, 1865; William H. White and Others to Gen. R. K. Scott, October 31, 1866; Milton Ford to General G. Thomas, May 6, 1867; Sarah Jenkins to Major Crawford, July 8, 1867; R. H. Cain to R. K. Scott, November 14, 1867, Letters Received, RG 393, DSP.

74. *Charleston News and Courier,* May 31, April 14, 1873.

75. *Charleston Courier,* April 19, June 28, 1867; *Charleston Daily Republican,* April 8, 1870.

76. *Charleston Courier,* September 24, 1867.

77. Powers, *Black Charlestonians,* p. 164.

78. Ibid.

79. Ibid., pp. 164–65.

80. *Charleston Courier,* July 6, 1866; July 4, 1867; July 6, 1867; December 31, 1867; January 2, 1868; July 6, 1868; January 3, 1871; July 5, 1871; January 2, 1872; July 5, 1872; *Charleston News and Courier,* January 2, 1875; *Charleston Daily Republican,* May 4, 1870.

81. Powers, *Black Charlestonians,* p. 164.

82. Taylor, *Travail and Triumph,* p. 189; Ira Berlin, *Slaves without Masters: The Free Negro in the Antebellum South* (New York: Pantheon Books, 1987), pp. 388–90; Williamson, *After Slavery,* p. 313; John F. Marszalek, ed., *The Diary of Miss Emma Holmes* (Baton Rouge: Louisiana State University Press, 1979), pp. 441–42; Iza Duffus Hardy, *Between Two Oceans; or, Sketches of American Travel* (London: Hurst and Blackett, 1884), pp. 305–306; *Charleston News and Courier,* December 8, 1874; February 8, March 2, March 3, 1875; February 19, 1876. The negative attitudes some blacks living in Charleston took toward the rural migrants were typical of the tendency among city dwellers in the North and the South during the nineteenth and twentieth centuries to give new arrivals a mixed reception. Leon F. Litwack, *Been in the Storm So Long: The Aftermath of Slavery* (New York: Vintage Books, 1980), pp. 315–16.

83. Litwack, *Been in the Storm So Long,* pp. 513–14; Botume, *First Days,* p. 59; Williamson, *After Slavery,* p. 316.

84. J. H. Rainey to G. M. Johnson, October 5, 1880, cited in Bernard Powers, "Black Charleston: A Social History, 1822–1885" (Ph.D. diss., Northwestern University, 1982), p. 171.

85. Jane Van Allen to Mr. Smith, February 16, 1867, American Missionary Association Papers, Duke University Library, Durham, N.C.

86. Sir George Campbell, *White and Black: The Outcome of a Visit to the United States* (New York: R. Worthington, 1879), p. 325.

87. Powers, *Black Charlestonians,* pp. 185–86.

88. Ibid., p. 185.

89. *Nation* 15, no. 372 (August 15, 1872): 106.

90. Powers, *Black Charlestonians,* p. 186.

91. George P. Rawick, ed., *The American Slave: A Composite Autobiography,* vol. 14, *South Carolina Narratives* (Westport, Conn.: Greenwood Press, 1972), pt. 4, p. 41.

92. Powers, *Black Charlestonians,* p. 186.

93. Ibid.

94. *New York Times,* July 4, 1874.

95. Williamson, *After Slavery,* p. 314.

96. Michael P. Johnson and James L. Roark, eds., *No Chariot Let Down: Charleston's Free People of Color on the Eve of the Civil War* (Chapel Hill: University of North Carolina Press, 1984), pp. 6–7.

97. Bernard Powers estimates that by 1880 the upper class of blacks in Charleston amounted to less than 2 percent of the black population. Powers, *Black Charlestonians,* p. 166.

98. Marszalek, *Diary of Miss Emma Holmes,* pp. 441–42; *Christian Recorder,* September 8, 1866; Powers, *Black Charlestonians,* pp. 219–20; Berlin, *Slaves without Masters,* pp. 388–89.

99. Taylor, *Travail and Triumph,* p. 189; Mamie G. Fields and Karen Fields, *Lemon Swamp and Other Places: A Carolina Memoir* (New York: The Free Press, 1983), pp. 13, 47, 63, 64; Septima P. Clark, *Echo in My Soul* (New York: E. P. Dutton, 1962), p. 18; Carter G. Woodson, *Free Negro Heads of Families in the United States in 1830* (Washington, D.C.: Association for the Study of Negro Life and History, 1925), p. lvii.

100. Williamson, *After Slavery,* p. 316.

101. Foner, *Reconstruction,* pp. 101–102; Joe M. Richardson, "Francis L. Cardozo: Black Educator during Reconstruction," *Journal of Negro Education* 48, no. 1 (Winter 1979): 73–83; Williamson, *After Slavery,* pp. 29, 30, 210, 211, 356, 357, 359, 365, 367, 383, 384; Thomas C. Holt, *Black over White: Negro Political Leadership in South Carolina During Reconstruction* (Urbana: University of Illinois Press, 1977), p. 21.

102. Williamson, *After Slavery,* pp. 312–13.

103. Berlin, *Slaves without Masters,* p. 391.

6. WE MUST HAVE OUR OWN HOUSE OF WORSHIP

1. Arnold H. Taylor, *Travail and Triumph: Black Life and Culture in the South since the Civil War* (Westport, Conn.: Greenwood Press, 1976), p. 143.

2. Charles Joyner, "If You Ain't Got Education: Slave Language and Slave Thought in Antebellum Charleston," in Michael O'Brien and David Moltke-Hansen, eds., *Intellectual Life in Antebellum Charleston* (Knoxville: University of Tennessee Press, 1986), pp. 266–68; Albert S. Thomas, *A Historical Account of the Protestant Episcopal Church in South Carolina, 1820–1957* (Columbia, S.C.: R. L. Bryan Company, 1957), pp. 35–36; *Proceedings of the Meeting in Charleston, S.C., May 13–15, 1845, on the Religious Instruction of the Negroes, Together with the Report of the Committee, and the Address to the Public* (Charleston, S.C.: B. Jenkins, 1845), pp. 9–10; Susan M. Fickling, "Slave-Conversion in South Carolina, 1830–1860" (M.A. thesis, University of South Carolina, 1924), pp. 28–29; Luther P. Jackson, "Religious Instruction of Negroes, 1830–1860, with Special Reference to South Carolina," *Journal of Negro History* 15, no. 1 (January 1930): 72, 111, 112; Andrew E. Murray, *Presbyterians and the Negro: A History* (Philadelphia: Presbyterian Historical Society, 1966), p. 138.

3. Peter Kolchin, *First Freedom: The Responses of Alabama's Blacks to Emancipation and Reconstruction* (Westport, Conn.: Greenwood Press, 1972), p. 108.

4. T. Erskine Clarke, "An Experiment in Paternalism: Presbyterians and Slaves in Charleston, South Carolina," *Journal of Presbyterian History* 53, no. 3 (Fall 1975): 228–30; Donald G. Mathews, "The Methodist Mission to the Slaves, 1829–1844," *Journal of American History* 1, no. 4 (March 1965): 615–31; *Public Proceedings Relating to Calvary Church, and the Religious Instruction of Slaves* (Charleston, S.C.: Miller and Browne, 1850), pp. 3–83; Rev. J. H. Thornwell, *The Rights and the Duties of Masters: Sermon Preached at the Dedication of a Church, Erected in Charleston, South Carolina: For the Benefit and Instruction of the Coloured Population* (Charleston, S.C.: Walker and James, 1850), p. 3; Jesse B. Barber, *Climbing Jacob's Ladder: The Story of the Work of the Presbyterian Church U.S.A. among the Negroes* (New York: Board of National Missions, 1952), p. 28; Fickling, "Slave-Conversion," pp. 29–48; John B. Adger, *My Life and Times, 1810–1899* (Richmond, Va.: The Presbyterian Committee of Publication, 1899), p. 165; Murray, *Presbyterians and the Negro,* p. 60; Jackson, "Religious Instruction," pp. 72–114; Robert F. Durden, "The Establishment of Calvary Protestant Episcopal Church for Negroes in Charleston," *South Carolina Historical Magazine* 65 (April 1964): 63–84.

5. Taylor, *Travail and Triumph,* p. 143; Murray, *Presbyterians and the Negro,* pp. 61–62; George N. Edwards, *A History of the Independent or Congregational Church of Charleston, South Carolina Commonly Known as Circular Church* (Boston: Pilgrim

Press, 1947), p. 86; Durden, "Establishment of Calvary Church," p. 65; J. Carleton Hayden, "Conversion and Control: The Dilemma of Episcopalians in Providing for the Religious Instructions of Slaves, Charleston, South Carolina, 1845–1860," *Historical Magazine of the Protestant Episcopal Church* 40, no. 2 (June 1971): 147.

6. Taylor, *Travail and Triumph*, p. 143.

7. Mathews, "Methodist Mission," p. 616.

8. Joyner, "If You Ain't Got Education," pp. 270–71; C. Eric Lincoln, *Race, Religion, and the Continuing American Dilemma* (New York: Hill and Wang, 1984), pp. 33, 71–72. For an excellent discussion on slave religion in the antebellum South, see Albert J. Raboteau, *Slave Religion: The Invisible Institution in the Antebellum South* (Oxford: Oxford University Press, 1978).

9. Lincoln, *Race, Religion*, pp. 32–33; E. Franklin Frazier, *The Negro Church in America* (New York: Schocken Books, 1974), pp. 31–32.

10. Lincoln, *Race, Religion*, p. 32–33; Taylor, *Travail and Triumph*, p. 143.

11. J. K. Robertson to Mrs. Smythe, June 28, 1865, A. T. Smythe Letters, South Carolina Historical Society, Charleston, S.C., quoted in Joel Williamson, *After Slavery: The Negro in South Carolina during Reconstruction, 1861–1877* (Chapel Hill: University of North Carolina Press, 1965), p. 180.

12. Henry M. Field, *Bright Skies and Dark Shadows* (New York: Charles Scribner's Sons, 1890), p. 114.

13. Kolchin, *First Freedom*, p. 110; Williamson, *After Slavery*, p. 194.

14. Bernard E. Powers, *Black Charlestonians: A Social History, 1822–1885* (Fayetteville: University of Arkansas Press, 1994), pp. 191–92.

15. Ibid., p. 192.

16. Kolchin, *First Freedom*, p. 110; Powers, *Black Charlestonians*, p. 194.

17. For excellent coverage of the Denmark Vesey insurrection, see John Lofton, *Insurrection in South Carolina: The Turbulent World of Denmark Vesey* (Yellow Springs, Ohio: Antioch Press, 1964); and John Lofton, *Denmark Vesey's Revolt: The Slave Plot That Lit a Fuse to Fort Sumter* (Kent, Ohio: Kent State University Press, 1983).

18. Harry V. Richardson, *Dark Salvation: The Story of Methodism As It Developed among Blacks in America* (Garden City, N.Y.: Doubleday, Anchor Press, 1976), p. 193; Wesley J. Gaines, *African Methodism in the South; or, Twenty-Five Years of Freedom* (Chicago: African Press, 1969), pp. 6–7; Taylor, *Travail and Triumph*, p. 146; Francis B. Simkins and Robert H. Woody, *South Carolina during Reconstruction* (Chapel Hill: University of North Carolina Press, 1932), pp. 385–86.

19. Simkins and Woody, *South Carolina during Reconstruction*, p. 386.

20. Clarence E. Walker, *A Rock in a Weary Land: The African Methodist Episcopal Church during the Civil War and Reconstruction* (Baton Rouge: Louisiana State University Press, 1982), pp. 72–73; *Christian Recorder*, June 3, 1865.

21. *Christian Recorder*, June 3, 1865.

22. Powers, *Black Charlestonians*, p. 200; *Charleston Courier*, May 31, 1865.

23. *Christian Recorder*, May 6, 1865.

24. Ibid., February 24, 1866.

25. Simkins and Woody, *South Carolina during Reconstruction*, pp. 386–87.

26. Mamie G. Fields and Karen Fields, *Lemon Swamp and Other Places: A Carolina Memoir* (New York: The Free Press, 1983), p. 35; Warren M. Jenkins, *Steps along the Way: The Origin and Development of the South Carolina Conference of the Central*

Jurisidiction of the Methodist Church (Columbia, S.C.: Socamead Press, 1967), pp. 4–6.

27. Leonard L. Haynes, Jr., *The Negro Community within American Protestantism, 1619–1844* (Boston: Christopher Publishing House, 1953), pp. 65–66; H. Shelton Smith, *In His Image But . . . : Racism in Southern Religion, 1780–1910* (Durham, N.C.: Duke University Press, 1972), pp. 243–44; Powers, *Black Charlestonians,* pp. 210–11; J. Carleton Hayden, "After the War: The Mission and Growth of the Episcopal Church among Blacks in the South, 1865–1877," *Historical Magazine of the Protestant Episcopal Church,* December 1972, pp. 426–27; Stiles Bailey Lines, "Slaves and Churchmen: The Work of the Episcopal Church among Southern Negroes, 1830–1860" (Ph.D. diss., Columbia University, 1960), pp. 2, 13, 405, and preface.

28. Simkins and Woody, *South Carolina during Reconstruction,* pp. 384–85.

29. Williamson, *After Slavery,* p. 199.

30. *Christian Recorder,* September 8, 1866.

31. Powers, *Black Charlestonians,* p. 211.

32. Ibid.; Williamson, *After Slavery,* pp. 199–200; *Christian Recorder,* September 8, 1866.

33. Kolchin, *First Freedom,* p. 109; Eric Foner, *Reconstruction: America's Unfinished Revolution, 1863–1867* (New York: Harper and Row, 1988), p. 89.

34. Minutes of the Southern Baptist Convention of 1866, quoted in Powers, *Black Charlestonians,* p. 191.

35. Taylor, *Travail and Triumph,* p. 145; Smith, *In His Image,* p. 227.

36. Minutes of the Charleston Baptist Association, 1867, p. 32, quoted in Powers, *Black Charlestonians,* p. 191.

37. Simkins and Woody, *South Carolina during Reconstruction,* p. 387.

38. Ibid., p. 387; *Christian Recorder,* October 21, 1865; February 24, 1866.

39. Smith, *In His Image,* pp. 237–38.

40. Simkins and Woody, *South Carolina during Reconstruction,* pp. 384–85, 392; Williamson, *After Slavery,* p. 199.

41. Powers, *Black Charlestonians,* p. 191.

42. Simkins and Woody, *South Carolina during Reconstruction,* pp. 384–85; Williamson, *After Slavery,* p. 199.

43. *Christian Recorder,* August 5, October 14, 1865.

44. Ibid., October 14, 1865.

45. Ibid., June 23, 1866.

46. Fields and Fields, *Lemon Swamp,* pp. 35–36; Jenkins, *Steps along the Way,* p. 6; Rev. W. Lawrence, *A Sketch of the History of the Reorganization of the South Carolina Conference, and of Centenary Church* (Charleston, S.C., 1885), pp. 12–13.

47. Lawrence, *A Sketch of the History,* pp. 12–13.

48. Ibid; *Christian Recorder,* September 8, April 28, 1866.

49. Fields and Fields, *Lemon Swamp,* p. 37.

50. E. J. Adams to Rev. G. Whipple, September 5, 1865, American Missionary Association Papers, Duke University Library, Durham, N.C. (hereafter, AMAP); Haynes, *The Negro Community,* p. 143; Powers, *Black Charlestonians,* p. 214.

51. Richard B. Drake, "The American Missionary and the Southern Negro, 1861–1888" (Ph.D. diss., Emory University, 1957), pp. 119–20; Powers, *Black Charlestonians,* p. 214.

52. Powers, *Black Charlestonians*, p. 214; F. L. Cardozo to Rev. M. E. Strieby, March 17, 1866; E. J. Adams to Rev. G. Whipple, September 5, 1865; S. M. Coles to Rev. M. E. Strieby, May 2, 1876, AMAP.

53. Powers, *Black Charlestonians*, p. 214. For an excellent work of scholarship that explores the fruitless efforts of the Congregationalist church to recruit Southern blacks during the Reconstruction period, see Joe M. Richardson, "The Failure of the American Missionary Association to Expand Congregationalism among Southern Blacks," *Southern Studies* 18, no. 1 (Spring 1979): 51–73. As late as the mid-twentieth century, it was unusual to find more than a handful of blacks in Congregationalist churches. Haynes, *The Negro Community*, p. 143.

54. *Christian Recorder*, June 3, 1865; Walker, *A Rock in a Weary Land*, pp. 73–74.

55. Walker, *A Rock in a Weary Land*, pp. 73–74.

56. *Christian Recorder*, June 3, 1865.

57. Walker, *A Rock in a Weary Land*, pp. 92–93; *Christian Recorder*, May 19, 1866.

58. Walker, *A Rock in a Weary Land*, p. 90.

59. Ibid., p. 90; *Christian Recorder*, July 8, 1865. Ironically, it was actually the M.E. Church North that discriminated on the basis of race. In Charleston, Rev. T. W. Lewis reserved New Bethel Church for whites, and if blacks went there they had to sit in the galleries as they had done during the antebellum years. Lewis designated Old Bethel Church for blacks. Walker, *A Rock in a Weary Land*, p. 74; *Christian Recorder*, June 3, 1865.

60. Walker, *A Rock in a Weary Land*, p. 74; *Christian Recorder*, June 3, 1865.

61. Ralph E. Morrow, *Northern Methodism and Reconstruction* (East Lansing: Michigan State University Press, 1956), p. 136.

62. August Meier and Elliott Rudwick, *From Plantation to Ghetto: An Interpretative History of American Negroes*, 3d ed. (New York: Hill and Wang, 1976), p. 142.

63. *Christian Recorder*, September 8, 1866.

64. Powers, *Black Charlestonians*, p. 215.

65. Ibid.

66. *Christian Recorder*, September 8, 1866. At the same time, it should come as no surprise that members of St. Mark's Church would apply for admission to the Diocesan Convention in 1875. Largely for racial reasons, however, they were refused entrance. Smith, *In His Image*, pp. 246–47; *Report upon the Application of St. Mark's Church (Coloured) To Be Admitted into Union with This Convention* (Charleston, S.C.: Walker, Evans and Cogswell, Printers, 1876), pp. 1–11; *Diocese of South Carolina in Convention, 1876 Report on Admission of St. Mark's* (Charleston, S.C.: Walker, Evans and Cogswell, 1876), pp. 3–22.

67. *Christian Recorder*, September 8, 1866; Powers, *Black Charlestonians*, p. 214.

68. Powers, *Black Charlestonians*, pp. 214–15; *Christian Recorder*, September 8, 1866.

69. Frazier, *Negro Church in America*, pp. 36–37; Taylor, *Travail and Triumph*, pp. 152–53; Powers, *Black Charlestonians*, pp. 216–17.

70. Thos. W. Cardozo to Rev. S. Hunt, June 23, 1865, AMAP; Clara M. DeBoer, "The Role of Afro-Americans in the Origins and Work of the American Missionary Association, 1839–1877" (Ph.D. diss., Rutgers University, 1973), p. 389.

71. Leon F. Litwack, *Been in the Storm So Long: The Aftermath of Slavery* (New York: Vintage Books, 1980), p. 467; George P. Rawick, ed., *The American Slave: A Composite*

Autobiography, vol. 2, *South Carolina Narratives* (Westport, Conn.: Greenwood Press, 1972), pt. 1, pp. 35–36.

72. *Charleston Courier,* March 26, 1867.

73. *Christian Recorder,* August 5, 1865.

74. Ibid., June 29, 1867.

75. Frazier, *The Negro Church in America,* pp. 39–40; Taylor, *Travail and Triumph,* p. 155; Powers, *Black Charlestonians,* p. 217; Minutes of Morris Street Baptist Church, January 8, 12, February 18, March 6, August 6, December 3, 1866; January 21, March 21, April 1, May 12, June 3, 1867, Avery Research Center for African-American History and Culture, College of Charleston, Charleston, S.C.

76. Minutes of Morris Street Baptist Church, March 6, April 2, July 9, October, November 8, 1866; April 1, 1867.

77. Frazier, *The Negro Church in America,* p. 40; Taylor, *Travail and Triumph,* p. 155; Powers, *Black Charlestonians,* p. 217; Minutes of Morris Street Baptist Church, May 12, 1867.

78. Taylor, *Travail and Triumph,* pp. 155–56.

79. Frazier, *The Negro Church in America,* p. 50.

80. Taylor, *Travail and Triumph,* pp. 156–57.

81. J. E. Hilary Skinner, *After the Storm; or, Jonathan and His Neighbours in 1865–1866* (London: Richard Bentley, 1866) 2:338; W. D. Harris, Teachers Monthly School Report, June 1868, Superintendent of Education, South Carolina, Teachers Monthly School Reports, Box 27, Bureau of Refugees, Freedmen, and Abandoned Land Records, National Archives, Washington, D.C.; James D. Anderson, *The Education of Blacks in the South, 1860–1935* (Chapel Hill: University of North Carolina Press, 1988), p. 8; *Christian Recorder,* September 29, 1866; *Charleston Courier,* June 28, 1867; Powers, *Black Charlestonians,* pp. 139, 146.

82. Carter G. Woodson, *The History of the Negro Church,* 2d ed. (Washington, D.C.: Associated Publishers, 1921), p. 273; Taylor, *Travail and Triumph,* p. 156; Frazier, *The Negro Church in America,* pp. 40–41.

83. Powers, *Black Charlestonians,* p. 217.

84. Minutes of Morris Street Baptist Church, January 12, 1866.

85. Powers, *Black Charlestonians,* pp. 217–18.

86. Frank [Francis] A. Rollin, *The Life and Public Services of Martin R. Delany, Sub-Assistant Commissioner Bureau Relief of Refugees, Freedmen, and of Abandoned Lands, and Late Major 104th U.S. Colored Troops* (Boston: Lee and Shepard, 1868), pp. 194–97; Williamson, *After Slavery,* p. 47; William C. Hine, "Frustration, Factionalism, and Failure: Black Political Leadership and the Republican Party in Reconstruction Charleston, 1865–1877" (Ph.D. diss., Kent State University, 1979), p. 33; *Charleston Courier,* April 3, 1865; Elizabeth H. Botume, *First Days amongst the Contrabands* (Boston: Lee and Shepard, 1893), pp. 172–73; Rupert Sargeant Holland, ed., *Letters and Diary of Laura M. Towne: Written from the Sea Islands of South Carolina, 1862–1884* (Cambridge, Mass.: The Riverside Press, 1912), p. 159; Benjamin Quarles, *The Negro in the Civil War* (New York: Russell and Russell, 1968), pp. 336–39.

87. *South Carolina Leader,* December 24, 1865; *Charleston Courier,* April 29, May 12, 1865; February 15, 1867.

88. *Christian Recorder,* August 8, 1865.

89. Peggy Lamson, *The Glorious Failure: Black Congressman Robert Brown Elliott and the Reconstruction in South Carolina* (New York: W. W. Norton, 1973), pp. 34–36; Simkins and Woody, *South Carolina During Reconstruction*, p. 55; Hine, "Frustration, Factionalism, and Failure," pp. 41–42.

90. *Charleston Courier,* March 22, 1865; Taylor, *Travail and Triumph,* p. 156.

91. *Charleston Courier,* March 27, 1867.

92. Powers, *Black Charlestonians,* p. 223; Walker, *A Rock in a Weary Land,* pp. 121–22; Williamson, *After Slavery,* pp. 206–207.

93. *Charleston News and Courier,* July 10, 1876.

94. Powers, *Black Charlestonians,* pp. 223–24; Williamson, *After Slavery,* pp. 206–207.

95. Powers, *Black Charlestonians,* pp. 223–24.

96. Rev. R. H. Cain to General Charles Devens, December 29, 1865, Department of the South Papers, National Archives, Washington, D.C. (hereafter, DSP).

97. Ibid.

98. Rev. R. H. Cain to R. K. Scott, November 14, 1867, DSP.

7. FREEDOM IS A CONSTANT STRUGGLE

1. Melinda Meek Hennessey, "Racial Violence during Reconstruction: The 1876 Riots in Charleston and Cainhoy," *South Carolina Historical Magazine* 86, no. 2 (April 1985): 101–102; Melinda Meek Hennessey, "To Live and Die in Dixie: Reconstruction Race Riots in the South" (Ph.D. diss., Kent State University, 1978), pp. 345–46. Racial violence during the Reconstruction period was intense throughout the South, and both blacks and whites were victims. For contemporary reports, see *New York Times,* January 28, April 23, May 10, 13, 16, 17, 18, 28, 1867; February 15, March 19, 1868; *New York Daily Tribune,* June 21, 1866; May 15, 16, 17, 24, 1867; *Charleston Courier,* March 10, April 24, 1866; September 30, 1867; January 16, 1868; O. Brown to Gen. O. O. Howard, June 29, 1865, Assistant Commissioner Letters Received, Bureau of Refugees, Freedmen, and Abandoned Lands Records, National Archives, Washington, D.C. (hereafter, FBP); Alrutheus Ambush Taylor, *The Negro in South Carolina during the Reconstruction* (New York: Russell and Russell, 1969), pp. 21–22; Annual Report of Outrages against Freed People by Whites for 1865, 1866, FBP; General A. Williams to Major E. S. Deane, December 31, 1866, FBP; John A. Carpenter, "Atrocities in the Reconstruction Period," *Journal of Negro History* 47, no. 4 (October 1962): 234–47; David M. Chalmers, *Hooded Americanism: The First Century of the Ku Klux Klan* (New York: Doubleday, 1965); Allen W. Trelease, *White Terror: The Ku Klux Klan Conspiracy and Southern Reconstruction* (New York: Harper and Row, 1971); Herbert Shapiro, "Afro-American Responses to Race Violence during Reconstruction," *Science and Society* 36, no. 2 (Summer 1972): 158–70; and George C. Rable, *But There Was No Peace: The Role of Violence in the Politics of Reconstruction* (Athens: University of Georgia Press, 1984).

2. *Charleston Courier,* December 29, 1865.

3. *Charleston Daily Republican,* March 28, 1871.

4. *Charleston News and Courier,* May 28, 1873.

5. Ibid., January 27, 1873.

6. Ibid., May 22, 1874; August 28, 1876.

7. Ibid., August 9, 1876.

8. Quoted in Francis B. Simkins and Robert H. Woody, *South Carolina during Reconstruction* (Chapel Hill: University of North Carolina Press, 1932), p. 67.

9. *Charleston Courier,* April 9, 1867; *Charleston Daily News,* April 9, 1867.

10. *Charleston Courier,* November 1, 1867.

11. *Charleston Daily News,* August 28, 1869.

12. *Charleston News and Courier,* July 4, 1877.

13. John F. Marszalek, ed., *The Diary of Miss Emma Holmes* (Baton Rouge: Louisiana State University Press, 1979), p. 455; Leon F. Litwack, *Been in the Storm So Long: The Aftermath of Slavery* (New York: Vintage Books, 1980), p. 147.

14. Rosser H. Taylor, *Antebellum South Carolina: A Social and Cultural History* (Chapel Hill: University of North Carolina Press, 1942), pp. 176–77.

15. *Charleston Daily News,* July 4, 1866; *Charleston Courier,* July 4, 6, 10, 1866.

16. Arney Robinson Childs, ed., *The Private Journal of Henry William Ravenel, 1859–1887* (Columbia: University of South Carolina Press, 1947), pp. 288–89; John Bennett to Gen. O. O. Howard, November 10, 1866, Department of the South Papers, National Archives, Washington, D.C. (hereafter, DSP).

17. *Charleston News and Courier,* November 19, 1877.

18. *Charleston Daily News,* July 9, 1866.

19. Bernard E. Powers, *Black Charlestonians: A Social History, 1822–1885* (Fayetteville: University of Arkansas Press, 1994), pp. 77–78; Col. William Gurney to Major E. H. Little, May 13, 1865; Col. William Gurney to Capt. R. Allison, May 14, 1865; Col. William Gurney to James Redpath, May 15, 1865; Col. William Gurney to Major W. L. M. Burger, May 17, 1865, DSP.

20. *New York Times,* July 24, 1865.

21. *Charleston Courier,* July 10, 1865; *New York Times,* July 16, 24, 1865; W. T. Bennett to James Redpath, July 12, 1865, FBP; Brig. General W. T. Bennett to Major W. L. M. Burger, July 13, 1865, DSP.

22. Hennessey, "Racial Violence," p. 102; *New York Times,* July 24, 1865.

23. *Charleston Courier,* July 12, 13, 14, 1865; *New York Times,* July 24, 1865.

24. *New York Times,* July 24, 1865; Brig. General W. T. Bennett to Major W. L. M. Burger, July 13, 1865; Capt. Charles Clinferman to Capt. Parker, July 14, 1865, DSP.

25. Hennessey, "Racial Violence," p. 102; *Charleston Daily News,* June 25, 1866; *Charleston Courier,* June 25, 1866.

26. Hennessey, "Racial Violence," p. 102; *Charleston Courier,* July 6, 1866.

27. Childs, *Private Journal,* p. 287; *Charleston Courier,* June 29, June 30, 1866; *Charleston Daily News,* June 26, July 6, 1866.

28. *Charleston Daily News,* June 26, 1866. For a complete record of testimony concerning the riot, see *Charleston Courier,* June 30, July 6, 1866; Report of the Brig. Major E. W. Everett, July 1866, DSP.

29. *Charleston Courier,* July 9, 1866.

30. E. H. Botume, *First Days amongst the Contrabands* (Boston: Lee and Shepard, 1893), p. 201; *Charleston Courier,* October 18, 1866.

31. Herbert Aptheker, *To Be Free: Studies in American Negro History* (New York: International Publishers, 1948), p. 160.

32. Ibid., p. 160.

33. William C. Hine, "The 1867 Charleston Streetcar Sit-Ins: A Case of Successful Black Protest," *South Carolina Historical Magazine* 77, no. 2 (April 1976): 111, 113.

34. Litwack, *Been in the Storm So Long*, p. 264.

35. *Charleston Courier,* March 27, 1867; Hine, "Charleston Streetcar Sit-Ins," p. 111.

36. *Charleston Courier,* March 27, 1867; *New York Times,* April 2, 1867.

37. *Charleston Courier,* March 27, 1867.

38. Ibid.

39. Hine, "Charleston Streetcar Sit-Ins," p. 112.

40. *Charleston Daily News,* April 2, 1867; *New York Daily Tribune,* April 2, 1867; *New York Times,* April 2, 5, 1867.

41. *New York Times,* April 5, 1867; *Charleston Daily News,* April 2, 1867.

42. Litwack, *Been in the Storm So Long*, p. 264.

43. *New York Times,* April 20, 1867.

44. Powers, *Black Charlestonians,* p. 235; Litwack, *Been in the Storm So Long,* p. 264; Hine, "Charleston Streetcar Sit-Ins," p. 114; John T. Trowbridge, *A Picture of the Desolated States and the Work of Restoration 1865–1868* (Hartford, Conn.: L. Stebbins, 1868), pp. 630–31; *Charleston Daily News,* May 4, 1867; *New York Daily Tribune,* May 4, 1867. Blacks in other cities also protested against the discriminatory policies of railway and streetcar companies. For coverage of their efforts to integrate streetcars in Richmond, Virginia, and Mobile, Alabama, see *New York Times,* April 21, 24, 1867; May 2, 8, 9, 1867.

45. Powers, *Black Charlestonians,* p. 235; Hine, "Charleston Streetcar Sit-Ins," p. 114; Joel Williamson, *After Slavery: The Negro in South Carolina during Reconstruction, 1861–1877* (Chapel Hill: University of North Carolina Press, 1965), p. 283.

46. *New York Daily Tribune,* May 6, 1867.

47. Hine, "Charleston Streetcar Sit-Ins," p. 111.

48. See, for example, editions of the *Charleston Courier* for the years 1866–1868; Whitelaw Reid, *After the War: A Southern Tour, May 1, 1865, to May 1, 1866* (Cincinnati: Moore, Wilstach, and Baldwin, 1866), p. 585; and *Charleston Daily Republican,* April 20, 29, 1870.

49. Williamson, *After Slavery,* pp. 340–44.

50. Powers, *Black Charlestonians,* p. 230.

51. Ibid.

52. Childs, *Private Journal,* p. 326.

53. *New York Times,* July 30, 1869.

54. *Charleston Daily News,* July 27, 1869; *New York Times,* July 28, 30, 1869.

55. *New York Times,* July 30, 1869.

56. Ibid.

57. *Charleston News and Courier,* July 10, 18, 1876.

58. Ibid., July 18, 1876.

59. Hennessey, "Racial Violence," p. 104; *Charleston News and Courier,* September 4, 6, 7, 1876.

60. Hennessey, "Racial Violence," pp. 104–105; *Charleston News and Courier,* September 7, 8, 1876.

61. *New York Times,* September 8, 1876.

62. Hennessey, "Racial Violence," p. 106; *New York Times,* September 8, 1876; *Charleston News and Courier,* September 7, 8, 9, 11, 12, 1876.

63. Myrta L. Avary, *Dixie after the War* (New York: Doubleday, Page and Company, 1906), p. 362; Williamson, *After Slavery,* p. 272.

64. *Charleston News and Courier,* September 7, 8, 9, 1876; Hennessey, "Racial Violence," p. 105.

65. *Charleston News and Courier,* September 9, 11, 1876.

66. Avary, *Dixie after the War,* p. 362.

67. Ibid.

68. Allen B. Ballard, *One More Day's Journey: The Story of a Family and a People* (New York: McGraw-Hill, 1984), p. 112; Williamson, *After Slavery,* p. 272.

69. Hennessey, "Racial Violence," p. 107.

70. *New York Times,* October 18, 1876.

71. Hennessey, "Racial Violence," p. 107; *New York Times,* October 18, 1876.

72. *New York Times,* October 18, 21, 31, 1876; *Charleston News and Courier,* October 18, 1876.

73. *Charleston News and Courier,* October 18, 1876.

74. Ibid.; Hennessey, "Racial Violence," pp. 108–109.

75. *New York Times,* October 18, 1876.

76. Hennessey, "Racial Violence," p. 110.

77. D. E. Huger Smith, *A Charlestonian's Recollections, 1846–1913* (Charleston, S.C.: Carolina Art Association, 1950), p. 154.

78. Hennessey, "Racial Violence," pp. 110–11; *New York Times,* November 9, 1876; *Charleston News and Courier,* November 9, 10, 21, 1876. For an extensive account of the November 8, 1876, Charleston riot, see Captain Royal T. Frank to Major Blackswith and others, November 18, 1876, DSP. Political violence occurred between blacks and whites during the Reconstruction period in other parts of South Carolina and throughout the South. See, for example, *Charleston Courier,* August 29, 30, 1867; November 9, 1876; *New York Times,* April 19, May 15, 1867; February 5, 1868; July 4, 1869; and *Charleston News and Courier,* November 9, 1876.

79. Hennessey, "Racial Violence," pp. 111–12.

EPILOGUE

1. William C. Hine, "Frustration, Factionalism, and Failure: Black Political Leadership and the Republican Party in Reconstruction Charleston, 1865–1877" (Ph.D. diss., Kent State University, 1979), p. 452.

2. Thomas Holt, "Negro State Legislators in South Carolina during Reconstruction," in Howard N. Rabinowitz, ed., *Southern Black Leaders of the Reconstruction Era* (Urbana: University of Illinois Press, 1982), pp. 236–37; Hine, "Frustration, Factionalism, and Failure," p. 452.

3. Hine, "Frustration, Factionalism, and Failure," p. 452.

4. William C. Hine, "Black Politicians in Reconstruction Charleston, South Carolina: A Collective Study," *Journal of Southern History* 49, no. 4 (November 1983): 559.

5. Hine, "Frustration, Factionalism, and Failure," p. 452.

6. Ibid., p. 453; Nell I. Painter, "Martin R. Delany: Elitism and Black Nationalism," in Leon F. Litwack and August Meier, eds., *Black Leaders of the Nineteenth Century* (Urbana: University of Illinois Press, 1988), pp. 165–68; Edmund L. Drago, *Initiative, Paternalism, and Race Relations: Charleston's Avery Normal Institute* (Athens: University of Georgia Press, 1990), p. 114.

7. Hine, "Frustration, Factionalism, and Failure," pp. 453–54.

8. Ibid., p. 455.

9. Ibid.

10. Thomas Holt, *Black over White: Negro Political Leadership in South Carolina during Reconstruction* (Urbana: University of Illinois Press, 1977), p. 124.

11. Ibid., pp. 123, 125.

12. Walter J. Fraser, Jr., *Charleston! Charleston! The History of a Southern City* (Columbia: University of South Carolina Press, 1989), p. 300; William L. Barney, *Battleground for the Union: The Era of the Civil War and Reconstruction, 1848–1877* (Englewood Cliffs, N.J.: Prentice-Hall, 1990), pp. 330–31; Drago, *Initiative, Paternalism, and Race Relations*, p. 80; Allen C. Guelzo, *The Crisis of the American Republic: A History of the Civil War and Reconstruction Era* (New York: St. Martin's Press, 1995), pp. 398–99; Eric Foner, *Reconstruction: America's Unfinished Revolution, 1863–1877* (New York: Harper and Row, 1988), pp. 579–82; Holt, *Black over White*, pp. 173–75.

13. Fraser, *Charleston! Charleston!* pp. 300–301.

14. Ibid., pp. 301–302, 308; Painter, "Martin R. Delany," p. 169; Foner, *Reconstruction*, pp. 607–608.

15. Fraser, *Charleston! Charleston!* pp. 307–308, 310.

16. Drago, *Initiative, Paternalism, and Race Relations*, pp. 114–15.

17. Ibid., p. 80.

18. Fraser, *Charleston! Charleston!* pp. 294–95.

19. Foner, *Reconstruction*, p. 535; Barney, *Battleground for the Union*, pp. 307–308; Bernard Powers, *Black Charlestonians: A Social History, 1822–1885* (Fayetteville: University of Arkansas Press, 1994), pp. 109–10, 120–21.

20. Loren Schweninger, *Black Property Owners in the South, 1790–1915* (Urbana: University of Illinois Press, 1990), pp. 182–83.

21. Victor Ullman, *Martin R. Delany: The Beginnings of Black Nationalism* (Boston: Beacon Press, 1971), p. 422.

22. Powers, *Black Charlestonians*, pp. 121–22.

23. Schweninger, *Black Property Owners*, pp. 150–51.

24. Foner, *Reconstruction*, p. 602.

25. Barney, *Battleground for the Union*, p. 308.

26. Tom W. Shick and Don H. Doyle, "The South Carolina Phosphate Boom and the Stillbirth of the New South, 1867–1920," *South Carolina Historical Magazine* 86, no. 1 (January 1985): 15.

27. Fraser, *Charleston! Charleston!* pp. 310–11; Powers, *Black Charlestonians*, p. 120.

28. Holt, *Black over White*, pp. 152.

29. Fraser, *Charleston! Charleston!* pp. 296–97, 307–308.

30. Foner, *Reconstruction*, p. 595.

31. Ibid., pp. 586–87.

32. Ibid., pp. 602–603.
33. Holt, *Black over White*, p. 153.
34. Foner, *Reconstruction*, p. 602.
35. Ibid.
36. Ibid.
37. Holt, "Negro Legislators in South Carolina," p. 241.
38. Foner, *Reconstruction*, p. 602.

BIBLIOGRAPHICAL ESSAY

This essay includes only the most significant sources I have used. I have chosen not to list every source in a formal bibliography, because most of my sources are cited in the Notes with full bibliographical details and often with commentary as well.

The private manuscript collections of white Southerners provide useful details about the living conditions of freedmen and social, political, and economic conditions in postwar Charleston and South Carolina. Among the most helpful were the Ellison Capers Papers and the A. L. Taveau Papers in Perkins Library at Duke University in Durham, North Carolina; the Elias Horry Deas Papers in the South Carolinian Library, University of South Carolina, Columbia; the Caroline Gilman Letters, A. T. Smythe Letters, and Jacob Schirmer Diary at the South Carolina Historical Society in Charleston; and the Elliott-Gonzales Papers, Gregorie-Elliott Papers, Wilmot S. Holmes Collection, Gabriel Manigault Papers, and N. R. Middleton Papers in the Southern Historical Collection at the University of North Carolina in Chapel Hill.

Population schedules of the manuscript censuses for 1850, 1860, and 1870 provided valuable material for studying residential, migration, and work-behavior patterns and such details of family relations as household composition, size of family, and naming patterns. These returns, available on microfilm in the National Archives in Washington, D.C., list each individual's age, color (white, mulatto, or black), gender, occupation, real property owned, personal property owned, literacy, and state of birth. Although the accuracy of returns depends on the skill and interest of numerous census takers and therefore undoubtedly contain some errors, they still provide the best overall picture of the population. A more detailed picture of residential patterns in Charleston at the beginning of the Civil War can be found in Frederick A. Ford, *Census of the City of Charleston, South Carolina, for the Year 1861, Illustrated by Statistical Tables, Prepared under the Authority of the City Council* (Charleston, S.C.: Evans and Cogswell, 1861). This is a city-commissioned census that is on microfilm at the South Carolina Historical Society in Charleston.

Published federal census data, also housed in the National Archives and scattered throughout the country in university libraries, supplements the manuscript census data. The published censuses helped to establish migration and residential patterns for 1850, 1860, and 1870 and provided mortality and crime figures, as well as occupation, property ownership, color, gender, state of birth, age, and literacy for 1860, 1870, 1890, and 1900. The most significant of these returns for this study were U.S. Bureau of the Census, *A Compendium of the Seventh Census of 1850* (Washington, D.C., 1854); U.S. Bureau of the Census, *The Statistics of the Population of the U.S. in 1870* (Washington, D.C., 1873); and U.S. Bureau of the Census, *Twelfth Census of the U.S. Population of 1900,* vol. 1 (Washington, D.C., 1901).

The extensive Records of the Bureau of Refugees, Freedmen and Abandoned Lands, Record Group 105, in the National Archives in Washington, D.C., describe local conditions pertaining to education, economics, politics, social life, and race relations. Also in the National Archives are the Department of the South Papers, Record Group 393, which provide invaluable insight into the civil affairs of freedmen, and Records of the Freedmen's Savings Bank, 1865–1874, Record Group 101. The bank records include personal data about depositors in Charleston and at other branches. Most depositor cards list residence, complexion, names of family members, and name of employer or occupation, along with signatures. Some early records also include the former slavemaster's name. These records helped to establish family relationships and to illuminate attitudes within families.

The American Missionary Association papers, in Perkins Library at Duke University in Durham, North Carolina, contain invaluable commentary on local conditions, race relations, and the interrelationships of missionaries with freedmen and with one another, especially in the immediate postwar period. These papers proved of paramount importance in analyzing the growth of institutions such as churches and schools in the black community.

Although black source material for this study is limited, a large collection of slave testimony recorded as a part of the Federal Writers' Project in the 1930s is available. The Federal Writers' Project interviews are reproduced in George P. Rawick, *The American Slave: A Composite Autobiography,* 19 vols. and supplements (Westport, Conn.: Greenwood Press, 1972). Slave narratives are also published in John W. Blassingame, ed., *Slave Testimony: Two Centuries of Letters, Speeches, Interviews, and Autobiographies* (Baton Rouge: Louisiana State University Press, 1977), and Norman R. Yetman, ed., *Life under the Peculiar Institution: Selections from the Slave Narrative Collection* (New York: Holt, Rhinehart and Winston, 1970). These slave narratives reveal the feelings and attitudes of former slaves toward wealthy blacks and the white population and are essential in understanding the relationship between former Charlestonian slaves and rural blacks who migrated to Charleston in the immediate postwar period. Moreover, they provide a picture of black economic, social, and religious life during the antebellum period.

NEWSPAPERS AND MAGAZINES

The local newspapers most useful for this study were the *Charleston Courier* (1865–1872), the *Charleston News and Courier* (1873–1878), and the *Charleston Daily News* (1866–1869). The *Charleston Daily Republican,* somewhat slanted toward the Republican party line, provided a useful counterweight to these largely Democratic papers. National periodicals and newspapers, including the *American Missionary Magazine* (1866, 1870), the *Christian Recorder* (1865–1867), *Nation* (1872), *National Freedman* (1865), and the *New York Daily Tribune* (1866–1867), the *New York Tribune* (1865, 1869, 1871), and the *New York Times* (1864–1865, 1867, 1869, 1874, 1876), also helped balance the perspectives of the local city dailies and were key sources of information on the daily economic, political, social, religious, and educational activities of freedmen. Most of them are housed at the Library of Congress in Washington, D.C.

PUBLISHED CONTEMPORARY ACCOUNTS

Published travel accounts, letters, memoirs, journals, and diaries by Northerners and Europeans who made excursions into the South during the period of this study are filled with comments on relations between blacks and whites and on the social and economic conditions and everyday lives of slaves and free blacks. Travel accounts are useful in ascertaining how former slaves perceived their relations with whites and how freedmen interacted with the wealthier class of blacks. Among the most insightful travel accounts that deal with racial and intraracial relations in Charleston and its environs during the antebellum period are Fredrika Bremer, *The Homes of the New World: Impressions of America,* 2 vols. (New York: Harper and Brothers, 1854); J. Benwell, *An Englishman's Travels in America: His Observations of Life and Manners in the Free and Slave States* (London: Binns and Goodwin, 1853); Adam Hodgson, *Letters from North America Written During a Tour in the United States and Canada,* 2 vols. (London: A. Constable and Company, 1824); Rev. G. Lewis, *Impressions of America and the American Churches* (New York: Negro Universities Press, 1968); Sir Charles Lyell, *Travels in North America in the Years 1841–42,* 2 vols. (New York: Wiley and Putnam, 1845); James Stuart, *Three Years in North America,* vol. 2 (Edinburgh:

Robert Cadell and Company, 1833); and James Redpath, *The Roving Editor; or, Talks with Slaves in Southern States* (New York: A. B. Burdick, 1859). The best travel accounts of the economic, social, and political activities of blacks during emancipation and Reconstruction are Sidney Andrews, *The South since the War as Shown by Fourteen Weeks of Travel and Observation in Georgia and the Carolinas* (Boston: Ticknor and Fields, 1866); Whitelaw Reid, *After the War: A Southern Tour, May 1, 1865 to May 1, 1866* (Cincinnati: Moore, Wilstach, and Baldwin, 1866); J. E. Hilary Skinner, *After the Storm; or, Jonathan and His Neighbours in 1865–1866* (London: Richard Bentley, 1866); Carl Schurz, *Report on the Condition of the South* (reprint, New York: Arno Press and the New York Times, 1969); J. H. Kennaway, *On Sherman's Track; or, The South after the War* (London: Seeley, Jackson, and Halliday, 1867); Robert Somers, *The Southern States since the War, 1870–1871* (reprint, Tuscaloosa: University of Alabama Press, 1965); and John T. Trowbridge, *The South: A Tour of Its Battle-Fields and Ruined Cities, a Journey through the Desolated States, and Talks with the People* (Hartford, Conn.: L. Stebbins, 1866). Diaries, journals, memoirs, and letters written by Northern whites who moved to the South as well as by white and black South Carolinians round out the picture provided by the writings of travelers to the South. The best of these are John W. Alvord, *Letters from the South Relating to the Condition of the Freedmen Addressed to Major General O. O. Howard* (Washington, D.C.: Howard University Press, 1870); Arney Robinson Childs, ed., *The Private Journal of Henry William Ravenel, 1859–1887* (Columbia: University of South Carolina Press, 1947); Elizabeth Hyde Botume, *First Days Amongst the Contrabands* (Boston: Lee and Shepard Publishers, 1893); Mamie Garvin Fields and Karen Fields, *Lemon Swamp and Other Places: A Carolina Memoir* (New York: The Free Press, 1983); Rupert Sargent Holland, ed., *Letters and Diary of Laura M. Towne: Written from the Sea Islands of South Carolina, 1862–1884* (Cambridge, Mass.: The Riverside Press, 1912); Septima Clark, *Echo in My Soul* (New York: E. P. Dutton, 1962); John F. Marszalek, ed., *The Diary of Miss Emma Holmes* (Baton Rouge: Louisiana State University Press, 1979); Elizabeth Ware Pearson, ed., *Letters from Port Royal, 1862–1868* (New York: Arno Press and the New York Times, 1969); D. E. Smith, *A Charlestonian's Recollections, 1846–1913* (Charleston, S.C.: Carolina Art Association, 1950); Daniel E. Huger Smith, Alice R. Huger Smith, and Arney R. Childs, eds., *Mason Smith Family Letters, 1860–1868* (Columbia: University of South Carolina Press, 1950); Frank [Francis] A. Rollin, *Life and Public Services of Martin R. Delany, Sub-Assistant Commissioner, Bureau Relief of Refugees, Freedmen, and of Abandoned Lands, and Late Major 104th U.S. Colored Troops* (Boston: Lee and Shepard, 1868); and C. Vann Woodward, ed., *Mary Chesnut's Civil War* (New Haven: Yale University Press, 1981).

THESES AND DISSERTATIONS

The most up-to-date study of black Charlestonians during the Reconstruction period is Bernard E. Powers, "Black Charleston: A Social History, 1822–1885" (Ph.D. diss., Northwestern University, 1982), subsequently published under the title *Black Charlestonians: A Social History, 1822–1885* (Fayetteville: University of Arkansas Press, 1994). This work contains invaluable bibliographical data. William C. Hine, "Frustration, Factionalism, and Failure: Black Political Leadership and the Republican Party in Reconstruction Charleston, 1865–1877" (Ph.D. diss., Kent State University, 1979), provides important material on the political activities of blacks in Charleston, particularly those who were members of the Republican Party. Walter B. Hill, "Family, Life, and Work Culture: Black Charleston, South Carolina, 1880 to 1910" (Ph.D. diss., University of Maryland at College Park, 1989), is an excellent source on black family structure. Melinda Meek Hennessey, "To Live and Die in Dixie: Reconstruction Race Riots in the South" (Ph.D. diss., Kent State University, 1978), is a superb study of race riots in the South during Reconstruction. Horace E. Fitchett, "The Free Negro in Charleston, South Carolina" (Ph.D. diss., University of Chicago, 1950), is a provocative piece of scholarship on free blacks and, though dated, remains a solid work on the subject. Josephine W. Martin, "The Educational Efforts of the Major Freedmen's Aid Societies and the Freedmen's Bureau in South Carolina, 1862–1870" (Ph.D. diss., University of South Carolina, 1971), chronicles the educational activities of aid societies and the Freedmen's Bureau in South Carolina, with a sizable amount of attention given to Charleston. It also emphasizes the zeal for education exhibited by numerous blacks. Michael Anthony Cooke, "The Health of Blacks during Reconstruction, 1862–1870" (Ph.D. diss., University of Maryland at College Park, 1983), shines some much needed light on the important question of the health status of blacks during Reconstruction. Two master's theses undertaken at the University of South Carolina, Susan M. Fickling, "Slave-Conversion in South Carolina, 1830–1860" (1924), and Burchill R. Moore, "A History of the Negro Public Schools of Charleston, South Carolina, 1867–1942" (1942), provide helpful information on the religious and educational activities of blacks.

GENERAL WORKS

Herbert Gutman, *The Black Family in Slavery and Freedom, 1750–1925* (New York: Vintage Books, 1976), is still the most thorough work on the black family during slavery and emancipation. Like other studies of slavery that were particularly useful for this project, it emphasizes the strength of the black family, despite the brutality and destructiveness of slavery. These other studies include John Blassingame, *The Slave Community: Plantation Life in the Antebellum South* (New York: Oxford University Press, 1979); Eugene Genovese, *Roll, Jordan, Roll: The World the Slaves Made* (New York: Pantheon Books, 1974); Robert W. Fogel and Stanley L. Engerman, *Time on the Cross: The Economics of American Negro Slavery* (Boston: Little, Brown, 1974); and Nathan Huggins, *Black Odyssey: The Afro-American Ordeal in Slavery* (New York: Pantheon Books, 1977). Two excellent works on urban slavery are Richard Wade, *Slavery in the Cities: The South, 1820–1860* (New York: Oxford University Press, 1964), and Claudia Dale Goldin, *Urban Slavery in the American South, 1820–1860* (Chicago: University of Chicago Press, 1976). Robert Starobin, *Industrial Slavery in the Old South* (New York: Oxford University Press, 1970), chronicles the horrible conditions of life for the slaves who worked in industry. Norrece T. Jones, Jr., *Born a Child of Freedom, Yet a Slave: Mechanisms of Control and Strategies of Resistance in Antebellum South Carolina* (London and Hanover, Conn.: Wesleyan University Press, 1990), details the various strategies of resistance employed by blacks in antebellum South Carolina.

The definitive work on free blacks in the South is Ira Berlin, *Slaves without Masters: The Free Negro in the Antebellum South* (New York: Pantheon Books, 1974). Marina Wikramanayake, *A World in Shadow: The Free Black in Antebellum South Carolina* (Columbia: University of South Carolina Press, 1973), is a superb study that illuminates the tenuous position occupied by Southern free blacks. Robert L. Harris, Jr., "Charleston's Free Afro-American Elite: The Brown Fellowship Society and the Humane Brotherhood," *South Carolina Historical Magazine* 82, no. 4 (October 1981): 289–310, explores the issue of color consciousness within the free black elite of Charleston and points out that among the elite blacks, those with dark complexions could not become members of the Brown Fellowship, a social group organized by the mulatto elite. Thus, they formed their own social group, the Humane Brotherhood. Michael Johnson and James Roark, eds., *No Chariot Let Down: Charleston's Free People of Color on the Eve of the Civil War* (Chapel Hill: University of North Carolina Press, 1984), is a series of edited letters by members of a free black family from Charleston. Most of the letters were written by James D. Johnson from Charleston to his brother-in-law and close friend who resided in Stateburg. The Ellison family letters recount the everyday occurrences of life within the free mulatto elite community in Charleston. The issue of black slaveowners has recently attracted much scholarly attention. Philip Burnham, "Black Slaveowners," in John A. Garraty, ed., *Historical Viewpoints*, vol. 1, *To 1877,* 7th ed. (New York: HarperCollins, 1995), 294–302, addresses the questions of why some blacks bought slaves, how their being black affected the slave-master relationship, and how free blacks in general related to the mass of those held in bondage. Michael Johnson and James Roark, *Black Masters: A Free Family of Color in the Old South* (New York: W. W. Norton, 1984), also addresses the relationship between black slaveowners and their slaves and provides much insight into the effects of the Charleston enslavement crisis on the city's mulatto aristocracy and the larger free black community. R. Halliburton, Jr., "Free Black Owners of Slaves: A Reappraisal," *South Carolina Historical Magazine* 76, no. 3 (July 1975): 129–42, argues that many black slaveowners were as capitalistic as most white slaveowners and as such treated their slaves first and foremost as property. By far, the best work on black slaveowners is Larry Koger, *Black Slaveowners: Free Black Slavemasters in South Carolina, 1790–1860* (Jefferson, N.C.: McFarland and Company, 1985). Koger offers a provocative reassessment of Carter G. Woodson's thesis that most black slaveowners had paternalistic relationships with their slaves and, as a consequence, generally treated them favorably. Using wills, tax rolls, census data, church records, probate records, and various manuscript collections, Koger presents a systematic analysis of black slaveowners, and his conclusions parallel the findings of Halliburton. Indeed, Koger notes, there was little or no difference in how black and white slaveowners treated their slaves.

The black wartime experience and the disintegration of slavery are covered superbly by several scholars. Black families in the American Civil War are discussed in Ira Berlin, Francine C. Carey, Stephen F. Miller, and Leslie S. Rowland, "Family and Freedom: Black Families in the American Civil War," *History Today,* January 1987, 9–15; Peter C. Ripley, "The Black Family in Transition: Louisiana, 1860–1865," *Journal of Southern History* 41, no. 3 (August 1975): 369–80; Paul D. Escott, "The Context of Freedom: Georgia's Slaves during the Civil War," *Georgia Historical Quarterly* 57, no. 1 (Spring 1974): 79–104; and Peter C. Ripley, *Slaves and Freedmen in Civil War Louisiana* (Baton Rouge: Louisiana State University Press, 1976). Black soldiers are dealt with in Benjamin Quarles, *The Negro in the Civil War* (New York: Russell and Russell, 1968); James M. McPherson, *The Negro's Civil War: How American Negroes Felt and Acted during the War for the Union* (New York: Pantheon Books, 1965); Dudley T. Cornish, *The Sable Arm: Negro Troops in the Union Army, 1861–1865* (New York: Longman's Green, 1956); Joseph T. Wilson, *The Black Phalanx: A History of the Negro Soldiers of the United States in the Wars of 1775–1812, 1861–1865* (New York: Arno Press and the New York Times, 1968); Manoj K. Joshi and Joseph P. Reidy, "To Come Forward and Aid in Putting Down This Unholy Rebellion: The Officers of Louisiana's Free Black Native Guard during the Civil War Era," *Southern Studies* 21, no. 3 (Fall 1982): 326–42;

Howard C. Westwood, "Captive Black Union Soldiers in Charleston—
What to Do?" *Civil War History* 28, no. 1 (March 1982): 28–44; and
Joseph T. Glatthaar, *Forged in Battle: The Civil War Alliance of Black
Soldiers and White Officers* (New York: Free Press, 1990).

Eric Foner, *Reconstruction: America's Unfinished Revolution, 1863–1877*
(New York: Harper and Row, 1988), is the most thorough synthesis of
the Reconstruction period. Foner presents blacks as central players in
the story of Reconstruction. W. E. B. Du Bois, *Black Reconstruction: An
Essay toward a History of the Part Which Black Folk Played in the Attempt to
Reconstruct Democracy in America, 1860–1880* (New York: Harcourt,
Brace, 1935), though published more than sixty years ago, is a classic
and must be read by those interested in the study of this period. The
best general work on blacks during emancipation and Reconstruction
in the South is Leon F. Litwack, *Been in the Storm So Long: The Aftermath
of Slavery* (New York: Vintage Books, 1980). It chronicles the countless
ways black men and women who were born into slavery perceived and
experienced freedom and how they acted on every level to help shape
their condition and future as freedpeople. An excellent work that
chronicles black life in the social, economic, religious, educational,
and political realms in postwar South Carolina is Alrutheus A. Taylor,
The Negro in South Carolina during the Reconstruction (New York: Russell
and Russell, 1969). But the definitive work on the social and economic
adjustments of freedmen after slavery on the state level is Joel Williamson, *After Slavery: The Negro in South Carolina during Reconstruction,
1861–1877* (Chapel Hill: University of North Carolina Press, 1965). It
provides excellent biographical data on black and white South Carolinians. The most up-to-date general history of Charleston, South
Carolina, is Walter J. Fraser, Jr., *Charleston! Charleston! The History of a
Southern City* (Columbia: University of South Carolina Press, 1989).
The chapter that covers the Reconstruction era is particularly insightful, and the thorough bibliography will benefit those interested in
studying South Carolina or Charleston history.

On the Freedmen's Bureau, the struggle by blacks to obtain land, and
other economic activities engaged in by blacks, see Martin Abbott, *The
Freedmen's Bureau in South Carolina, 1865–1872* (Chapel Hill: University
of North Carolina Press, 1967); George R. Bentley, *A History of the
Freedmen's Bureau* (New York: Octagon Books, 1970); Claude F. Oubre,
Forty Acres and a Mule: The Freedmen's Bureau and Black Land Ownership
(Baton Rouge: Louisiana State University Press, 1982); James T.
Currie, "Benjamin Montgomery and the Davis Bend Colony," *Prologue*
10, no. 1 (Spring 1978): 5–21; Stephen Joseph Ross, "Free Soil, Free
Labor, Free Men: John Eaton and the Davis Bend Experiment," *Jour-
nal of Southern History* 44, no. 2 (May 1978): 213–32; Janet Sharp
Hermann, *The Pursuit of a Dream* (New York: Oxford University Press,

1981); Carl R. Osthaus, *Freedmen, Philanthropy, and Fraud: A History of the Freedmen's Savings Bank* (Urbana: University of Illinois Press, 1976); Jacqueline Jones, *Labor of Love, Labor of Sorrow: Black Women, Work and the Family, from Slavery to the Present* (New York: Vintage Books, 1985); Loren Schweninger, "Slave Independence and Enterprise in South Carolina, 1780–1865," *South Carolina Historical Magazine* 93 (April 1992): 101–25; Loren Schweninger, *Black Property Owners in the South, 1790–1915* (Urbana: University of Illinois Press, 1990); and William C. Hine, "Black Organized Labor in Reconstruction Charleston," *Labor History* 25, no. 4 (Fall 1984): 504–17. The best overview of the impact of emancipation on the South's economy is Roger L. Ransom and Richard Sutch, *One Kind of Freedom: The Economic Consequences of Emancipation* (Cambridge: Cambridge University Press, 1977).

By far the most thorough work on black politicians during Reconstruction is Thomas Holt, *Black over White: Negro Political Leadership in South Carolina during Reconstruction* (Urbana: University of Illinois Press, 1977). It concentrates on the origins and development of black political leadership at the state level. Holt details and analyzes the aims and objectives of black political leaders, as well as the initiatives they undertook to make their goals a reality. Encompassed in his work is valuable biographical data on South Carolina's black political leaders. William C. Hine, "Black Politicians in Reconstruction Charleston, South Carolina: A Collective Study," *Journal of Southern History* 49, no. 4 (November 1983): 555–84, surveys the backgrounds of some of Charleston's black politicians. Howard N. Rabinowitz, ed., *Southern Black Leaders of the Reconstruction Era* (Urbana: University of Illinois Press, 1982), presents several excellent profiles of black Reconstruction politicians. Peggy Lamson's *The Glorious Failure: Black Congressman Robert Brown Elliot and the Reconstruction in South Carolina* (New York: Norton Books, 1973), is a creditable work. Okon Uya's *From Slavery to Public Service: Robert Smalls, 1839–1915* (New York: Oxford University Press, 1971), presents a very plausible interpretation of the life of Robert Smalls. Nell I. Painter, "Martin Delany: Elitism and Black Nationalism," in Leon F. Litwack and August Meier, eds., *Black Leaders of the Nineteenth Century* (Urbana: University of Illinois Press, 1988), 149–71, is a provocative analysis of the political views of Martin Delany.

There is a wealth of fine literature on black education. Although Robert E. Butchart, *Northern Schools, Southern Blacks, and Reconstruction: Freedmen's Education, 1862–1875* (Westport, Conn.: Greenwood Press, 1980), and Robert C. Morris, *Reading, Riting, and Reconstruction: The Education of Freedmen in the South, 1861–1870* (Chicago: University of Chicago Press, 1981) are both excellent, they focus on the efforts of Northern whites to educate Southern freedmen and overlook the activities of freedmen to educate themselves. The definitive work on black education is James D. Anderson, *The Education of Blacks in the South, 1860–1935* (Chapel Hill: University of North Carolina Press, 1988). It offers a detailed analysis of the efforts of blacks to establish and maintain schools. A chapter by Herbert Gutman titled "Schools for Freedom: The Post-Emancipation Origins of Afro-American Education," in Ira Berlin, ed., *Herbert G. Gutman: Power and Culture—Essays on the American Working Class* (New York: The New Press, 1987), 260–97, also highlights the efforts by blacks to support their own educational endeavors. Edmund Drago, *Initiative, Paternalism, and Race Relations: Charleston's Avery Normal Institute* (Athens: University of Georgia Press, 1990), presents a history of Charleston's Avery Normal Institute and provides excellent and extensive biographical data on black Charlestonians. Some of the best work on black education appears in journal articles. Three of the most significant are Martin Abbott, "The Freedmen's Bureau and Negro Schooling in South Carolina," *South Carolina Historical Magazine* 47, no. 2 (April 1956): 65–81; C. W. Birnie, "The Education of the Negro in Charleston Prior to the Civil War," *Journal of Negro History* 12, no. 1 (January 1927): 13–21; and Luther P. Jackson, "The Educational Efforts of the Freedmen's Bureau and Freedmen's Aid Societies in South Carolina, 1862–1872," *Journal of Negro History* 8, no. 1 (January 1923): 1–40.

E. Franklin Frazier, *The Negro Church in America* (New York: Schocken Books, 1974), and Carter G. Woodson, *The History of the Negro Church* (Washington, D.C.: The Associated Publishers, 1921), are two of the many excellent works available on the religious life of blacks. The definitive work on the religious activities of blacks during the antebellum period is Albert Raboteau, *Slave Religion: The Invisible Institution in the Antebellum South* (Oxford: Oxford University Press, 1978). Numerous general studies proved helpful to this project. The impact of race on religion is assessed in C. Eric Lincoln, *Race, Religion, and the Continuing American Dilemma* (New York: Hill and Wang, 1984), and a detailed analysis of the role of racism in Southern religion is offered in H. Shelton Smith, *In His Image But . . . . : Racism in Southern Religion, 1780–1910* (Durham, N.C.: Duke University Press, 1972). The most thorough studies of various religious denominations and their relationships to blacks include George Singleton, *The Romance of African Methodism: A Study of the African Methodist Episcopal Church* (New York: Arno Press and the New York Times, 1968); A. Knighton Stanley, *The Children Is Crying: Congregationalism among Black People* (Philadelphia: The Pilgrim Press, 1979); Harry V. Richardson, *Dark Salvation: The Story of Methodism as It Developed among Blacks in America* (Garden City, N.Y.: Doubleday, Anchor Press, 1976); T. Erskine Clarke, "An Experiment in Paternalism: Presbyterians and Slaves in Charleston, South Carolina," *Journal of Presbyterian History* 53, no. 3 (Fall 1975): 223–38;

Robert F. Durden, "The Establishment of Calvary Protestant Episco-
pal Church for Negroes in Charleston, South Carolina," *South Carolina
Historical Magazine* 65, no. 1 (January 1964): 63–84; and J. Carleton
Hayden, "After the War: The Mission and Growth of the Episcopal
Church among Blacks in the South, 1865–1877," *Historical Magazine of
the Protestant Episcopal Church,* December 1973, 403–27. Clarence E.
Walker, *A Rock in a Weary Land: The African Methodist Episcopal Church
during the Civil War and Reconstruction* (Baton Rouge: Louisiana State
University Press, 1982), is probably the best book on the black church
during the Civil War and Reconstruction.

INDEX